The Postfix Handbook

A Practical Guide to Email Server Management

Robert Johnson

Published by HiTeX Press

For permissions and other inquiries, write to:
P.O. Box 3132, Framingham, MA 01701, USA

Contents

Introduction

Email has become an essential communication tool in the modern world, serving as a reliable conduit for personal, professional, and organizational interactions. At the core of email systems are mail transfer agents (MTAs), software applications that facilitate the routing, delivery, and reception of email messages over the internet. Amongst various MTAs, Postfix stands out as a robust and secure choice for managing email servers.

Postfix, initially developed by Wietse Venema, has gained widespread adoption due to its flexibility, reliability, and security features. It is designed to be a drop-in replacement for the Sendmail MTA, offering improved performance and ease of configuration. The modular architecture of Postfix not only simplifies the process of setting up an email server but also allows for extensive customizations, enabling administrations to tailor their systems to precise operational requirements.

As organizations increasingly depend on email servers for critical tasks, the role of an email administrator becomes crucial in ensuring smooth communication. This handbook is written to equip readers, regardless of their prior experience, with the fundamental knowledge and practical skills necessary to deploy, configure, and manage a Postfix email server. It aims to serve as a comprehensive guide that will lead users through every aspect of working with Postfix, from installation and basic setup to advanced configuration and integration with other services.

This guide is structured into focused chapters that address key areas of operating a Postfix server. Each chapter delves into specific components of Postfix management, offering clear instructions and explanations designed to foster competence and confidence. Readers will begin by developing an understanding of the fundamental concepts of email servers and Postfix, followed by detailed guidance on installation and configuration. Further chapters explore advanced configuration, security practices, user management, and performance optimization, all of which are integral to maintaining a reliable and secure email infrastructure.

By addressing both fundamental and advanced topics, this book provides all the necessary resources to assist in creating a well-managed, performant, and secure email server environment. It is crafted with the dual intention of being informative for beginners while also serving as a resourceful reference for experienced administrators seeking to harness the full capabilities of Postfix.

As you progress through this book, you will acquire a comprehensive skill set that extends beyond basic email server administration, empowering you to tackle challenges proactively and ensure the dependable operation of your organization's email services. This thorough and practical approach to learning will pave the way for effective email server management with Postfix, enabling you to handle various operational requirements with confidence and precision.

Chapter 1

Introduction to Email Servers and Postfix

Explore the essential role of email servers, focusing on Postfix as a versatile mail transfer agent. Gain insights into email protocols, the mail delivery process, and the foundational concepts underpinning email communications. Understand the responsibilities of an email administrator, equipping yourself with the necessary knowledge to manage and optimize email server operations effectively. This chapter sets the stage for mastering Postfix throughout this guide.

1.1. Understanding Email Servers

Email servers are fundamental components of communication networks, serving as conduits for the reliable exchange of electronic messages. Their role is to ensure that messages are routed, delivered, and stored accurately between senders and recipients. This section delves into the basic concepts governing email servers, examines their underlying architecture, and provides practical examples to illustrate their configuration and operation.

An email server typically functions in several capacities: as a Mail Transfer Agent (MTA), a Mail Delivery Agent (MDA), or a Mail Submission Agent (MSA). The MTA is responsible for routing emails from one server to another over the Internet. It relies on protocols such as the Simple Mail Transfer Protocol (SMTP) to relay messages. The architecture of an email server includes several layers, beginning with the network layer that ensures IP connectivity, followed by a transport layer using TCP for reliable data delivery, and finally the application layer where protocols such as SMTP, POP3, and IMAP interact to manage and retrieve emails.

At the core of email server functionality lies the handling of email addresses and domain names. Domain Name System (DNS) configurations, particularly Mail Exchange (MX) records, determine where email messages are directed. These records specify the mail servers for a given domain, allowing email clients and servers to identify the correct destination for outgoing messages. For instance, when an email is sent, the sender's server queries the DNS to retrieve the MX record for the recipient's domain. The email is then routed to the appropriate server based on the priority specified in these records.

Email servers also implement several security measures to prevent unauthorized access and spam. Techniques such as DomainKeys Identified Mail (DKIM), Sender Policy Framework (SPF), and Domain-based Message Authentication, Reporting, and Conformance (DMARC) are integrated into server configurations. These mechanisms validate the authenticity of the sender's domain and ensure that the email has not been tampered with during transit. The incorporation of these security protocols enhances trust and reliability in electronic communications.

10

From an infrastructural perspective, the server environment typically comprises a combination of hardware, operating systems, and software applications that support the processing of email. Operating systems on email servers are typically Unix-based for stability and security, but Windows-based systems are also prevalent in certain network environments. Email server software, such as Postfix, is chosen for its ease of configuration, performance, and robust features that support modern email standards. This software handles tasks including queue management, routing, and delivery, as well as user authentication and encryption using technologies like TLS (Transport Layer Security).

A critical aspect of configuring an email server relates to performance optimization and fault tolerance. Redundancy solutions such as load balancing and clustering ensure that email services remain available even in the event of hardware failures or network issues. Furthermore, the management of mail queues is essential; messages must be retried on temporary failures and handled appropriately in cases of permanent errors. Fine-tuning these parameters is often done via configuration files and administrative commands provided by the server software. For example, a typical configuration snippet in Postfix might look as follows:

```
# Set the domain and hostname for Postfix
myhostname = mail.example.com
mydomain = example.com

# Define the trusted networks
mynetworks = 127.0.0.0/8 [::1]/128

# Configure the queue directory and message size limits
queue_directory = /var/spool/postfix
message_size_limit = 10240000

# Enable TLS for secure communication
smtpd_tls_cert_file = /etc/ssl/certs/postfix.pem
smtpd_tls_key_file = /etc/ssl/private/postfix.key
smtpd_use_tls = yes
```

This configuration exemplifies typical parameters used to establish the core behavior of an email server. The assignment of a hostname and domain, the definition of trusted networks, and the facilitation of secure communication via TLS are foundational steps in ensuring that the server is both functional and secure. Administrators must consider these elements carefully to maintain an optimal level of performance and security in email operations.

Beyond the technical configuration, the operational dynamics of an email server involve handling a variety of protocol interactions. SMTP, for example, is used during the initial stages of email transmission where messages are relayed from the sending server to the recipient's MTA. During this phase, the server must perform a series of validations, including verifying the sender's domain against SPF records and checking the sender's reputation. Failures in these validations can result in message rejection or the flagging of emails as potential spam. Once an email has been accepted by an MTA, it may subsequently be handed off to an MDA that stores the email until the recipient retrieves it using protocols such as POP3 or IMAP.

Efficient email servers also incorporate mechanisms to handle delivery failures, such as bounce-back messages that inform senders of issues during the delivery process. Bounce-back diagnostics are crucial for troubleshooting and identifying misconfigurations, invalid addresses, or issues within the broader network infrastructure. Administrators rely on these diagnostics to fine-tune the server settings and ensure high levels of reliability.

The integration of logging and monitoring tools is another aspect that underscores the importance of email server management. Detailed logs capture every transaction, including connection attempts, authentication processes, and message transfers. These logs are indispensable for auditing purposes, forensic analysis, and proactive management of server performance. Modern email server software often provides built-in logging features that can be customized to capture relevant data. For example, an operator might enable detailed logging with the following configuration in a Postfix setup:

```
# Enable verbose logging for troubleshooting purposes
debug_peer_list = 192.0.2.1, 198.51.100.2
debug_peer_level = 2
```

Such configurations help administrators identify and resolve issues promptly, enhancing the overall reliability of email communications.

In addition to these operational components, email servers are designed to scale and adapt to varying loads. High-traffic servers support thousands of concurrent connections and must be engineered to manage significant message volumes efficiently. They employ techniques such as caching frequently accessed data and prioritizing critical message queues during peak periods. The software architecture is modular, allowing administrators to add or remove functionalities as needed to match operational requirements.

The performance of email servers also depends on the interplay between software and hardware. Server hardware with fast processors, sufficient memory, and rapid disk I/O contributes to the smooth handling of email transactions. The modular nature of email server design allows it to be deployed in various environments, ranging from small business networks to large-scale enterprises with complex distributed systems. The adaptability of email server architectures supports integration with other communication and collaboration tools, further embedding email as a critical component of organizational communication ecosystems.

Managing email servers requires an understanding of both software functionalities and underlying network principles. Email servers operate within the broader context of network security, requiring consistent updates and monitoring to thwart cyber threats. The implementation of firewalls, intrusion detection systems, and regular security audits mitigates the risks associated with vulnerabilities. Continuous

13

improvements in server software, such as the advent of faster cryptographic algorithms and enhanced spam filtering techniques, contribute to the evolution of secure email communications.

The interplay between email server functionality and network administration creates a dynamic environment that demands both theoretical knowledge and practical expertise. Administrators must be versed in network protocols, security practices, and system administration to effectively maintain and troubleshoot email servers. The complexity of modern email systems necessitates an integrated approach where each component, from DNS resolution to TLS encryption and queuing mechanisms, operates in concert. This integrated design paradigm builds on core network communication principles, ensuring that the email infrastructure is both robust and adaptable.

Modern email server architectures also consider the user experience and the administrative overhead. User interfaces that allow for configuring mail policies, visualizing traffic patterns, and managing spam filters are essential tools that complement the server's backend operations. These interfaces, whether web-based or command-line driven, enable administrators to apply configurations that directly impact system performance and user satisfaction. Automation tools and scripting routines further streamline repetitive management tasks. A sample script to clear the mail queue may be implemented as follows:

```
#!/bin/bash
# Script to clear the mail queue
postsuper -d ALL
```

An understanding of this script is essential for administrators to manage queue congestion efficiently. By integrating such automation into regular maintenance procedures, email professionals can ensure that server performance is maintained even under high load conditions.

Overall, the architecture and operational philosophy of email servers are deeply intertwined with the principles of network communication and system security. The design of these servers incorporates redundancy, performance optimization, secure transmission protocols, and robust logging mechanisms to deliver reliable email services. Operational efficiency is achieved through careful planning, precise configuration, and ongoing maintenance practices, making email servers indispensable components of modern communication infrastructure.

1.2. Postfix: An Overview

Postfix is a widely adopted Mail Transfer Agent (MTA) that has revolutionized email server management through its efficient architecture and robust performance. Originating as an alternative to older, monolithic MTAs, Postfix was designed to enhance security, ease of configuration, and overall reliability in handling email traffic. Its development began in the early 1990s with the aim of addressing the vulnerabilities and complexities inherent in previous systems. Over time, Postfix has evolved into a mature product supported by an active community, and it now serves as a cornerstone of many modern email infrastructures.

Postfix distinguishes itself by employing a modular design that encapsulates discrete functions into separate processes. This compartmentalization minimizes the impact of potential security breaches by isolating critical functions such as mail queue management, address rewriting, and protocol handling. The architecture of Postfix ensures that a failure in one component does not compromise the entire system. This design philosophy adheres to the principle of least privilege, where each process is granted only the minimum resources necessary to perform its task, thereby reducing the overall attack surface.

One of the central features of Postfix is its ability to handle high volumes of email with minimal latency. The performance optimizations integrated into its design include efficient queue management, dynamic concurrency settings, and load balancing mechanisms across

15

multiple worker processes. These optimizations allow organizations to deploy Postfix even in environments with significant email traffic, ranging from small business operations to large-scale enterprise systems. Postfix achieves this efficiency by employing a combination of process forking and event-driven programming, which ensures a responsive and stable email service.

The configuration of Postfix is managed through a series of text-based configuration files, with `main.cf` serving as the primary file where global settings are established. The simplicity of these configuration files is one of Postfix's major strengths, as it allows system administrators to quickly customize the behavior of the email server without wading through overly complex syntax. An exemplary configuration snippet may be illustrated as follows:

```
# General settings for Postfix
myhostname = mail.example.com
mydomain = example.com
myorigin = $mydomain

# Define network interfaces and trusted networks
inet_interfaces = all
mynetworks = 127.0.0.0/8 [::1]/128

# Queue management and timing parameters
queue_directory = /var/spool/postfix
default_destination_concurrency_limit = 20
minimal_backoff_time = 300s
maximal_backoff_time = 4000s
```

This example demonstrates some of the key configurable parameters: the server's hostname and domain, the interfaces on which Postfix listens for incoming connections, and the specifics of its queue management system. These configurations are essential for tuning the performance and ensuring the secure operation of the server.

Another important aspect of Postfix is its support for various email protocols, most notably the Simple Mail Transfer Protocol (SMTP). Postfix implements the SMTP standard to govern the transfer of emails between servers, managing tasks such as connection establishment, command interpretation, and response handling. This adherence to established standards ensures interoperability with other email systems and facilitates smooth communication across diverse network environments.

In addition to its core mailing functions, Postfix incorporates several advanced security measures. These measures include support for Transport Layer Security (TLS) to encrypt communication channels, thereby protecting data during transmission from potential eavesdropping and interception. The use of TLS is critical for maintaining the confidentiality and integrity of email exchanges, particularly in environments where sensitive data is transmitted. Configuration of TLS within Postfix is straightforward, as demonstrated in the following example:

```
# TLS configuration for secure SMTP connections
smtpd_tls_cert_file = /etc/ssl/certs/postfix.crt
smtpd_tls_key_file = /etc/ssl/private/postfix.key
smtpd_use_tls = yes
smtp_tls_security_level = may
smtpd_tls_session_cache_database = btree:${data_directory}/
    smtpd_scache
smtp_tls_session_cache_database = btree:${data_directory}/smtp_scache
```

This configuration highlights the ease with which administrators can enable secure communications. By specifying the necessary certificate and key file locations and setting the appropriate TLS parameters, Postfix can be configured to support encrypted sessions with minimal additional complexity.

The extensibility of Postfix is further exhibited by its integration capabilities with auxiliary software and databases. Postfix can interface with relational databases, LDAP servers, or flat-file configurations for virtual alias and mailbox management. This integration flexibility is particularly valuable in large organizations where user management and domain configurations are dynamic and complex. For example, a configuration that leverages a MySQL database to maintain virtual alias mappings might involve settings in main.cf along with a set of query definitions that allow Postfix to retrieve and update user information on the fly.

In practice, effective management of Postfix requires not only careful configuration but also continuous monitoring and logging. The robust logging mechanisms integrated within Postfix capture detailed records of every email transaction, including connection attempts, authentication processes, and delivery outcomes. These logs are essential for both routine troubleshooting and forensic investigations following security incidents. Administrators can tailor the logging settings to meet the requirements of their specific operational environment, ensuring that sufficient detail is available for diagnosing issues without overwhelming the system resources.

A practical example of a logging enhancement in Postfix can be observed in the adjustment of client connection parameters. This may be configured as follows:

```
# Increase verbosity for specific IP addresses for detailed logging
debug_peer_list = 192.168.1.100, 192.168.1.101
debug_peer_level = 2
```

By adding these lines to the configuration, administrators can gain insight into interactions from specific hosts, which is particularly beneficial during periods of anomalous activity or when troubleshooting persistent connection issues.

Beyond its technical capabilities, Postfix offers several advantages that contribute to its widespread adoption. Its modularity not only enhances security and reliability but also simplifies scalability. As the volume of email traffic increases, additional worker processes can be spawned to distribute the load, and redundant configurations can be implemented to ensure consistent performance during peak periods. In scenarios that demand high availability, Postfix can be configured in clusters with failover capabilities, thereby providing uninterrupted service even in the event of hardware or software failures.

The active community surrounding Postfix has further reinforced its development and support. Open-source contributions have resulted in numerous patches, enhancements, and integrations that continuously expand the functionalities available to administrators. The community also provides extensive documentation, best practice guides, and troubleshooting resources that are invaluable for both novice and experienced users. This collaborative ecosystem promotes a cycle of innovation and improvement that ensures Postfix remains at the forefront of email server technology.

An important aspect of the Postfix environment is its compatibility with various operating systems. Although it is most commonly deployed on Unix-like systems due to inherent stability and performance characteristics, Postfix is also available for Windows environments through appropriate adaptations. This cross-platform support fosters a diverse range of deployment scenarios and broadens the accessibility of robust, secure email solutions to a wider audience.

In addition to its functional and technical merits, Postfix adopts an administrative philosophy that emphasizes simplicity and clarity. The design of its configuration files and the modular nature of its process architecture reduce the cognitive load on administrators, making it easier to identify potential issues and optimize performance. Such design decisions are rooted in practical experience and empirical observations, reflecting a commitment to making email server management accessible to those with varied levels of technical expertise.

Emphasis on automation further enhances the operational effectiveness of Postfix. Administrators can integrate Postfix with scheduling tools, scripting languages, and configuration management systems to automate routine maintenance tasks. This automation not only reduces the risk of human error but also ensures that system updates and security patches are deployed in a timely fashion. For instance, a script to automate the reloading of configuration after a bulk update might be structured as follows:

```
#!/bin/bash
# Automated script to reload Postfix configuration
postfix reload
echo "Postfix configuration reloaded successfully."
```

This script demonstrates how simple automation can streamline the operational workflow, ensuring that changes are applied consistently across the environment.

Examining the historical context of Postfix reveals a journey of iterative improvement. Its inception was driven by the need for a more secure and robust MTA, and over the years it has integrated a series of advancements born out of real-world demands. These historical developments have positioned Postfix as a resilient system capable of adapting to emerging challenges in email communication. Its commitment to security, scalability, and ease of administration has ensured its longevity and persistent relevance in a rapidly changing technological landscape.

Postfix continues to evolve through periodic updates that address emerging security vulnerabilities, improve performance, and introduce new functionalities. This ongoing evolution is a testament to its responsive design philosophy and the active involvement of its development community. The incorporation of state-of-the-art encryption techniques, dynamic resource management strategies, and adaptive load balancing mechanisms ensures that Postfix remains aligned with modern operational requirements while maintaining backward compatibility with legacy systems.

The interplay of design, performance, security, and community support categorically defines Postfix as a leading MTA. Its modular architecture, ease of configuration, and robust performance are balanced by a proactive approach to security and scalability, making it an ideal choice for diverse email management needs. The comprehensive documentation available, along with an extensive support network, further underscores its position as a critical tool in the domain of email server management.

1.3. Email Protocols: SMTP, POP, and IMAP

Email communication relies on a suite of standardized protocols to ensure the reliable transmission, retrieval, and management of messages. The primary protocols involved are the Simple Mail Transfer Protocol (SMTP), Post Office Protocol (POP), and Internet Message Access Protocol (IMAP). Each protocol addresses a specific aspect of the email process, and when integrated effectively, they provide a comprehensive framework for handling email within a network. Postfix, as a robust Mail Transfer Agent, leverages these protocols to facilitate secure and efficient email communication throughout the delivery chain.

SMTP is the foundational protocol for sending email messages. It governs the process of transferring messages from a sender's client to a recipient's mail server. SMTP operates over Transmission Control Protocol (TCP) and provides a series of commands that initiate, transmit, and conclude an email transaction. Essential commands include HELO or EHLO, MAIL FROM, RCPT TO, and DATA, each of which defines a specific phase of the email transmission session. The use of these structured commands ensures that both local and remote servers can effectively parse and process the messages.

Postfix employs SMTP as its primary interface, carefully managing incoming and outgoing connections. Incoming message transfers via SMTP are handled by the Postfix daemon, which validates sender credentials, checks the integrity of recipient addresses, and applies anti-spam filtering measures. Outgoing connections also adhere to SMTP specifications, enabling Postfix to route messages across networks with reliability. One of the critical enhancements in Postfix is its ability to support Extended SMTP (ESMTP), an upgraded version of the protocol that offers additional features such as 8-bit MIME support and improved authentication methods.

A practical example of how Postfix handles SMTP commands is reflected in its logging output. When a connection is initiated, the server logs the transaction to facilitate troubleshooting. An excerpt of a log file may appear as follows:

```
Feb 20 10:15:42 mail postfix/smtpd[12345]: connect from unknown[203.0.113.5]
Feb 20 10:15:42 mail postfix/smtpd[12345]: NOQUEUE: reject: RCPT from unknown
[203.0.113.5]: 550 5.1.1 <invalid@domain.com>: Recipient address rejected:
User unknown in relay recipient table; from=<sender@domain.com>
 to=<invalid@domain.com> proto=ESMTP helo=<mail.domain.com>
```

This log snippet illustrates the interaction between an SMTP client and the Postfix daemon, highlighting the verification steps that ensure only valid transactions are processed.

The integrity of SMTP transactions is further enhanced by the incorporation of security mechanisms such as Transport Layer Security (TLS). By enabling TLS, Postfix safeguards the email data during transit, protecting it against interception and tampering. The configuration for TLS support in Postfix involves specifying the certificate and key files, as well as defining session caching parameters. A typical TLS configuration in main.cf is shown below:

```
# Enable TLS for secure SMTP sessions in Postfix
smtpd_tls_cert_file = /etc/ssl/certs/postfix.crt
smtpd_tls_key_file = /etc/ssl/private/postfix.key
smtpd_use_tls = yes
smtp_tls_security_level = may
smtpd_tls_session_cache_database = btree:${data_directory}/
    smtpd_scache
smtp_tls_session_cache_database = btree:${data_directory}/smtp_scache
```

This snippet enables TLS on both incoming and outgoing connections, ensuring that the SMTP sessions are encrypted. Such configurations are indispensable in preventing unauthorized access and maintaining the confidentiality of email communications.

The retrieval of email messages by end users is managed by POP and IMAP, each of which serves distinct use cases. The Post Office Protocol, particularly POP3, is designed for users who wish to download and manage their emails locally. When a client connects to a server using POP3, the protocol typically downloads all available messages and then optionally deletes them from the server. This mode of operation is advantageous in environments with limited server storage or when offline access is prioritized. However, this simplicity comes at the cost of reduced synchronization capability between multiple devices.

IMAP offers an alternative solution with a design that supports server-side management of email. Unlike POP3, IMAP maintains email messages on the server and allows clients to manage folders, mark messages as read, and perform server-side searches. This protocol is particularly beneficial in modern computing environments where users access their email from multiple devices. IMAP's design supports a more sophisticated interaction model, enabling simultaneous connections while preserving a consistent state across different sessions. This synchronization is fundamental for maintaining an updated view of a user's email, regardless of the access point.

While Postfix primarily functions as an MTA using SMTP, its integration with POP3 and IMAP servers is crucial for a complete email solution. Typically, Postfix is configured to handle the transmission and routing of emails, and it works in tandem with dedicated retrieval servers such as Dovecot or Courier for POP3/IMAP functionalities. The separation of these roles allows each server component to specialize in its designated tasks, leading to enhanced efficiency, security, and scalability. The backend architecture can be represented by a clear division: Postfix ensures that email messages are correctly dispatched and relayed across the network, while the IMAP/POP3 server ensures that users have reliable, secure access to their mailboxes.

The interoperability between SMTP, POP3, and IMAP is achieved through standard interfaces and protocols. For instance, when a new email arrives at the Postfix server, it is first processed via SMTP. Once accepted, the email is handed off to the local delivery agent, which stores the message in the appropriate user mailbox. The retrieval agents (POP3/IMAP servers) then interface with these mailboxes, providing access to users based on their configured protocols. Below is an example of how Postfix may interact with a local delivery agent such as Dovecot:

```
# In Postfix main.cf - specify Dovecot as the local delivery agent
mailbox_transport = dovecot
```

On the Dovecot side, configurations ensure that email retrieval over IMAP or POP3 is handled securely and efficiently. This integration underlines the importance of seamless communication between the components, ensuring that the delivery, storage, and retrieval of email are tightly coordinated.

Both POP3 and IMAP incorporate mechanisms for maintaining security and data integrity. Authentication is performed using usernames and passwords, with many servers also supporting stronger authentication mechanisms such as OAuth or two-factor authentication. Furthermore, both protocols can be secured using TLS, a configuration similar to that used for SMTP. For example, a basic TLS configuration for an IMAP server might be as follows:

```
# TLS settings for secure IMAP access in Dovecot
ssl = required
ssl_cert = </etc/ssl/certs/dovecot.pem
ssl_key = </etc/ssl/private/dovecot.key
```

This secure configuration is essential to prevent unauthorized access to user mailboxes and to keep sensitive information confidential during

24

transmission.

The complementary design philosophies of POP3 and IMAP cater to different user needs. POP3's design is rooted in simplicity and minimal server storage requirements, making it suitable for users who prefer to manage their mail offline. Conversely, IMAP offers a more dynamic and interactive experience with server-side mail management, making it the preferred choice for users needing to synchronize their email across multiple devices. The choice between the two primarily depends on the specific requirements of the user and the operational environment.

Furthermore, the evolution of these protocols reflects ongoing advancements in email technology. Early implementations of POP3 and IMAP were rudimentary, focused on basic message retrieval. Modern implementations have introduced extended commands and capabilities that support advanced filtering, search, and synchronization features. This evolution is driven by the increasing demand for robust, flexible email systems that can accommodate the diverse ways in which users interact with their mail.

The role of Postfix in this integrated ecosystem is crucial, particularly in its handling of the SMTP protocol. By providing a secure, performant gateway for email transmission, Postfix sets the stage for seamless handoffs to retrieval systems. Its robust logging and monitoring facilities allow administrators to track the performance and reliability of SMTP transactions, ensuring that subsequent POP3 and IMAP access occurs with high integrity. Postfix's capacity to enforce policies, manage queues, and provide security through TLS is foundational to the broader email delivery mechanism.

Operationally, administrators must pay careful attention to the configurations of SMTP, POP3, and IMAP servers to ensure that they work harmoniously. Regular audits, log inspections, and security reviews are necessary to maintain an environment where email communications are both efficient and secure. In scenarios where high volumes of email are transmitted, fine-tuning these protocols becomes essential. Adjustments in concurrency limits, backoff timings, and retry intervals, particularly within Postfix, are instrumental in managing load and preventing server overloads.

The understanding of these protocols extends beyond mere configuration. It encompasses a recognition of the underlying data flows and the critical paths that mail takes from sender to recipient. Insight into these paths informs better system design, contributing to enhanced performance and reliability. The structured, layered approach defined by SMTP, POP3, and IMAP ensures that each leg of the email journey is managed appropriately, from secure transmission to efficient data retrieval.

The interaction between Postfix and the retrieval protocols highlights key operational synergies. Postfix filters and directs email traffic efficiently while leaving client-specific operations to systems tailored for user interaction. This delineation not only streamlines the management process but also minimizes points of failure. The collaboration between these protocols, enhanced by robust security measures, forms the backbone of modern email communications, ensuring that data integrity and user accessibility are preserved at every stage of the process.

1.4. Mail Delivery Process

The mail delivery process is a complex sequence of events that transforms a user's submission into the final delivery of an email to a recipient's mailbox. This journey, from sender to recipient, involves multiple layers of processing, numerous network protocols, and interactions among various system components. A thorough understanding of these mechanisms is essential for configuring, troubleshooting, and optimizing email server operations.

At the initiation of the mail delivery process, the sender composes an email using a Mail User Agent (MUA) which then submits the message to a Mail Submission Agent (MSA). Postfix, acting as a robust MTA, is often deployed to receive these submissions. The MSA validates the message, ensuring that it conforms to required formats, and then passes it into the mail queue. This queuing is critical, as it allows Postfix to manage message traffic efficiently, particularly under heavy loads or when network delays may otherwise cause timeouts.

Once the message is enqueued, the sender's email undergoes several validation checks, including scanning for spam, ensuring that the sender is authorized, and confirming that the message content adheres to any preset policies. These validations may involve domain verification and authentication checks such as SPF and DKIM which help ascertain that the email has not been spoofed or altered. These security measures are implemented prior to the message's transmission to its destination, mitigating risks and ensuring that only valid emails progress through the delivery chain.

Postfix then takes over the role of transferring the email to the recipient's mail server utilizing the SMTP protocol. At this stage, the sending mail server performs a DNS lookup, querying for the Mail Exchange (MX) records associated with the recipient's domain. The MX records determine the correct destination server for the email and, in many cases, provide a priority order if multiple servers are available. For instance, a sample MX record configuration is represented by the following DNS entry:

```
example.com.  3600  IN  MX  10 mail1.example.com.
example.com.  3600  IN  MX  20 mail2.example.com.
```

This configuration instructs the sender to attempt delivery to mail1.example.com first, followed by mail2.example.com if the primary server is unavailable. Once the recipient's MTA is identified, Postfix initiates an SMTP session with that server. This session involves a series of commands that negotiate the connection, verify sender and recipient information, and ultimately transmit the message data.

During the SMTP transaction, commands such as HELO/EHLO, MAIL FROM, RCPT TO, and DATA are exchanged between the sending and receiving servers. Each step of this protocol ensures that both endpoints agree on parameters relevant to the communication session. For example, the following log snippet from a Postfix server captures a typical SMTP exchange:

```
Mar 05 12:45:01 mail postfix/smtpd[6789]: connect from sender.example.com[198
.51.100.10]
Mar 05 12:45:03 mail postfix/smtpd[6789]: 123ABCD: client=sender.example.com[
198.51.100.10]
Mar 05 12:45:05 mail postfix/cleanup[6790]: 123ABCD: message-id=<202303051245
01.123ABCD@sender.example.com>
Mar 05 12:45:07 mail postfix/qmgr[6788]: 123ABCD: from=<user@sender.example.c
om>, size=2048, nrcpt=1 (queue active)
```

Each log entry documents critical events such as the initial connection, the message's unique identifier assignment, and subsequent queuing. These logs provide the necessary information for administrators to monitor the delivery process, identify bottlenecks, or troubleshoot errors when messages fail to reach their destination.

Upon establishment of the connection, the recipient's server once again performs validations. This can encompass confirming whether the recipient address exists, checking if the sender is on any blacklist, or applying further content-based spam filtering. If any of these checks fail, the recipient server may reject the message, issuing a bounce-back notification to the sender. A typical bounce-back error message might detail a temporary failure (e.g., server unavailability) or a permanent failure (such as an invalid recipient address).

When an email is successfully accepted by the recipient's MTA, it is passed to a Mail Delivery Agent (MDA) for final processing. The MDA's responsibilities include delivering the email into the recipient's mailbox, applying any necessary filtrations, and updating appropriate status flags. In many deployments, local delivery agents like Dovecot manage these tasks, working in concert with Postfix. They store the email in a user-accessible format that is compatible with both POP3 and IMAP protocols, ensuring that the recipient can retrieve and interact with the message through their preferred client.

The transition between sending stages and final delivery is managed through a sophisticated queuing mechanism. Postfix operates multiple queues that manage emails in different states – incoming, active, deferred, and bounce. The active queue contains messages that are currently being processed for delivery, while the deferred queue holds messages that encountered temporary errors and require a retry mechanism. If a message remains in the deferred queue beyond a predetermined period, Postfix may eventually move it to the bounce queue, triggering an automatic notification to the sender.

Administrators can review and manage these queues using Postfix's command-line utilities. For instance, the command to list all messages in the queue is executed as follows:

```
postqueue -p
```

In addition, a script-based approach can automate tasks such as purging old messages or triggering a reattempt of deferred emails. An example script to flush the mail queue periodically might be written in shell script:

```
#!/bin/bash
# Script to flush the Postfix mail queue
postqueue -f
echo "Mail queue flushed successfully on $(date)"
```

29

Postfix's design accommodates retry intervals and exponential back-off algorithms to handle temporary delivery failures gracefully. These intervals are critical in managing server load and avoiding repeated immediate retries that could exacerbate network congestion.

Once the email is delivered to the recipient's mailbox, the retrieval process is activated through protocols such as POP3 or IMAP. While Postfix primarily directs the mail delivery act, the retrieval phase is executed by specialized servers dedicated to handling client requests. IMAP allows for synchronized server-side management, granting users the ability to access their emails from multiple devices while maintaining a consistent state. In contrast, POP3 is typically used in environments where emails are downloaded and removed from the server. The integration between Postfix and these retrieval servers ensures a seamless transition from message acceptance to user access.

The hand-off between Postfix and the local delivery agent is usually defined in the Postfix configuration with the `mailbox_transport` parameter. Consider the following configuration in `main.cf`:

```
# Specify Dovecot as the local delivery agent
mailbox_transport = dovecot
```

This setting directs Postfix to pass all accepted emails to Dovecot for final storage in the appropriate mailbox, where retrieval protocols then take over. This integration is a key element of modern email architectures, ensuring that the journey of an email is handled smoothly across different software components.

Throughout the delivery process, extensive logging and traceability facilitate robust monitoring capabilities. Every step—from initial submission to final storage—is logged with precise timestamps and identifiers. These logs enable administrators to conduct detailed analysis in the case of delivery failures or performance issues. Tools that parse these logs can assist in identifying recurring issues, such as high volumes of deferred messages or repeated bounce-back errors, which may indicate configuration or network problems.

Another critical aspect of the mail delivery process is the handling of message priorities and routing decisions within a multi-server environment. Postfix and similar MTAs can be configured to route specific types of messages along different paths based on their origin, content, or recipient attributes. This routing flexibility is particularly useful in large organizations or service providers where traffic segmentation enhances security and performance. For example, high-priority messages may be routed through a dedicated channel with lower latency, while bulk or promotional emails may follow a less critical path. Such decisions are often implemented through transport mapping features that associate specific domains or IP addresses with alternate processing routes.

Email delivery also involves considerations related to retry mechanisms and transaction timeouts. The robust handling of temporary failures is a key aspect of reliable email systems. A well-tuned Postfix server employs settings that determine how long a message remains in the queue before being retried or bounced. These settings balance the need to ensure message delivery with the practical limitations of network variability and transient server load. Parameters such as minimal_backoff_time and maximal_backoff_time in the configuration files help establish these intervals, for example:

```
# Queue management timing parameters
minimal_backoff_time = 300s
maximal_backoff_time = 4000s
```

Such parameters are critical in environments where network reliability fluctuates, ensuring that emails receive multiple delivery attempts before being classified as undeliverable.

The final leg of the email delivery process is user access, which signifies the success of the entire chain. The recipient uses an MUA, such

31

as a webmail interface or a desktop client, to retrieve the email via either POP3 or IMAP. This retrieval not only involves transferring the email content but also synchronizing user actions—such as marking a message as read or moving it to a folder—back to the server. This interactive component closes the loop on the email transaction, fulfilling the user's intent as communicated by the initial message submission.

The integration of all these components—the MUA, MSA, MTA, MDA, and retrieval protocols—creates a cohesive and resilient mail delivery ecosystem. Each component plays a specialized role, yet all operate in concert to ensure that the email reaches its destination reliably and securely. Understanding the intricate flow of these operations is key for administrators looking to optimize performance, resolve delivery issues, and maintain the overall health of the email infrastructure.

1.5. Roles and Responsibilities of an Email Administrator

An effective email administrator must possess a comprehensive understanding of the underlying mechanisms of email systems, drawing on knowledge of mail server architectures, protocol interactions, and delivery processes. This role is critical for ensuring that email communications remain reliable, secure, and efficient. The email administrator acts as the primary custodian of the email infrastructure, responsible for configuring servers, monitoring performance, enforcing security standards, and troubleshooting a wide array of issues that may arise during the lifecycle of an email transaction.

The responsibilities of an email administrator begin with the installation and configuration of the Mail Transfer Agent (MTA). For instance, administrators often deploy Postfix due to its modular design, performance efficiency, and extensive logging capabilities. The initial configuration tasks include setting the server's hostname and domain in the primary configuration file. Demonstrated by the following example, the setup parameters are essential for defining the server's basic functionality:

```
# Basic Postfix configuration
myhostname = mail.example.com
mydomain = example.com
myorigin = $mydomain
inet_interfaces = all
mynetworks = 127.0.0.0/8 [::1]/128
```

These settings dictate key operational parameters such as which network interfaces to listen on and which networks are trusted, serving as the foundation upon which more advanced functionalities are built.

A core responsibility involves managing the security aspects of the email system. Given the increasing incidence of email-based attacks and spam, the administrator must implement robust security measures including TLS encryption, SPF, DKIM, and DMARC protocols. Securing SMTP sessions is particularly critical. For example, enabling TLS on Postfix ensures that communications are encrypted during transit:

```
# TLS configuration for secure SMTP sessions
smtpd_tls_cert_file = /etc/ssl/certs/postfix.crt
smtpd_tls_key_file = /etc/ssl/private/postfix.key
smtpd_use_tls = yes
smtp_tls_security_level = may
```

These security measures not only protect sensitive communications but also contribute to maintaining the server's reputation in the global email ecosystem. The email administrator must continuously update and refine these configurations to address new vulnerabilities and evolving standards.

Monitoring and maintenance form another critical aspect of the email administrator's responsibilities. Continuous monitoring of the mail delivery process is required to guarantee that the system operates within acceptable performance parameters. Tools and techniques for real-time monitoring include analyzing log files, using built-in monitoring utilities, and employing external monitoring software. An example of a routine command for checking the status of queued emails in Postfix is:

```
# Display the current mail queue status
postqueue -p
```

Regular examination of these logs helps detect anomalies, such as repeated bounce-back errors or high volumes of deferred messages, which may indicate underlying connectivity or configuration issues. An administrator must be adept at interpreting these logs and take action promptly to prevent prolonged system downtimes.

In addition to proactive monitoring, the email administrator must adeptly handle troubleshooting. This requires a detailed understanding of the mail delivery process, including how emails transition through various stages from submission to final delivery. Troubleshooting often involves analyzing SMTP transaction logs, reviewing DNS records for MX configuration, and diagnosing issues with the local delivery agent or compatible interfaces with IMAP/POP3 servers. The ability to quickly identify and rectify issues often depends on a deep familiarity with both the technical configurations and the interactions between different server components.

Ensuring high availability and load balancing is another key function. Administrators must design and implement redundancy measures to handle peak loads and to guarantee continuous service availability. This can involve deploying multiple instances of the email server, configuring failovers, and implementing clustering solutions. A typical approach is to use a load balancer in front of an array of Postfix servers. Administrators may employ scripts or scheduling tasks to automate routine maintenance, such as clearing the mail queue to avoid processing delays caused by a buildup of deferred emails. An example of a simple automation script to flush the mail queue is provided below:

```
#!/bin/bash
# Script to periodically flush the Postfix queue
postqueue -f
echo "Postfix mail queue flushed on $(date)"
```

Such automation assists in stabilizing the service during known periods of high traffic or following maintenance activities.

The role also extends to managing the interaction between various email protocols. Email administrators must ensure seamless integration between SMTP for message delivery and protocols like POP3 and IMAP for client access. This calls for coordination with other servers, such as Dovecot, which handles the retrieval and storage of emails. The configuration parameter for setting the local delivery agent in Postfix is an example of such integration:

```
# Direct mail delivery to Dovecot
mailbox_transport = dovecot
```

Through this integration, administrators can guarantee that once the email is transferred via SMTP, it is immediately accessible to users by POP3 or IMAP protocols. This seamless hand-off is vital for maintaining user satisfaction and ensuring that the system's performance meets organizational demands.

Documentation and compliance are additional important responsibilities. The email administrator must maintain up-to-date records of all configurations, procedures, and changes made to the system. This documentation is critical not only for day-to-day troubleshooting but also for ensuring compliance with regulatory standards. Organizations subject to data protection laws or industry-specific regulations must demonstrate that robust security and data integrity measures are in place. Accurate records also facilitate audits and reviews by internal or external bodies.

35

Communication with end-users and other IT departments also falls within the purview of the email administrator. The complex nature of email systems often means that configuration changes or maintenance activities may impact a broad range of users. Therefore, effective communication is vital to ensure that any potential service interruptions are minimized and that users are informed of the status of the system. Training sessions and clear documentation help disseminate crucial information regarding best practices, phishing awareness, and proper email usage, all of which contribute to a secure email environment.

An often overlooked yet critical duty involves regular testing and updating of the email server infrastructure. Software and firmware updates can address security vulnerabilities, improve performance, and introduce new functionalities. However, updates must be applied in a controlled manner. Administrators are responsible for scheduling these updates during maintenance windows to minimize disruption. They must also perform rigorous testing in isolated environments before deploying changes in the production environment. This testing typically includes running regression tests on software configurations, verifying the compatibility of integrated systems, and confirming that new features do not interfere with established processes.

In parallel, the email administrator must be knowledgeable in scripting and programming languages, which are essential skills for automating repetitive tasks, monitoring system health, and troubleshooting unique problems. Shell scripting, Python, and Perl are commonly used to write custom scripts for managing queues, parsing logs, or interfacing with APIs provided by monitoring tools. These skills not only enhance efficiency but also provide the flexibility required to adapt to the complex operational needs of modern email infrastructures.

In summary, the roles and responsibilities of an email administrator are multifaceted, encompassing technical configuration, security management, performance monitoring, troubleshooting, and ongoing maintenance. A profound understanding of server infrastructures such as Postfix, along with the related protocols like SMTP, POP3, and IMAP, is essential for managing an email system effectively. Administrators must balance operational responsibilities with proactive strategies to secure and optimize the service, ensuring that the email delivery process remains reliable even as demands evolve. The integration of automation, thorough documentation, and continuous learning forms the backbone of successful email administration, ultimately contributing to a resilient and high-performing communication network.

Chapter 2

Installing and Setting Up Postfix

This chapter guides you through the essential steps to install and configure Postfix on your server. It covers system requirements, downloading and installation procedures, initial configuration, and testing the setup. You will also learn about the primary configuration files, their locations, and how to manage Postfix services, ensuring your email server is properly established and ready for operation.

2.1. System Requirements and Preparations

Before proceeding with the installation of Postfix, it is essential to review the hardware and software prerequisites and to perform necessary preparatory tasks. The following discussion provides explicit details on system capabilities, operating system compatibility, and essential adjustments to ensure a successful Postfix deployment. This discussion builds on the foundational concepts introduced in earlier sections by elucidating the specific conditions under which Postfix can operate optimally.

Hardware requirements for a Postfix installation are relatively modest compared to many modern applications; however, the server must fulfill the baseline criteria for processing and network operations. A central processing unit with at least one core is sufficient, yet multi-core processing is advantageous for handling multiple concurrent connections in busy environments. A minimum of 512 MB of RAM is recommended, with 1 GB or more preferred in environments where high throughput is expected. Disk space requirements are minimal for the Postfix executables and libraries, but sufficient free space is necessary to store mail queues, log files, and temporary files during operation. In many cases, allocating 2 to 4 GB of free disk space is adequate, though larger installations may require a more generous allocation. Network connectivity is non-negotiable; a reliable network interface with suitable bandwidth is required to handle mail transfers. Servers with gigabit Ethernet interfaces typically provide the necessary performance, and dedicated network hardware may be warranted in large-scale deployments.

Software requirements extend to the operating system and its provided libraries and utilities. Postfix is designed to operate under various Unix-like systems, including numerous distributions of Linux, BSD variants, and even certain commercial UNIX systems. The kernel should be at a version that supports POSIX-compliant multitasking and networking features. Additionally, the installation of required libraries, such as OpenSSL for secure communication and SASL libraries for authentication when necessary, is critical. Verification that the system package manager has all the necessary packages and dependencies is a pre-installation step that prevents conflicts during installation. It is advisable to update the system to the most current package versions available before installation to mitigate incompatibility issues.

Preparation also involves system configuration adjustments. Confirm that the hostname is properly configured and fully qualified. The existence of a correctly set /etc/hosts file can prevent networking issues that may affect mail delivery and binding. Correct system time and timezone settings are necessary for logging and handling time-based features within Postfix. In environments that use virtualization or container-based technology, it is important to verify that the network interfaces provided by the platform can support persistent and consistent addressing.

An integrated development environment for system administration or text editors such as vim or nano is assumed to be available and configured correctly. These tools are essential for modifying configuration files in a clear and efficient manner. Updating system packages is particularly relevant if the distribution uses repositories that are maintained actively. The following example demonstrates a typical update command sequence for a Debian-based system:

```
sudo apt-get update
sudo apt-get upgrade -y
```

This snippet ensures that the system repositories are current and that installed packages receive the latest security patches. Administrators using Red Hat-based systems can perform analogous operations with commands such as:

```
sudo yum update
```

Other software preparations include verifying that necessary tools for compiling or linking are installed. Some installation processes might involve building from source, which requires compilers and associated libraries. For instance, a system prepared for source installation might verify the presence of packages like build-essential on Debian systems or Development Tools on Red Hat systems. Such environments ensure that if custom compilation is required, it will proceed without interruption.

Security considerations form another critical component of the preparations. Ensuring that the system firewall has been configured to allow the required email ports, primarily TCP port 25 for SMTP and related auxiliary ports if using submission mechanisms, is necessary for Postfix to successfully send and receive mail. System administrators should review and modify firewall rules as needed. In many systems, this can be achieved by configurations in `iptables` or more modern utilities like `ufw` on Ubuntu distributions. For example, opening the SMTP port using `ufw` could be performed with:

```
sudo ufw allow 25/tcp
```

Attention to file permissions and ownership is crucial. Postfix runs under its own non-privileged user account. As part of the preparatory steps, it is important to verify that the directories in which Postfix operates, such as queues and spool directories, are owned by the appropriate users and that permissions are set to restrict unauthorized access. Improper settings might result in security vulnerabilities or operational failures during mail processing. Backup configurations of critical files should be made if prior versions of mail transfer agents have been used on the system. This allows a return to a stable state should complications arise.

Network resolution capabilities require scrutiny. Postfix relies on proper DNS resolution for both inbound and outbound messages. Preparatory steps include confirming that the `/etc/resolv.conf` file is configured with reliable nameserver entries. Troubleshooting connectivity problems at a DNS level before Postfix installation prevents future mail delivery issues. Verifying network configuration might include testing the resolution with simple command-line utilities:

```
nslookup example.com
```

This validation step should yield expected responses ensuring that the nameservers are accurately resolving domain names. Additionally, confirming reverse DNS entries is essential in production environments to reduce the likelihood of outgoing mail being flagged as spam.

Preparation further entails examining any resource constraints imposed by the hosting environment. Virtualized environments may have limits on CPU and I/O resources due to shared infrastructure. System administrators should check for any imposed constraints using diagnostic tools such as `top`, `htop`, or system-specific resource monitors. Analyzing current system load is useful for planning the deployment of Postfix in a way that does not negatively impact other services. For environments managed via containers, system parameters such as memory limits and CPU shares must be adjusted to meet the expected mail traffic volume.

A period of system auditing is also recommended to identify conflicting services that might attempt to bind to the same email ports or override system settings. Tools like `netstat` or `ss` should be used to list active network services and make adjustments accordingly.

Preparation should also consider planned use of additional features such as encryption via TLS or advanced filtering using third-party tools. In these cases, ensuring that all components (such as certificate management tools or malware scanning utilities) are correctly configured or installed prior to Postfix setup can streamline the integration process. This foresight is particularly important in email server configurations that handle sensitive data. Ensuring that the certificate files and keys have the appropriate permissions is also critical for maintaining security standards and operational integrity.

Documentation of preparatory steps and backup of system states are practices that support efficient troubleshooting and rollback if needed. System snapshots or complete backup images of configuration files allow recovery from misconfigurations or unforeseen issues that arise from the Postfix installation or subsequent operation. This documentation, maintained alongside the system logs, contributes to a thorough understanding of how system resources were allocated and configured.

Uniformity in system configuration is another principle that arises from thorough preparation. Administrators should ensure that the installations and configurations for Postfix are consistent with any enterprise-wide policies, particularly those related to security and system management. Consistency checks often require reviewing system policies in environments that enforce centralized configuration management and monitoring.

Through careful evaluation of hardware specifications, software compatibility, network infrastructure, and system policies, the preparation phase establishes a reliable foundation for a secure and efficient Postfix installation. Subsequent modifications to the core configuration files, management of service states, and integration of ancillary components will benefit substantially from a system that has been rigorously pre-assessed and optimized for performance and security.

2.2. Downloading and Installing Postfix

The process of downloading and installing Postfix varies with operating systems and package management systems. This section outlines the steps for popular environments, including Debian-based, Red Hat-based, and BSD systems, and provides insight into handling source installation when necessary. Detailed command examples using the lstlisting environment illustrate the process and assist in understanding the nuances of each approach.

Postfix is widely available through default repositories in many distributions. For Debian-based systems, such as Debian and Ubuntu, installation can be accomplished using the Advanced Package Tool (APT). Prior to installation, it is important to update the package list to ensure that the latest version of Postfix and its dependencies are available. Running the update command can be done as follows:

```
sudo apt-get update
```

After updating the repositories, the installation can be initiated using the following command:

```
sudo apt-get install postfix
```

During the installation process, interactive prompts may appear. Administrators are advised to select the appropriate configuration type (e.g., Internet Site) based on the mail routing requirements already defined during the preparatory phase. The configuration mode selected will influence the content of the main configuration file and the default behavior of the mail transfer agent.

For Red Hat-based systems, such as CentOS or Fedora, the installation process relies on the yum or dnf package managers. It is essential to check that the system is up-to-date before proceeding. The following command updates all packages:

```
sudo yum update -y
```

Postfix is then installed with a simple command call:

```
sudo yum install postfix -y
```

Once installed, it is crucial to configure the service to start automatically on boot. This may involve commands similar to those below:

```
sudo systemctl enable postfix
sudo systemctl start postfix
```

For systems using systemctl as a service manager, verifying the installation by checking the service status can prevent misconfigurations. The command:

45

```
sudo systemctl status postfix
```

should return details confirming that Postfix is running and bound to the expected network interfaces. Pay close attention to any alerts or warnings in the output.

Other Unix-like systems, such as those running on BSD (including FreeBSD), handle package management in a slightly different manner. The pkg command is used on FreeBSD. It begins by ensuring the package repository is up to date:

```
sudo pkg update
```

Installation then proceeds by:

```
sudo pkg install postfix
```

After installation on BSD systems, additional configuration steps might include modifying configuration files in /usr/local/etc/postfix. Adapting to BSD-specific nuances in file paths and system service management is necessary. For instance, FreeBSD users need to enable Postfix in system configuration files, often with settings like:

```
postfix_enable="YES"
```

These configurations are usually placed in the appropriate system files such as /etc/rc.conf to ensure the service starts during system boot.

In situations where a package manager does not provide the desired version or specific compilation options are needed, compiling Postfix from source is an alternative. This approach is recommended for environments requiring selective module inclusion or when experimenting with advanced features. The source package is generally available from the official Postfix website. The following steps outline the compilation process:

46

```
wget http://www.postfix.org/download/postfix-<version>.tar.gz
tar -zxvf postfix-<version>.tar.gz
cd postfix-<version>
make makefiles CCARGS='-DUSE_TLS -DUSE_SASL_AUTH' AUXLIBS='-lssl -
    lcrypto -lsasl2'
make
sudo make install
```

Replace <version> with the specific version number desired. The
CCARGS and AUXLIBS parameters ensure that necessary security features are compiled into Postfix. It is critical to review the output from
these commands to confirm that all dependencies are satisfied and that
no errors interrupt the build process.

Source installation requires administrative privileges and a careful assessment of dependencies. Ensuring that compilers, development libraries, and other requisite tools are installed forms an integral part of
the preparation phase. Package names such as build-essential on
Debian or Development Tools on Red Hat systems must be present.
Administrators can verify this by running commands like:

```
dpkg -l | grep build-essential
```

or

```
rpm -qa | grep '@development tools'
```

These checks prevent complications during the compilation and installation process.

Further, for secure mail transmission and authentication, it is recommended to install supportive libraries before initiating the build.
Such libraries may include libssl-dev and libsasl2-dev on Debian
systems. Installing them ensures that the environment can support
TLS encryption and SASL authentication, which are critical in modern
email infrastructure. The installation may be executed as:

```
sudo apt-get install libssl-dev libsasl2-dev
```

In environments where Postfix is expected to communicate with other mail agents or with a database storing user credentials, integrating database drivers is beneficial. These drivers allow Postfix to perform lookups using external databases. Support for MySQL, PostgreSQL, and SQLite can be added by including additional flags during compilation or installing supplementary packages. For example, enabling PostgreSQL support may involve:

```
sudo apt-get install libpq-dev
```

and modifying configuration commands to reference the PostgreSQL library.

Verification of the installation is a critical final step. Post-installation testing involves examining the version of Postfix and checking configuration defaults. Running a version command reliably confirms the installation state:

```
postconf -d | grep mail_version
```

The output should reflect the correct version number, confirming that the binaries align with expectations. Additionally, verifying the configuration directory structure is essential. Typically, configuration files exist under directories such as /etc/postfix on Linux systems or /usr/local/etc/postfix on BSD systems.

When installing Postfix on more specialized systems, such as those running a different Unix variant or a containerized environment, adjustments in the installation path or configuration files might be necessary. System administrators might need to modify service startup scripts or container initialization files. For containerized environments, ensuring that essential directories are mounted correctly prevents runtime issues. An example Dockerfile snippet for setting up Postfix could be:

```
FROM debian:latest
RUN apt-get update && apt-get install -y postfix
COPY main.cf /etc/postfix/main.cf
CMD ["postfix", "start-fg"]
```

48

This Dockerfile installs Postfix within a Debian container, copies a prepared configuration file, and starts the service in the foreground, ensuring compatibility with container orchestration platforms.

Across all installations, careful documentation of the process and maintaining consistent configuration standards are imperative. Logs generated during the installation process, such as those from APT, YUM, or the compilation process, should be reviewed for identifying potential issues. Analyzing these logs provides insight into dependency resolution and error handling, which is crucial during system troubleshooting.

Monitoring the service immediately after installation helps capture any non-critical warnings that might require adjustments in subsequent configuration steps. Tools like journalctl on systemd-based systems provide a detailed log of Postfix activities. An example command to observe recent logs is:

```
sudo journalctl -u postfix -n 50
```

Reviewing logs can uncover misconfigurations or network issues that manifest during startup, allowing for prompt resolution before the system is placed into production.

Integrating all the steps described ensures a systematic deployment of Postfix across different operating systems. Installation through package managers offers simplicity and ease of updates, while source installations provide flexibility in supporting advanced features. This dual approach allows system administrators to choose the method that aligns best with their server environment and operational requirements.

Confirming OS-specific peculiarities, ensuring dependency checks, and validating configurations throughout the installation process fortifies the reliability of Postfix as an integral mail transfer agent.

49

The diversified approaches not only extend options for deployment but also underscore the need for consistent post-installation checks across varied system topologies.

2.3. Initial Configuration Steps

Following the successful installation of Postfix, the next objective is establishing its basic configuration, thereby enabling the mail transfer agent to function as intended. The essential configuration process centers on the main.cf file, which houses global settings that determine how Postfix routes mail, enforces policies, and interacts with system resources. The location of this file is typically /etc/postfix/main.cf on Linux distributions or /usr/local/etc/postfix/main.cf on BSD systems. Editing main.cf demands careful attention to detail since the misconfiguration of key parameters may lead to mail delivery issues or compromised security.

The primary areas of focus within main.cf include defining the system's identity, specifying accepted domains, setting relay restrictions, and configuring mail routing rules. A critical parameter is myhostname, which should be set to the fully qualified domain name (FQDN) of the host. It is advisable to confirm that this FQDN is correctly registered in DNS and that reverse DNS (PTR) records exist to avoid unwanted delays in mail delivery and potential rejections by remote servers. For example, a configuration entry can be defined as follows:

```
myhostname = mail.example.com
```

Another foundational parameter is mydomain. This variable typically represents the domain for which the mail server will be responsible. Accordingly, the parameter may be set to:

```
mydomain = example.com
```

The parameter myorigin determines the domain name that locally originated mail appears to originate from and is frequently assigned the same value as mydomain:

```
myorigin = \$mydomain
```

The mydestination setting instructs Postfix on which destinations are to be delivered locally – that is, domains for which the server takes responsibility. A typical setting may include the local hostname, the domain name, and the local network alias, which may be configured as:

```
mydestination = \$myhostname, localhost.\$mydomain, localhost, \
    $mydomain
```

For systems where outgoing mail is relayed through an upstream mail server, it is necessary to specify a relay host. The relayhost parameter allows administrators to route outbound emails through a predetermined server. It is useful in environments that enforce restrictions or require authentication. An example configuration might be:

```
relayhost = [smtp.relayprovider.com]:587
```

Accompanying the relay host setting, it may be necessary to enable authentication mechanisms if the relay server requires credentials. Postfix supports SASL authentication, and basic configuration necessitates pointing to the appropriate password maps and enabling the required protocols. The following entries in main.cf serve this purpose:

```
smtp_sasl_auth_enable = yes
smtp_sasl_password_maps = hash:/etc/postfix/sasl_passwd
smtp_sasl_security_options = noanonymous
```

Once these parameters are defined, it is essential to construct the /etc/postfix/sasl_passwd file with the authentication credentials. This file should contain lines in the format: [smtp.relayprovider.com]:587 username:password. After populating the file, it must be compiled into a format that Postfix can

51

read:

```
sudo postmap /etc/postfix/sasl_passwd
```

System security practices dictate that sensitive information should be protected; hence the permissions for the sasl_passwd file should be restricted:

```
sudo chmod 600 /etc/postfix/sasl_passwd /etc/postfix/sasl_passwd.db
```

Several additional settings refine the behavior of the Postfix daemon. The parameter inet_interfaces controls which network interfaces the server listens on. For a server that is intended to receive mail only on localhost, this can be set to:

```
inet_interfaces = loopback-only
```

Alternatively, for full network access, it can be configured as:

```
inet_interfaces = all
```

Another vital configuration descriptor is the mynetworks parameter, which defines the list of trusted networks allowed to relay mail without authentication. A typical local network might be specified as follows:

```
mynetworks = 127.0.0.0/8, [::1]/128
```

For environments with additional internal IP ranges, these can be appended accordingly. Postfix administrators must be cautious with this parameter since overly broad definitions may allow unauthorized relay usages, potentially turning the server into an open relay, which is a common vector for spam distribution.

Logging and debugging are important aspects of initial setup. Configuring the verbosity and format of log output can aid in troubleshooting potential issues during mail processing. The default logging behavior is often sufficient, but administrators may choose to adjust the debug parameters temporarily for diagnostic purposes. For instance, increasing the verbosity of SMTP transactions is possible by modifying the following fields:

```
debug_peer_level = 2
smtp_connect_timeout = 30s
```

After making configuration changes, it is necessary to reload the Postfix service. This step updates the running configuration without interrupting existing sessions. The reload command is generally executed as follows:

```
sudo systemctl reload postfix
```

Or, in systems that utilize traditional service commands:

```
sudo service postfix reload
```

It is advisable to verify the running configuration using the postconf command. This command summarizes the current settings, allowing an administrator to inspect and confirm that all parameters have been correctly applied. For example:

```
postconf | grep '^myhostname\|^relayhost'
```

The output should match the intended configuration values, affirming that the settings have been successfully integrated.

In addition to the primary configuration file, the master.cf file controls the daemon processes that Postfix runs. Although the default configuration in master.cf typically suffices for minimal installations, there are scenarios where customizing service definitions can enhance performance or security. Each service definition within master.cf details process attributes such as the command to execute, listening ports, and operational parameters. For instance, if an administrator intends to modify the SMTP service to incorporate TLS support or change its operational parameters, the corresponding line can be adjusted. Example modifications in master.cf might appear as:

```
smtp      inet  n       -       y       -       -       smtpd
```

```
-o smtpd_tls_security_level=encrypt
```

Such inline service definitions force Postfix to encrypt sessions even if client capabilities are limited. Adjustments to master.cf should be made judiciously; each change requires validation through the reloading of the configuration followed by a review of the logs to ensure that no service disruptions occur.

During initial testing of the configuration, it is advisable to send test emails internally as well as externally. Using command-line utilities such as sendmail or mail ensures that the default queue processing, error handling, and SMTP authentication settings are correctly established. A simple test message can be sent with the following command:

```
echo "Test email body" | mail -s "Postfix Test" recipient@example.com
```

Following the dispatch, reviewing the mail logs using tools like tail assists in confirming that the message was processed appropriately. Output from recent mail transactions may be observed as follows:

```
sudo tail -n 50 /var/log/mail.log
```

Inspection of the log file should reveal successful connections, proper authentication (if applicable), and confirmation of mail queue processing. Any errors noted in the log will indicate areas that require revision in the configuration files.

Security configurations remain a focal point post-installation. Beyond basic authentication and network restrictions, it is essential to validate that Postfix correctly enforces policies for outbound connections. For example, configuring header checks to prevent spoofing is achievable via regular expression definitions in external files. Such files are integrated via the header_checks parameter:

```
header_checks = regexp:/etc/postfix/header_checks
```

Content within the referenced file /etc/postfix/header_checks

54

might include rules to reject emails with forged sender addresses. After editing, the file should be processed into the required format using the postmap command. Consistent review of these policy rules is instrumental in maintaining a secure email environment.

Initial configuration further benefits from testing various mail scenarios. Simulated inbound and outbound email transmissions help in verifying that all relay and routing decisions are made in accordance with the defined rules. It is prudent to simulate errors, such as sending mail from unauthorized networks, to ensure that Postfix appropriately denies the request. Each rejection and acceptance recorded in the logs confirms that the configuration is functioning as designed.

Finally, documenting every change made during the initial configuration phase yields benefits for future troubleshooting and maintenance. This documentation should include copies of the modified files, records of any custom settings, and a log of troubleshooting steps. The benefit of such documentation becomes especially evident when planning upgrades or integrating additional features such as spam filters and antivirus scanners. Integrative configurations are easier to implement when a clear baseline of the default settings is preserved.

By methodically addressing hostname resolution, domain settings, relay configurations, security policies, and service definitions, the system is aligned for reliable operation. A correctly configured Postfix installation underpins an efficient and secure email service, facilitating robust mail routing with minimal downtime and enhanced protection against unauthorized usage.

2.4. Testing the Installation

After configuring Postfix, systematic testing is crucial for verifying that the mail system is operating as expected. Testing encompasses verifying both basic and advanced functionalities such as sending and receiving emails, handling relays, verifying authentication, and ensuring secure communication. The testing process integrates practical command-line utilities, log reviews, and network diagnostics, which together provide a robust framework for assessing the health of the installation.

One of the primary tests is to send a simple email message using the command-line utilities installed with Postfix. The sendmail interface is a common tool for this purpose. Administrators can craft a simple message from the terminal to verify that the message is handled correctly by the mail queue. For example, the following command sends an email to a local user:

```
echo "This is a test email from Postfix." | sendmail -v user@example.
   com
```

The output from sendmail typically provides verbose details about message delivery steps including handshakes, queue creation, and final dispatch. This output is fundamental in confirming that the basic communication channels are active.

For systems that use the mail command, a test email can also be dispatched using:

```
echo "Postfix installation test." | mail -s "Test Email" user@example
   .com
```

Following the test dispatch, examining the mail log files is an essential step in verifying that emails are correctly processed. The log files, generally located in /var/log/mail.log on many Linux distributions, capture detailed information about each transaction. To review the mail service logs, an administrator may use:

```
sudo tail -n 50 /var/log/mail.log
```

This command displays the most recent 50 lines of the log file, which

56

should include entries confirming successful connections, authentication details (if applicable), and the eventual relay of messages. Successful log entries often contain key phrases such as "status=sent" or "queued as", indicating that the email has been processed.

A complementary method for testing is to use the `telnet` command to simulate an SMTP session. This approach facilitates a hands-on review of how Postfix handles connection requests and command responses. If connecting via `telnet` to the SMTP port (typically port 25) on the host, the following sequence illustrates a basic interaction:

```
telnet localhost 25
EHLO localhost
MAIL FROM:<sender@example.com>
RCPT TO:<recipient@example.com>
DATA
Subject: Postfix Test

This is a test message.
.
QUIT
```

This manual session verifies that the SMTP dialog is functioning correctly by emulating a simple mail transfer. The responses from the server, such as "250 OK" after each command, indicate that the system is processing the commands accurately. Any deviation from expected responses highlights areas that require additional troubleshooting.

For environments in which authentication has been configured, testing SASL integration is essential. Administrators can simulate an authenticated session by using command-line tools that support SMTP authentication. While manual testing via `telnet` is possible by sending appropriate authentication commands, tools like swaks (Swiss Army Knife for SMTP) simplify this process. An example command using swaks to test an authenticated session is:

```
swaks --to recipient@example.com --from sender@example.com --server
    localhost --auth LOGIN --auth-user sender@example.com --auth-
    password secret
```

The output from swaks provides a detailed transcript of the authentication and email dispatch process. This transcript should confirm that credentials are accepted and that the email message follows through successfully. Such testing validates the store and processing of credentials in the /etc/postfix/sasl_passwd file and confirms that associated security restrictions are in place.

TLS encryption is another critical component in ensuring secure mail transmission. Testing for TLS requires verifying that the Postfix server can negotiate encrypted connections. This can be done by connecting to the server with openssl s_client:

```
openssl s_client -starttls smtp -connect localhost:25
```

This command initiates a connection to the Postfix server and attempts to establish a TLS session. The output from openssl s_client includes certificate details and information about the negotiated cipher. An absence of certificate errors and a successful handshake indicate that TLS is configured properly. Verifying these settings is critical especially when the server is intended for production use, as encrypted connections protect against eavesdropping and man-in-the-middle attacks.

Another important testing method involves examining the status of the Postfix service through system-level utilities. Commands such as:

```
sudo systemctl status postfix
```

provide a snapshot of the current state of the service, including its uptime and any recent error messages. If the system uses traditional service management, the following command may be used:

```
sudo service postfix status
```

Such status outputs should indicate that Postfix is active and running normally. Should any errors or failure indications appear, they offer the first clues for troubleshooting further. In this context, using

58

`journalctl` on systemd-based systems also allows for more detailed log investigations:

```
sudo journalctl -u postfix --since "1 hour ago"
```

This command retrieves system logs for Postfix, offering deeper insight into issues that may have occurred during recent operations.

Testing the configuration also involves confirming that native file permissions and mailbox directories are correctly set up. Misconfigured file permissions can lead to failures in queue management or delivery issues. Administrative commands such as:

```
sudo postconf -n
```

yield a summary of non-default Postfix configurations which can be checked against expected values. Reviewing this output ensures that no unintended configuration items exist. Additionally, ensuring that directories like `/var/spool/postfix` have the correct ownership and permissions is fundamental to the secure operation of the mail server.

Simulated error testing serves as an integral aspect of post-installation verification. For example, intentionally sending an email from an unauthorized domain or through a network not included in the `mynetworks` setting allows administrators to confirm that proper rejection and logging are in place. Such tests, while deliberately producing errors, validate that security safeguards are effective. The rejection responses, when inspected in the log files, demonstrate that Postfix is correctly enforcing relay restrictions.

In some cases, administrators may opt to create custom test scripts to automate a series of SMTP transactions. These scripts can be executed periodically to verify that Postfix continues to run as expected. An example Python script using the `smtplib` library is as follows:

```python
import smtplib
from email.mime.text import MIMEText
```

```
msg = MIMEText("This is an automated test from Postfix.")
msg['Subject'] = 'Automated Test Email'
msg['From'] = 'sender@example.com'
msg['To'] = 'recipient@example.com'

try:
    server = smtplib.SMTP('localhost', 25)
    server.ehlo()
    server.sendmail(msg['From'], [msg['To']], msg.as_string())
    server.quit()
    print("Test email sent successfully.")
except Exception as e:
    print("Error sending test email:", e)
```

Executing this script provides an automated approach to not only test the SMTP connection but also simulate repeated transactions to gauge performance under load. The output of the script, whether successful or not, informs administrators about the robustness of transport mechanisms.

Integration of these testing mechanisms into a continuous monitoring strategy adds resilience to the email system. Regularly scheduled tests ensure that changes in configuration, system updates, or new security policies do not inadvertently disrupt mail services. For instance, incorporating these tests into a cron job can help maintain operational oversight:

```
*/10 * * * * /usr/local/bin/test_postfix.sh >> /var/log/postfix_test.
    log 2>&1
```

This cron entry runs a test script every ten minutes and logs the output to a dedicated file for future reference. Examining the log file regularly helps in early detection of anomalies such as intermittent connection failures or unauthorized access attempts.

Testing also extends to ensuring that Postfix handles various delivery scenarios appropriately. This includes internal email routing, external relaying, and bounce-back scenarios when recipient addresses are invalid. Simulating these conditions allows administrators to verify that

60

error messages are correctly generated and that bounce messages are routed appropriately. Analyzing the header information and delivery timestamps can reveal discrepancies that might indicate deeper configuration issues.

Careful documentation of the testing process and its results is advised for ongoing system maintenance. Logs of test execution, combined with configuration snapshots, provide a historical record that can be useful during troubleshooting or when planning upgrades. Documentation should capture not only successful transactions but also the details of any errors encountered and the steps taken to remedy them.

Systematic and rigorous testing of the Postfix installation confirms that the settings applied in previous steps are operational. It serves as both a safeguard against configuration drift and a proactive measure to ensure continuous mail service reliability. The procedures described here collectively establish a dependable framework for verifying that Postfix is fully operational and that all integrated components, from TLS encryption to authentication mechanisms, are performing as intended. Run failed with status: failed

2.5. Starting and Stopping Postfix Service

Controlling the Postfix service is a fundamental operation that ensures the mail transfer agent (MTA) operates reliably in production as well as in development environments. Effective service management encompasses starting, stopping, restarting, and reloading the Postfix service, each of which plays a critical role in managing changes and troubleshooting potential issues. This section details the essential commands and methodologies used to control the service, leveraging both modern systemd utilities and traditional service management scripts where applicable.

The primary utility in contemporary Linux distributions is `systemctl`, which is used to manage system services under systemd. The command to start the Postfix service is:

```
sudo systemctl start postfix
```

Starting the service initiates all defined Postfix processes in the background, and this command is particularly useful after an installation or when the system reboots. Always verifying that the service has initiated correctly is a prudent step; the status command provides immediate feedback on the operational state:

```
sudo systemctl status postfix
```

The output indicates whether Postfix is active or inactive, lists its process ID(s), and displays any error messages that may point to initialization issues.

Stopping the Postfix service is equally critical, especially during maintenance windows or when applying configuration changes. It is advisable to gracefully stop the service to allow the processing of ongoing transactions before shutting down the service completely. With systemd, the stop command is used as follows:

```
sudo systemctl stop postfix
```

Stopping ensures that the daemon processes cease accepting new connections while completing active transactions. In environments where the legacy SysVinit system is used, a similar command exists:

```
sudo service postfix stop
```

Restarting the service is a common operation following configuration adjustments or system updates. A restart sequence stops the active service and starts a new instance, thereby applying any new settings contained in the configuration files. With systemd, the command is:

```
sudo systemctl restart postfix
```

For distributions still dependent on older system management frameworks, the restart operation is similarly carried out using:

```
sudo service postfix restart
```

It is important to note that restarting the service follows a full shutdown and initiation cycle, momentarily interrupting service. In environments with high mail traffic, alternative approaches such as reloading the configuration may be preferable.

The reload functionality is designed to update the configuration parameters without halting active connections. This minimizes disruptions and allows changes to take effect immediately. In systemd, the reload procedure is executed as:

```
sudo systemctl reload postfix
```

Alternatively, if the service management environment is based on SysVinit scripts, a similar reload command is available:

```
sudo service postfix reload
```

Reloading is particularly advantageous when adjustments to the main.cf or master.cf files are made. It is advisable to always check the configuration for syntax or logic errors before reloading the service. Verification of configuration files can be performed with the postconf utility, as in:

```
postconf -n
```

This command displays only the non-default parameters, allowing administrators to quickly verify that changes are correctly applied without reloading the complete settings list.

In multi-service environments or systems that use containerized deployments, custom scripts and orchestration tools may be used to control the Postfix service. For instance, Docker containers running Postfix typically include a startup script that integrates the service start command with additional health-check logic. A sample Dockerfile snippet that starts Postfix in a container is:

```
FROM debian:latest
RUN apt-get update && apt-get install -y postfix
COPY main.cf /etc/postfix/main.cf
CMD ["postfix", "start-fg"]
```

In this example, the `start-fg` command runs Postfix in the foreground, which is suitable for environments managed by container orchestration platforms. This approach simplifies integration with external monitoring tools that track container logs and health indicators.

Beyond simple start and stop operations, monitoring the Postfix service ensures ongoing reliability. Regularly checking the status with commands such as:

```
sudo systemctl status postfix
```

or using `journalctl` to review system logs:

```
sudo journalctl -u postfix --since "5 minutes ago"
```

helps detect any emerging issues such as service crashes or failure to restart upon configuration errors. It is also recommended to inspect the mail log file, usually located at `/var/log/mail.log`, to corroborate the operational logs with the system status.

Understanding the difference between a restart and a reload is integral to Postfix service management. A restart halts all active processes and initiates new ones, thereby ensuring that all changes are incorporated. However, this operation temporarily disrupts mail processing. Conversely, a reload signals the active processes to re-read their configuration files while continuing to process active connections. In systems where uptime is critical, deploying a reload rather than a restart reduces service disruption and maintains a consistent state for mail delivery.

In scenarios where Postfix experiences issues on startup or displays irregular behavior in the logs, administrators may need to perform a series of investigative steps. A common approach involves stopping the service, performing configuration verification, and then starting it anew. For example, it is beneficial to first check for syntax errors in the configuration files:

```
postfix check
```

This command scans the configuration and queues for potential issues. Resolving errors identified during the check can prevent the service from failing to start or causing interruptions during mail processing.

From an operational standpoint, incorporating these commands into automated scripts can enhance the manageability of the mail system. System administrators may include service control in scheduled maintenance scripts or integrate them into server monitoring platforms such as Nagios, Zabbix, or Prometheus. An example shell script to verify service status and restart if necessary is:

```
#!/bin/bash
STATUS=$(systemctl is-active postfix)
if [ "$STATUS" != "active" ]; then
    echo "Postfix is $STATUS. Attempting restart..."
    sudo systemctl restart postfix
    if [ $? -eq 0 ]; then
        echo "Postfix restarted successfully."
    else
        echo "Failed to restart Postfix. Please check logs."
    fi
else
    echo "Postfix is running normally."
fi
```

Such scripts can be scheduled via cron jobs, ensuring that the mail service is self-healing and that administrators are alerted immediately when manual intervention is required.

Differences in underlying system architecture also influence service control commands. For example, on BSD systems, managing Postfix relies on updating system configuration files, such as enabling the service in /etc/rc.conf. A typical BSD configuration might include the following line:

```
postfix_enable="YES"
```

After setting this parameter, starting and stopping Postfix generally mirrors the Linux command approach, though the specific commands may differ slightly based on the BSD variant's service management framework.

When managing a production environment, detailed logging and active monitoring become indispensable. Postfix logs provide not only a record of all mail transactions but also the diagnostics necessary to troubleshoot startup and shutdown sequences. Reviewing logs immediately after a restart or reload can reveal transient errors or warnings that might otherwise be overlooked. It is not uncommon to observe intermittent errors during restarts, which may indicate a need for further configuration tuning or even hardware resource adjustments.

Ensuring that service control commands are executed with the appropriate privileges is also crucial. Most administrative commands for starting, stopping, or restarting Postfix require elevated privileges, and using sudo ensures that these commands are executed with the necessary authority. In highly secured environments, permission models might restrict even administrative users from executing such commands without additional authentication steps, necessitating careful review of security policies.

Integration with configuration management tools like Ansible, Puppet, or Chef further enhances control over the Postfix service. These tools allow centralized management of service states across a fleet of servers. For example, an Ansible playbook task to restart Postfix may resemble the following:

```
- name: Restart Postfix service
```

```
service:
  name: postfix
  state: restarted
```

Such tasks ensure that administrators can deploy uniform configurations and execute service restarts across multiple systems simultaneously, thereby reducing human error and ensuring operational consistency.

Documenting operational procedures, including the specific commands and their expected outputs, aids in establishing best practices for system administration. Clear documentation ensures that new team members or system administrators can quickly become proficient in managing the Postfix service. Every procedure—from initial service start and runtime monitoring to controlled shutdowns and restarts—should be meticulously recorded and periodically reviewed to incorporate changes from software updates or evolving operational requirements.

The commands and methods delineated above constitute a comprehensive framework for managing the Postfix service effectively. Mastering these techniques guarantees that the MTA remains responsive to configuration changes, is capable of recovering from transient errors, and maintains a high level of service availability. Whether operating in a small-scale environment or a large, distributed system, the ability to control Postfix systematically is essential for ensuring a stable and secure email infrastructure.

Chapter 3

Basic Configuration of Postfix

This chapter delves into configuring key Postfix settings, starting with critical files like main.cf and master.cf. It covers domain and host configurations, transport and relay settings, and the creation of mail aliases. By understanding queue management and implementing basic security, you'll establish a robust foundation for your email server, ensuring efficient mail handling and enhanced security from the outset.

3.1. Understanding Main.cf and Master.cf

The Postfix mail server relies on two primary configuration files, `main.cf` and `master.cf`, to define its operational behavior. These files determine everything from mail routing policies to the behavior of individual daemons. In this section, we explore the structure, content,

69

and interplay of these configurations, discussing how they contribute to a robust and manageable mail system. This discussion builds on previous content regarding basic settings and domain configurations, extending that foundational understanding to the core operational parameters of Postfix.

The `main.cf` file is the central configuration file of Postfix. It specifies global parameters and policies that govern the behavior of the mail server. The file is written in a simple key-value format where each parameter is set on a separate line. Parameters may include mail routing rules, security settings, performance tuning options, and general system parameters. Because `main.cf` is responsible for directing the overall behavior of Postfix, its settings must be crafted with precision. A typical entry might resemble the following:

```
myhostname = mail.example.com
mydomain = example.com
myorigin = $mydomain
inet_interfaces = all
mydestination = $myhostname, localhost.$mydomain, localhost,
    $mydomain
```

Each directive in this snippet plays a crucial role. For instance, `myhostname` defines the fully qualified domain name of the server, while `mydomain` and `myorigin` set the parameters for mail origin addresses. The parameter `inet_interfaces` controls the network interfaces Postfix listens on, and `mydestination` lists the domains for which the server should accept mail. The flexible nature of these settings allows administrators to tailor the server to both small-scale and enterprise-level environments.

In addition to defining basic mail routing, `main.cf` offers extensive control over security and performance. Parameters such as `smtpd_tls_cert_file` and `smtpd_tls_key_file` enable Transport Layer Security (TLS) for encrypted mail delivery, ensuring the secure exchange of email between servers. Similarly, the configuration may include directives related to access control and rejection policies, helping to mitigate spam and unauthorized access. Within `main.cf`, an administrator could enforce policies by using parameters like:

```
smtpd_banner = $myhostname ESMTP
smtpd_recipient_restrictions = permit_mynetworks,
    reject_unauth_destination
```

Here, the `smtpd_banner` provides a custom greeting message during SMTP sessions, while `smtpd_recipient_restrictions` specifies a sequence of checks to ensure that mail is only accepted from authorized networks. A careful balance between flexibility and security is achieved by correctly ordering these restrictions.

Unlike `main.cf`, which focuses on global policies and parameter definitions, the `master.cf` file details the daemon processes and service configurations that run in the background. This file essentially acts as a process supervision table where each line corresponds to a service that Postfix can run. The file lists commands, arguments, and configurations for each daemon, allowing tailored control over service behavior. A typical excerpt from `master.cf` is:

```
smtp       inet  n       -       n       -       -       smtpd
submission inet  n       -       n       -       -       smtpd
smtps      inet  n       -       n       -       -       smtpd
```

Each of these entries specifies that the SMTP, submission, and SMTPS services are handled by the `smtpd` daemon. The fields in each line indicate the service name, the socket type, the number of processes, chroot settings, process limits, and the command to execute. Working with `master.cf` enables the administrator to adjust resource allocation and modify daemon behavior, critical functions in high-load environments where performance is paramount.

The relationship between `main.cf` and `master.cf` is integral to the functioning of Postfix. While `main.cf` sets out the parameters and global policies that govern mail processing, `master.cf` defines the ac-

71

tual mechanisms by which these policies are implemented. Consider a scenario where a system administrator must enable TLS encryption for incoming connections. The corresponding settings in main.cf ensure that TLS is supported, but it is the definition of the SMTP daemon in master.cf that enforces the implementation. In such a case, both configuration files must be modified in harmony. A typical adjustment could involve setting trust and restriction parameters in main.cf, followed by verifying that the corresponding service in master.cf references the appropriate executable options.

Postfix's modular design means that administrators may need to customize individual services without altering the global mail policies. The flexibility inherent in separating these configurations enables targeted adjustments. The master.cf file includes the ability to override default command-line parameters for daemons. If services need to be restarted with different resource limits or additional logging options, an administrator can modify the specific service line directly. For example:

```
pickup     fifo  n          -        n     60     1       pickup -v
```

This configuration not only defines the pickup service as a FIFO queue process but also appends a verbose flag (-v) to assist with debugging. The use of detailed logging can be essential during periods of system troubleshooting or performance tuning. The specificity offered by master.cf facilitates granular control over individual components, making it a vital tool for system administrators seeking to optimize their mail servers.

Both main.cf and master.cf support comments, allowing administrators to document configuration decisions. Each comment begins with a # symbol, and careful annotation helps maintain clarity as configurations evolve over time. A well-commented configuration file reduces the likelihood of errors during future modifications. For example:

```
# Set the primary hostname for this mail server.
myhostname = mail.example.com

# Define domains for which this server will accept mail.
mydestination = $myhostname, localhost, example.com
```

Consistent documentation in these files is critical, particularly in environments where multiple administrators manage the server over time. The clear delineation of parameters and service definitions minimizes the risk of misconfiguration.

The syntactical simplicity of these configuration files belies their deep influence on the behavior of Postfix. While the key-value style of main.cf ensures that parameter settings are explicit and easily modified, the structured format of master.cf offers a transparent look at the process management of the mail system. This design allows administrators to perform both routine maintenance and in-depth performance tuning without the overhead of a more complex configuration management system. The explicitness of these files reduces ambiguity and fosters a clear understanding of how email flows through the system.

Experienced administrators often implement conditional configurations based on network or load conditions. Although Postfix's configuration does not natively support conditional statements, the use of multiple configuration files combined with include directives allows for modular setups. For instance, an administrator can maintain separate configuration files for testing and production environments, referencing these files within main.cf as needed. This technique helps manage complexity while preserving system reliability. Consolidated configuration management practices contribute to a scalable and adaptable mail system.

When making changes to either configuration file, it is essential to reload the Postfix daemon to apply updates. This process can be executed with the command:

```
postfix reload
```

Reloading the configuration ensures that updated parameters and modified service definitions take effect immediately. Reliable application of changes is crucial in production environments, giving administrators the flexibility to adapt the server to evolving requirements without requiring a full service restart that might disrupt mail delivery.

The interplay between main.cf and master.cf reflects the broader principle of modularity in system configuration. Each file serves a distinct yet complementary role, with main.cf establishing the policy framework and master.cf defining the operational pathways. Mastery of both files is foundational to effective email server management, as even minor misconfigurations can yield significant implications for mail delivery, security, and overall system performance.

Maintaining a balance between flexibility and stability is intrinsically linked to the precision involved in editing these configuration files. Administrators must evaluate the impact of each parameter in context, considering both current needs and future scalability. The intentional separation of global policy (main.cf) from daemon configurations (master.cf) allows administrators to isolate and address issues efficiently. Each file contributes to the overall reliability and maintainability of the mail system, emphasizing the importance of thorough understanding in managing large-scale implementations.

By integrating detailed annotations, properly formatted entries, and a keen awareness of both file structures, administrators can effectively manage complex mail server tasks. The guidance provided by these configuration files supports not only the immediate operation of the server but also lays the groundwork for future enhancements as administrative needs evolve. The robust design philosophy of Postfix, visible in the separation of responsibilities between main.cf and master.cf, provides both the precision and scope necessary for modern mail systems.

The careful curation of these two configuration files demonstrates that robust email management is a function of clear parameter definitions and well-structured process management. Through deliberate modifications and a comprehensive understanding of the configuration syntax, administrators can optimize mail routing and process handling, ensuring a mail server that consistently performs under varied operating conditions. The cumulative understanding of these mechanisms enhances the administrator's ability to design, implement, and refine a secure and efficient mail processing system.

3.2. Configuring Domains and Hosts

Configuring domains and hosts is a critical aspect of Postfix administration, as it determines how incoming and outgoing mail is treated, routed, and delivered. In a Postfix server, domains and hostnames are set primarily through parameters in the `main.cf` file. These parameters include, but are not limited to, `myhostname`, `mydomain`, `myorigin`, and `mydestination`. The proper configuration of these parameters distinguishes between external mail delivery and internal mail routing, ensuring that messages are correctly classified and handled according to domain-specific policies.

A central parameter is `myhostname`, which defines the fully qualified domain name (FQDN) of the mail server. This parameter is used as the primary identity of the server when it interacts with external systems. For example:

```
myhostname = mail.example.com
```

In this configuration, `mail.example.com` must resolve through DNS and have valid MX records defined. The DNS records ensure that mail

75

sent to addresses within the example.com domain can locate the correct mail server. A complementary parameter is mydomain, which sets the primary domain name for the server. Often, this is set explicitly or derived from myhostname, as shown below:

```
mydomain = example.com
```

The myorigin parameter controls the domain that appears in email addresses for outgoing mail. This is particularly important when the server processes mail from local users and ensures that outgoing messages have a consistent domain. For instance:

```
myorigin = $mydomain
```

Another essential parameter is mydestination. This list defines the domains for which the Postfix server should accept mail as local delivery. Proper configuration of mydestination distinguishes local domains from those intended for relay. Consider the following example:

```
mydestination = $myhostname, localhost.$mydomain, localhost, example.
    com
```

In this configuration, mail addressed to any of the defined names is delivered locally. However, if mail is received for a domain not listed here, Postfix treats it as a candidate for relay, subject to relay policies defined elsewhere in the configuration.

Advanced configurations may require the separation of internal and external domains. For organizations operating multiple domains or handling subdomains, the use of parameters such as virtual_mailbox_domains proves advantageous. This parameter allows the administrator to define a set of domains that are processed as virtual mailboxes rather than traditional local accounts. A typical configuration might appear as follows:

```
virtual_mailbox_domains = example.com, sub.example.com
```

Here, both the primary domain and its subdomain are designated for

76

virtual mailbox handling, enabling the server to store mail in dedicated mailbox directories corresponding to each domain. This is particularly useful for hosting services where users from distinct domains require isolated mail storage.

The `transport` table is another important mechanism for managing domain-specific mail delivery. This table allows administrators to define different delivery transport methods for distinct domains. For instance, mail for one domain might be delivered locally, while another domain requires a relay to an external server. A sample entry in the transport table is:

```
example.net   smtp:[relay.example.net]
```

This configuration instructs Postfix to use the SMTP protocol to relay mail for `example.net` to another server at `relay.example.net`. To integrate this table with the main configuration, the following line is added to `main.cf`:

```
transport_maps = hash:/etc/postfix/transport
```

After editing the transport file, it is necessary to compile it using the `postmap` command:

```
postmap /etc/postfix/transport
```

This command creates the required binary hash file that Postfix utilizes for efficient lookup during mail processing.

For systems managing a large number of domains or employing policy-based routing, the use of canonical maps, such as `sender_canonical_maps` and `recipient_canonical_maps`, provides additional flexibility. These maps are useful when rewriting email addresses as messages pass through the mail server. A canonical mapping might transform a local username to a properly formatted email address by appending the appropriate domain name:

```
user1      user1@example.com
```

77

```
user2       user2@example.com
```

To enable canonical mapping in Postfix, the following configuration is added:

```
sender_canonical_maps = hash:/etc/postfix/sender_canonical
```

After modifying the canonical mappings, the postmap command is again used to compile these maps. Integration of canonical maps into the overall configuration is essential when operating in environments where email address rewriting is required for compatibility with external systems or when ensuring consistency in internal email representations.

The configuration of domains and hosts is also influenced by external factors, such as Domain Name System (DNS) settings and the proper formation of mail exchange (MX) records. For proper external mail delivery, the mail server must have valid DNS entries. This includes an MX record for the domain, pointing to the FQDN defined in myhostname. For example, the DNS configuration might include:

example.com.	IN	MX	10	mail.example.com.
mail.example.com.	IN	A	192.0.2.1	

These DNS entries ensure that mail sent to example.com correctly finds the mail server and that the IP address associated with the server is resolvable by other mail systems. The interplay between DNS and Postfix configuration cannot be overstated, as misconfigured DNS records often lead to mail delivery failures or security vulnerabilities.

Customization of hostnames also plays a significant role in the identification and management of mail servers. When a mail server processes mail from multiple domains or operates as part of a cluster of servers, the hostname must be managed carefully to avoid conflicts. The system hostname, typically set in the operating system, should align with the myhostname parameter in Postfix. A mismatch can result in incon-

78

sistent behavior, especially during TLS certificate negotiations where the certificate common name must match the server's advertised hostname.

When configuring DNS and hostnames, administrators may incorporate additional checks or scripts to verify that the server is correctly identified across network interfaces. A typical diagnostic command to ensure proper hostname resolution is:

```
hostname -f
```

This command returns the server's fully qualified domain name, which should match the value specified in myhostname. Discrepancies here might indicate underlying configuration issues in the operating system or in the network DNS settings.

Further granular control over host configurations is possible by segregating configuration directives based on the interface used for specific mail flows. For example, separate configurations can be applied for mail received on the external interface versus internal network interfaces. Postfix allows administrators to adjust parameters dynamically, using separate settings for different mail flows. Although Postfix does not support conditional configurations directly within main.cf, the use of multiple configuration files and include directives can simulate conditional behavior in complex deployments.

For multi-domain hosting, administrators should consider employing the virtual aliasing system. The virtual alias mapping enables redirection of mail addressed to one domain to a different address, facilitating scenarios such as shared hosting environments or domain migrations. A virtual alias file might contain entries structured as follows:

```
info@example.com      user1
support@example.com   user2
```

To activate these mappings, the configuration in main.cf is updated:

```
virtual_alias_maps = hash:/etc/postfix/virtual
```

Subsequent compilation of the virtual alias file ensures that Postfix leverages these mappings during mail delivery:

```
postmap /etc/postfix/virtual
```

Optimizing the configuration of domains and hosts is not limited to file edits and DNS records. Administrators must also consider the security and policy implications of how domains are managed. Enforcing strict controls on which domains are accepted for local delivery can mitigate the risk of unauthorized use of the mail server, reducing exposure to spam relay and other malicious activities. For instance, by carefully managing the mydestination and relay_domains parameters, it is possible to create a firewall-like effect that limits which domains are trusted.

relay_domains explicitly lists domains for which the server is willing to relay mail. This is particularly useful when handling trusted partners or remote servers that require reliable mail routing without compromising security. An illustrative configuration might include:

```
relay_domains = partnerdomain.com, anothertrusted.com
```

In addition to explicit domain listings, administrators should incorporate robust logging and monitoring practices to track domain-specific mail flows. Logging settings in Postfix can be tuned to capture detailed information about the processing of mail for various domains, providing critical insights during troubleshooting or performance tuning. For example, increasing verbosity for specific mail flows may reveal misconfigurations or malicious activity.

The configuration of domains and hosts demands that every change be tested in a controlled environment before deployment in a production system. This practice minimizes downtime and ensures that mail routing continues uninterrupted across both internal and external channels. Administrators often script the configuration validation process using tools such as postfix check, which verifies syntax and consistency across configuration files:

```
postfix check
```

Successful validation of the configuration contributes to the overall stability and reliability of the mail server.

The interplay between domain settings and the server's overall identity plays a fundamental role in the functionality of the entire email system. As previous sections have introduced the role of the primary configuration files, the current discussion emphasizes the fine-tuning required to ensure that both internal communications and external mail deliveries are managed effectively. By understanding how to set and customize domains and hostnames, administrators can balance operational requirements with security protocols, ensuring that each message is handled according to its intended path.

A comprehensive understanding of DNS configurations, combined with precise settings in Postfix's various configuration files, empowers administrators to build scalable environments. As mail volume increases, the importance of correctly configured domains and hostnames becomes increasingly pronounced. The catalog of configuration parameters available in Postfix allows operators to adapt to changing requirements and to incorporate best practices that safeguard mail delivery integrity.

The detail-oriented approach to configuring domains and hosts illustrates the necessity of a holistic management strategy. Each parameter serves a distinct purpose, yet they interact collectively to define the operational profile of the mail server. Through rigorous configuration management, systematic testing, and continuous monitoring, the Postfix server can be tailored to accommodate both the routine and exceptional demands of modern email communication.

81

3.3. Defining Transport and Relay Settings

Transport and relay settings in Postfix are crucial for controlling how email is delivered and forwarded within and outside the organization. Transport maps enable administrators to override the default delivery mechanism for specific domains or addresses, while relay settings determine when and how Postfix hands off outgoing mail to remote servers. The interplay of these configurations allows for sophisticated routing policies that enhance both performance and security.

At the heart of configuring transport rules is the transport table. This table maps domain names or email addresses to specific transport methods, allowing the administrator to control the delivery process on a granular level. The mapping file is typically located at /etc/postfix/transport, and its configuration follows a simple key-value format. For example, to specify that mail destined for example.net should be relayed via a different SMTP server, one might add the following entry:

```
example.net     smtp:[relay.example.net]
```

This entry informs Postfix that when mail for the domain example.net is encountered, it should use the SMTP transport method and explicitly relay the message to the server relay.example.net. The square brackets indicate that Postfix should bypass MX record lookups for the destination, using the IP address specified by the relay server instead. Once the transport file is updated, it must be compiled into a hash database using the postmap command:

```
postmap /etc/postfix/transport
```

Integration of the transport map into the main configuration file is accomplished by adding or updating the following directive in the main.cf file:

```
transport_maps = hash:/etc/postfix/transport
```

82

This directive directs Postfix to consult the hash database when determining the appropriate transport for delivering each message. Through transport maps, administrators can effectively segregate mail flow, redirecting specific traffic to alternative delivery paths, third-party MX servers, or even applying specialized handling for sub-domains.

Relay settings complement transport maps by governing which mail is forwarded to external networks. The relay mechanism in Postfix typically comes into play when mail does not belong to a domain that the server hosts locally. Two key parameters, `relayhost` and `relay_domains`, control this behavior. The parameter `relayhost` sets an external server to which all outgoing mail not intended for local delivery is sent. A basic configuration might appear as follows:

```
relayhost = [smtp.relayprovider.com]:587
```

Here, the use of square brackets and the explicit port designation (587) indicate that all non-local mail is relayed through the specified SMTP server. This approach centralizes outbound mail handling, often enabling additional security, logging, or policy enforcement by the relay provider.

In environments where selective relaying is more appropriate, the `relay_domains` parameter provides finer control. It allows administrators to specify a list of domains that are eligible for relaying. This is particularly useful in scenarios where the mail server is used solely for sending mail for certain trusted domains, while rejecting relaying requests for unapproved destinations. Consider the following configuration:

```
relay_domains = example.org, partner.com
```

This entry ensures that only mail addressed to `example.org` and `partner.com` will be relayed outside the local network. Messages sent to any other domain will be subject to the default handling rules, which might include local delivery or further routing according to the transport maps.

Security is a primary concern when configuring relay settings. Open relays, which allow arbitrary users to have their emails sent through the server, are a common vulnerability exploited by spammers. Postfix counteracts this risk by carefully enforcing recipient restrictions. The smtpd_recipient_restrictions directive in main.cf is typically configured to validate that the sender of a message is authorized to use the relay function. A common setup might include the following restrictions:

```
smtpd_recipient_restrictions =
    permit_mynetworks ,
    reject_unauth_destination ,
    permit_sasl_authenticated
```

In this configuration, mail from trusted networks is allowed, while unauthenticated requests for destinations outside of configured domains are rejected. The inclusion of permit_sasl_authenticated permits authenticated users to relay mail irrespective of network origin, granting flexibility while maintaining a secure perimeter against abuse.

When configuring relay settings, it is common to use transport maps in combination with sender or recipient restrictions to create robust policies. For instance, an organization might designate internal traffic to follow one path while applying a different relay for external traffic based on sender authentication. By combining transport rule definitions with authentication policies, an administrator can design mail flows that segregate traffic types efficiently. Detailed logging is recommended when implementing such complex routing strategies. Increasing logging verbosity during initial deployment helps in diagnosing issues, and the following command can be used to monitor mail flow:

```
postfix set-permissions
```

Alongside logging, testing the configurations is integral to ensuring the desired behavior. Postfix provides a built-in command to validate its configuration files without interrupting service, which is especially useful when deploying updates to transport and relay rules:

```
postfix check
```

Administrators can further simulate mail flow by sending test messages and scrutinizing log files, typically located in /var/log/mail.log or /var/log/maillog. Automated scripts can assist in comparing expected relay behavior against actual logs, highlighting misconfigurations quickly.

For environments that require dynamic routing, administrators might also integrate policy servers with Postfix. In such scenarios, external policy servers are queried during the SMTP dialogue to determine if a message should be relayed or what transport it should use. Policy delegation involves the use of Postfix's built-in support for external programs, which can be configured in the master.cf file to intervene in the SMTP session. For instance, the following configuration excerpt demonstrates how a policy service might be used:

```
policy    unix  -      n      n      -      0      spawn
    user=postfix argv=/usr/local/bin/policy-service
```

In the above configuration, the policy service is spawned for each incoming SMTP connection. The external script or application (/usr/local/bin/policy-service) is then responsible for implementing complex, real-time decisions about message relaying and transport selection. Such setups are particularly useful in large organizations or service providers where relay decisions may depend on current network loads or external threat intelligence. It is imperative that such policy services are thoroughly tested and optimized to handle the expected volume with minimal delay.

Additionally, Postfix supports the use of recipient-dependent and sender-dependent relay settings. These configurations allow differences in handling based on the origin or destination of messages. For instance, an administrator can specify different relay hosts for different senders using the `sender_dependent_relayhost_maps` parameter. An example configuration is as follows:

```
sender_dependent_relayhost_maps = hash:/etc/postfix/sender_relay
```

An entry in `/etc/postfix/sender_relay` might look like this:

```
user@example.com     [smtp.specialrelay.com]:587
```

After updating the file, compilation via:

```
postmap /etc/postfix/sender_relay
```

This setup directs mail from a specific sender to a designated relay, thereby enabling differentiated handling based on message origin. Similar mechanisms exist for recipient-dependent configurations. Using such specialized maps provides administrators with a high degree of control, facilitating custom relay paths for priority clients or load balancing among multiple relay servers.

For relay configurations to be optimized, it is essential that the transport and relay settings are considered in conjunction with DNS configurations. Correct DNS entries, particularly MX records and A records, are essential for ensuring that the routing decisions driven by the transport maps correspond to the actual network topology. Testing tools such as `dig` or `nslookup` help verify that DNS configurations align with the intended transport rules. An example command to verify an MX record might be:

```
dig MX example.net
```

This command returns the mail exchange records for the domain `example.net`, ensuring that the DNS settings and the transport maps function in harmony.

The process of defining both transport and relay settings is iterative.

Administrators must continuously assess performance, reliability, and security. In high-volume environments, tuning parameters such as connection timeouts, fallback routing paths, and error handling policies become critical to maintaining overall service integrity. As load increases, making incremental adjustments and thoroughly monitoring the impact can mitigate potential bottlenecks before they affect production operations.

Finally, documentation of relay and transport configurations is fundamental to long-term maintainability. Detailed comments within configuration files, consistent naming conventions in mapping files, and a clear audit trail of configuration changes contribute to a robust operational posture. The careful structuring of transport and relay rules provides a reliable framework that supports both current operational demands and future growth, ensuring that mail routing and delivery remain efficient, secure, and adaptable to changing network conditions. Run failed with status: failed

3.4. Managing Queues and Delivery Settings

The operation of Postfix involves processing, queuing, and ultimately delivering mail messages. A clear understanding of how mail queues are managed and how delivery parameters are adjusted is essential for achieving optimal performance and reliability. Postfix separates its message processing into distinct queues, each serving a specific phase in the delivery process. These queues include the incoming, active, deferred, and hold queues. Tuning the parameters associated with each queue allows administrators to manage load, prioritize urgent messages, and troubleshoot delivery issues.

Postfix's configuration for managing queues is primarily controlled through parameters in `main.cf`. The parameter `queue_directory` specifies where Postfix stores its queues. A typical setting might appear

87

as follows:

```
queue_directory = /var/spool/postfix
```

Setting a custom queue directory can be beneficial in environments with disk space constraints or where dedicated storage performance is required. Administrators must ensure that the specified directory has appropriate permissions and sufficient capacity to handle peak loads.

Several key parameters determine how messages move through the various queues. minimal_backoff_time and maximal_backoff_time control the retry intervals for messages in the deferred queue. These parameters balance the need to recover from transient failures with the necessity of not overwhelming remote systems with rapid retries:

```
minimal_backoff_time = 300s
maximal_backoff_time = 4000s
```

By adjusting these values, administrators can control the time interval between successive delivery attempts. A shorter interval might be suitable in a stable network environment, whereas a longer interval can reduce network load during periods of congestion or when communicating with slow-responding recipient servers.

The message lifetime in queues is determined by the max_idle parameter, which sets the maximum time a message may remain in a queue without activity before Postfix attempts redelivery. This parameter ensures that messages do not linger indefinitely, providing a mechanism to eventually reattempt delivery or bounce the message back to the sender after excessive delays. An example configuration might include:

```
max_idle = 7d
```

In scenarios of high message volume where immediate delivery is critical, administrators might consider reducing the max_idle period. However, this adjustment should be carefully balanced against the alert algorithms and retry mechanisms inherent in Postfix.

88

Active queue management is another essential consideration. The `active_queue_lifetime` parameter governs the lifespan of a message in the active queue. This queue is responsible for scheduling messages that are ready for delivery. If the processing rate is not well-tuned, the active queue may experience a backlog, potentially delaying high-priority messages. An example active queue lifetime might be set as:

```
active_queue_lifetime = 300s
```

Optimizing the active queue can involve fine-tuning the `qmgr_delay` parameter, which dictates the delay between queue management iterations. Modifying this delay can lead to a smoother message flow through the system, particularly under fluctuating load conditions. For example:

```
qmgr_delay = 300s
```

In addition to queue-specific parameters, overall delivery settings can be adjusted to influence the post-processing of emails. Parameter `default_destination_concurrency_limit` defines how many simultaneous connections Postfix allows per destination. A higher concurrency value can be advantageous when delivering to destinations that support multiple connections but may be detrimental if the recipient server imposes strict connection limits. A sample configuration line might be:

```
default_destination_concurrency_limit = 20
```

Similarly, the parameter `max_delivery_attempts` defines how many times Postfix will attempt to deliver a message before considering it undeliverable. In contexts where transient errors are common, an increased number of attempts may improve the likelihood of eventual delivery. However, excessive retries could clog the deferred queue and delay the processing of subsequent messages. An administrator may set this value as follows:

```
max_delivery_attempts = 5
```

Another crucial aspect of performance tuning is managing the rate at which messages are delivered. The `default_dest_rate_delay` parameter introduces a delay between deliveries to the same destination, which can help reduce the load on the recipient's server and avoid triggering rate limiting or spam detection systems. For example:

```
default_dest_rate_delay = 1s
```

For more granular control, the `destination_rate_delay` map can be employed to specify rate delays per destination. This feature is particularly useful in environments where some partners or domains have known performance constraints. A sample map might look like:

```
partner.com    5s
trusted.net    0s
```

Once this map is established, it is integrated into the configuration with the following directive:

```
destination_rate_delay = hash:/etc/postfix/destination_rate_delay
```

After modifying the file, it must be compiled using:

```
postmap /etc/postfix/destination_rate_delay
```

These adjustments ensure that mail delivery is balanced against the responsiveness and capacity of external systems.

Queue management also extends to the handling of deferred mail. Messages that cannot be delivered promptly are moved to the deferred queue. Administrators can configure parameters such as `defer_transports` to control which transport methods are subject to deferral. For example, an organization might wish to defer messages sent via certain protocols while ensuring that others are delivered immediately. A sample configuration could be:

```
defer_transports = error
```

This configuration indicates that messages encountering transient errors in specific transports are deferred rather than being permanently rejected. Monitoring the size and composition of the deferred queue is essential. Tools such as `mailq` and `postqueue -p` provide administrators with diagnostic output detailing the status of pending messages. Regular review of these outputs can highlight patterns of delay and pinpoint configuration or network issues that require intervention.

Advanced queue management involves custom handling for bulk mail traffic versus interactive, real-time communication. The `initial_destination_concurrency_limit` parameter is designed for new destinations and can be adjusted separately from the standard concurrency limit to hasten the establishment of connections without overwhelming target servers. An example setting might be:

```
initial_destination_concurrency_limit = 2
```

This lower limit allows the system to probe remote servers for connection capabilities gradually, after which the limit is increased based on successful deliveries. Such strategies help maintain a balance between aggressive processing and cautious connection formation.

Managing the retry mechanisms within Postfix also involves an understanding of its internal work queue structure. The `minimal_backoff_time` parameter, mentioned earlier, governs the pace at which redelivery attempts are retried. In conjunction with parameters like `maximal_queue_run_time`, administrators can limit the total duration that a particular mail item is actively processed in a single run before being re-queued. This mechanism prevents long-running job delays from adversely affecting the throughput of the entire mail system. A corresponding configuration line might be:

```
maximal_queue_run_time = 3600s
```

The coordination of these parameters is key to avoiding queue congestion. For example, if a high volume of deferred messages builds up due to network congestion, the server's performance can degrade significantly. Systematic adjustments based on real-time monitoring and periodic performance audits enable the mail system to adapt to varying loads without causing inadvertent delays.

Monitoring tools and logging play an indispensable role in queue management. Postfix logs delivery attempts, deferred messages, and errors in detailed log files such as /var/log/mail.log. Administrator scripts can analyze these logs to provide insights into queue trends and adherence to delivery parameters. In production environments, custom monitoring solutions that integrate with system performance dashboards allow administrators to set alerts based on queue sizes or unusual delivery delays.

Regular maintenance of the mail queue is an operational best practice. Flushing the queue using the postfix flush command can expedite the processing of pending messages once underlying issues are resolved. Additionally, periodic cleanup tasks may be necessary to remove stale or undeliverable messages, thus preventing the accumulation of obsolete data that could impair performance. The following command is often used in scheduled maintenance:

```
postsuper -d ALL deferred
```

Implementing such routines helps maintain a lean and efficient queue structure, ensuring that system resources are allocated to current and active messages.

Effective management of Postfix queues and delivery settings requires careful synchronization of multiple configuration parameters. Adjustment of retry intervals, concurrency limits, and delivery delays forms the backbone of optimizing mail processing. Detailed attention to the structure and behavior of each queue stage enhances responsiveness and reliability, enabling the mail system to cope with varying loads and transient issues. By incorporating robust monitoring and maintenance practices, administrators can ensure that the mail system operates within optimal thresholds, delivering messages promptly while minimizing the risk of overdue deliveries.

3.5. Configuring Basic Security Settings

Securing a Postfix mail server is a critical task that involves multiple layers of defense to protect against unauthorized access and mail abuse. Basic security settings are implemented in the main.cf file, and they include measures such as Transport Layer Security (TLS) encryption, authentication, access control, and logging. These settings build on prior configuration sections, ensuring that the mail system is not only efficient and flexible but also resilient against a variety of threats.

A primary layer of defense is the integration of TLS encryption. TLS secures the communication channels between mail servers and clients by encrypting the data transmitted during SMTP sessions. To enable TLS in Postfix, administrators must specify the certificate and key files. The following example illustrates common TLS directives:

```
smtpd_use_tls = yes
smtpd_tls_cert_file = /etc/ssl/certs/postfix_cert.pem
smtpd_tls_key_file = /etc/ssl/private/postfix_key.pem
smtpd_tls_security_level = may
smtpd_tls_protocols = !SSLv2,!SSLv3,!TLSv1
smtpd_tls_mandatory_protocols = TLSv1.2 TLSv1.3
smtpd_tls_auth_only = yes
```

In this configuration, smtpd_use_tls enables TLS for incoming connections, while the certificate and key files provide the credentials required for encryption. The smtpd_tls_security_level parameter is set to may to negotiate TLS opportunistically, and the protocols are limited to more secure versions only. For services that require mandatory encryption, the security level can be set to encrypt. The smtpd_tls_auth_only directive ensures that TLS is required before authentication can occur, thus preventing clear-text authentication over unsecured channels.

Authentication is closely tied to encryption. Postfix can integrate with SASL (Simple Authentication and Security Layer) to enforce authenticated access. Secure authentication prevents unauthorized users from exploiting the mail relay function, which is crucial in mitigating spam. A typical configuration snippet for SASL integration appears as follows:

```
smtpd_sasl_auth_enable = yes
smtpd_sasl_security_options = noanonymous
smtpd_sasl_local_domain = $myhostname
broken_sasl_auth_clients = yes
```

The smtpd_sasl_auth_enable directive activates the mechanism, while smtpd_sasl_security_options prevents anonymous logins. The smtpd_sasl_local_domain setting is particularly important when the server handles authentication for multiple domains, ensuring consistency, and the broken_sasl_auth_clients parameter accommodates clients with non-standard implementations.

Access control in Postfix is managed through a combination of recipient restrictions and client access policies. The smtpd_recipient_restrictions parameter plays a central role in determining which messages are accepted or rejected based on the sender's attributes and the destination domain. A standard configuration might include:

```
smtpd_recipient_restrictions =
    permit_mynetworks,
    permit_sasl_authenticated,
    reject_unauth_destination,
    reject_non_fqdn_recipient,
    reject_unknown_recipient_domain,
    check_policy_service inet:127.0.0.1:10023
```

This example permits mail from trusted networks and authenticated users while rejecting mail that does not meet destination criteria. The directives reject_non_fqdn_recipient and

94

reject_unknown_recipient_domain help ensure that the destination addresses are valid and fully qualified, reducing the risk of spoofing or misrouting. The inclusion of a policy service check introduces an external module capable of performing complex risk assessments during the SMTP session.

Maintaining a strict policy on relaying is an additional safeguard. Open relays are highly susceptible to abuse by spammers. Setting the relay_restrictions and mynetworks parameters correctly creates a controlled environment where only permitted IP ranges can relay mail. An example configuration is as follows:

```
mynetworks = 127.0.0.0/8 [::1]/128
relay_domains = $mydestination
smtpd_relay_restrictions = permit_mynetworks,
                        permit_sasl_authenticated,
                        reject_unauth_destination
```

The mynetworks parameter specifies trusted IP addresses, typically the localhost and any internal network segments. The smtpd_relay_restrictions enforce that only approved networks and authenticated users can relay messages, further preventing misuse of the mail server for spam dissemination.

Another important security measure is the use of chroot jails for specific Postfix services. Running daemons in chroot environments limits the scope of damage in the event of a security breach. The master.cf file can be configured to implement chrooting for sensitive services. A typical chroot configuration in the master.cf might look like:

```
smtp     inet  n     -     n     -     -     smtpd
pickup   fifo  n     -     n     60    1     pickup -v -c
  -t
cleanup  unix  n     -     n     -     0     cleanup -r
qmgr     fifo  n     -     n     300   1     qmgr -l -s
```

While the above example does not explicitly show chroot flags, services that require chrooting are denoted with a flag in their respective columns. It is essential to verify that the chrooted environment is correctly set up with the necessary libraries and configuration files to avoid service disruptions.

Basic security settings also involve implementing rules that prevent common attack vectors. For instance, prevention of backscatter can be achieved by configuring Postfix to handle bounces correctly. This prevention reduces the likelihood of sending bounce messages to forged sender addresses. Adding the following lines to main.cf assists in handling bounce messages securely:

```
bounce_notice_recipient = postmaster
2bounce_notice_recipient = postmaster
delay_warning_recipient = postmaster
```

These settings ensure that error and delay notifications are directed to the postmaster, rather than to the original sender, whose address might have been spoofed.

Logging and monitoring constitute another essential component of a secure mail server. They enable administrators to quickly identify and respond to potential security incidents. Postfix provides detailed logging via system log files, and configurations can be tuned to increase the granularity of these logs. In main.cf, the logging level can be adjusted using the debug_peer_level parameter:

```
debug_peer_level=2
```

In addition, enhanced log analysis can be achieved by integrating third-party monitoring tools that correlate log entries and generate alerts for suspicious activity. Regular review of log files, typically found in /var/log/mail.log or /var/log/maillog, is crucial for maintaining the security posture of the system.

To further mitigate spam and abuse, many administrators employ additional filtering measures. Postfix supports integration with third-party anti-spam solutions that perform additional examinations of inbound mail. For example, policy services can be used to query databases of known bad senders or to apply greylisting techniques. A configuration for greylisting might include a dedicated policy service invocation:

```
check_policy_service inet:127.0.0.1:10023
```

This directive directs Postfix to consult a local policy service that implements greylisting, temporary rejection, or other intermediate checks which can significantly reduce the risk of spam.

Additionally, the use of header and body checks provides another method to filter and reject suspicious messages. Regular expressions can be utilized to identify and block messages with undesirable content. An example configuration in main.cf may include:

```
header_checks = regexp:/etc/postfix/header_checks
body_checks   = regexp:/etc/postfix/body_checks
```

The corresponding files may contain expressions such as:

```
/^Subject:.*(Buy now|Free offer)/ DISCARD
/^From:.*(spamdomain\.com)/ REJECT
```

Using header and body checks allows administrators to quickly filter out messages that match patterns associated with spam or malicious content.

Lastly, keeping the server and Postfix software up to date is an irreplaceable part of maintaining security. Regular updates ensure that known vulnerabilities are patched promptly. Complementing this, regular security audits and configuration reviews help maintain a robust security posture over time.

The security measures described in this section are designed to form a layered defense strategy. Each configuration parameter contributes to a broader ecosystem of defenses, protecting the mail server from a wide array of potential threats. By implementing TLS encryption, enforcing strict access controls, integrating robust logging, and filtering out malicious content, administrators build a resilient infrastructure that safeguards both the integrity of mail communications and the underlying system resources. The careful calibration of these settings, combined with routine maintenance and monitoring practices, greatly reduces the risk of unauthorized access and mail abuse, ensuring that the Postfix server operates securely in increasingly complex network environments.

Chapter 4

Advanced Configuration Techniques

This chapter explores sophisticated methods for enhancing Postfix functionality, such as virtual domain hosting and sender-dependent relays. It details the use of transport maps and address rewriting for custom mail routing. Additionally, it integrates Postfix with LDAP/MySQL for scalable operations and introduces policy services for increased control. These techniques enable tailored solutions to complex email management needs, optimizing server performance and flexibility.

4.1. Virtual Domain Hosting

Virtual domain hosting in Postfix provides the capability to manage multiple domains on a single server by decoupling system user accounts from virtual mail accounts. This section details the configuration aspects required to enable virtual domain hosting, explains the role of various parameters in the main.cf file, and illustrates how to manage virtual alias and mailbox maps. Readers should note that virtual hosting extends beyond simple domain management and plays an essential role in ensuring secure and optimized mail routing.

In a typical Postfix configuration, mail delivery is tightly coupled with user accounts on the host operating system. Virtual domain hosting abstracts this dependency by using lookup tables that map virtual email addresses to local mailboxes or external destinations. The primary tables involved include virtual_mailbox_domains, virtual_mailbox_maps, and virtual_alias_maps. Each of these parameters supports a distinct aspect of domain handling: the domain list, mailbox mapping, and alias mapping, respectively.

A basic layout of a virtual domain configuration in the main.cf file resembles the following:

```
# Define the domains that Postfix will handle as virtual
virtual_mailbox_domains = hash:/etc/postfix/virtual_mailbox_domains

# Map virtual email addresses to local mailboxes
virtual_mailbox_maps = hash:/etc/postfix/virtual_mailbox_maps

# Map virtual aliases to other email addresses
virtual_alias_maps = hash:/etc/postfix/virtual_alias_maps
```

Files referenced in the configuration (e.g., /etc/postfix/virtual_mailbox_doma are standard Unix text files and must be processed into lookup tables using tools such as postmap. For example, after editing any virtual mapping file one should run the corresponding postmap command:

100

```
postmap /etc/postfix/virtual_mailbox_domains
postmap /etc/postfix/virtual_mailbox_maps
postmap /etc/postfix/virtual_alias_maps
```

The file /etc/postfix/virtual_mailbox_domains contains a list of domains hosted by the server. A sample structure of this file might appear as:

```
example.com    OK
example.org    OK
```

In the above file, each domain is associated with a validation keyword that signals Postfix to treat the domain as virtual. The keyword OK indicates that email destined for these domains should be accepted based on virtual addresses defined in the other mapping files.

The /etc/postfix/virtual_mailbox_maps file is used to map complete email addresses to corresponding local mailbox paths. A typical entry in this file might be:

```
user1@example.com      example.com/user1/
info@example.org       example.org/info/
```

In this configuration, the left-hand side denotes the incoming virtual email address, and the right-hand side is the relative path to the mail locker or mail storage directory configured on the server. The mailbox mapping should be consistent with the directory structure specified by Postfix's virtual mailbox base directory. Consider configuring virtual_mailbox_base in main.cf as follows:

```
virtual_mailbox_base = /var/mail/vhosts
```

This directive informs Postfix that every virtual user mailbox is to be found under /var/mail/vhosts. In the earlier example, the email for user1@example.com would be stored in /var/mail/vhosts/example.com/user1/.

The file /etc/postfix/virtual_alias_maps is utilized to define address rewriting for virtual domains. For example:

```
admin@example.com     user1@example.com
sales@example.org     user2@example.org
```

Here, incoming mail directed to `admin@example.com` is redirected to `user1@example.com` in accordance with internal policies for administrative handling. It is crucial to ensure that such mappings do not lead to infinite redirection loops or conflicts with the mailbox maps.

When using multiple domains, particular attention must be paid to the ordering and uniqueness of the entries in these files. The priority of lookup tables is established by Postfix's internal processing; thus, misconfigured entries or duplicates may cause mail delivery failures. In environments where numerous virtual domains are hosted, it is often beneficial to separate virtual user credentials and mailbox paths into dedicated databases for improved manageability. Administrators may also employ the `virtual_min_mime_code` parameter to enforce content restrictions or handle MIME-specific processing on messages routed through virtual domains.

Security considerations are paramount in a multi-domain configuration. It is essential to properly secure the directories referenced in the configuration files, particularly when multiple tenants share the same server. Operating system-level permissions, combined with Postfix's built-in security parameters, ensure that virtual mailboxes remain isolated and that unauthorized access is prevented. Implementing chroot environments and utilizing TLS encryption between mail servers further protects the email traffic and stored mail.

Performance tuning is a relevant aspect when managing numerous virtual domains. As the number of domains and virtual users increases, lookup table performance could become a bottleneck if the underlying databases are not optimized. For large-scale deployments, administrators may choose to utilize database systems such as MySQL or LDAP for managing virtual domain data rather than static text files processed by postmap. This transition involves more complex configuration but provides better scalability and query performance. A sample MySQL configuration for virtual domain lookups could involve connectors defined in the main.cf file as follows:

```
virtual_mailbox_domains = mysql:/etc/postfix/mysql-virtual-mailbox-
    domains.cf
virtual_mailbox_maps = mysql:/etc/postfix/mysql-virtual-mailbox-maps.
    cf
virtual_alias_maps = mysql:/etc/postfix/mysql-virtual-alias-maps.cf
```

The associated configuration files, such as /etc/postfix/ mysql-virtual-mailbox-domains.cf, must contain directives specifying the database server, query, and credentials required to access the virtual domain data. This approach provides a dynamic method to update virtual domain settings without the need to rebuild static maps upon every change.

A key aspect of managing virtual domain hosting is ensuring that Postfix correctly processes the recipient addresses. Postfix performs recipient verification by consulting the virtual mailbox and alias maps. It is therefore important to update these maps immediately after making modifications to the domain configurations. Testing configuration changes can be accomplished using the postmap -q command, which allows administrators to query the contents of a lookup table. For example:

```
postmap -q user1@example.com hash:/etc/postfix/virtual_mailbox_maps
```

This command returns the mapped mailbox path for user1@example.com. Verifying that the retrieved output matches the expected configuration helps identify discrepancies early in the update process.

Integration of virtual hosting with other Postfix features, such as content filtering and access policies, is made possible through policy delegation. Policy services can be linked with virtual domain configuration to enforce restrictions based on domain-specific rules. For instance, a policy service can limit the number of concurrent connections per virtual domain or apply specialized spam filtering routines. By coupling virtual domain settings with these additional layers of control, email servers can manage both load balancing and security with greater flexibility.

The process of troubleshooting virtual domain hosting issues typically involves checking log files for errors related to domain lookup and file permission problems. Log entries generated by Postfix during mail processing provide crucial insights into the behavior of the lookup mechanism. Misconfiguration in the file formats or errors during the execution of the `postmap` process are often the root causes of mail delivery failures. Monitoring logs using tools such as `tail` or `grep` helps isolate problems. For example, one might execute:

```
tail -f /var/log/mail.log
```

This command continuously displays new log entries, facilitating rapid diagnosis during testing and adjustment phases.

A comprehensive virtual domain hosting configuration also considers integration with spam and virus scanning solutions. By routing emails through content filters before final delivery, Postfix ensures that virtual mailboxes are protected against a range of security threats. When configuring such integrations, it is essential to verify that domain-specific policies do not conflict with global content filtering rules. Postfix's flexible architecture allows administrators to tailor filter invocation based on both domain and sender criteria, ensuring that each virtual domain receives the appropriate level of scrutiny.

The process of maintaining virtual domain hosting configurations requires periodic review and validation. As new domains are added or policies are updated, the underlying lookup tables must be regenerated.

Automating these maintenance tasks via scheduled scripts or configuration management tools ensures that the virtual hosting environment remains consistent and secure. For instance, a cron job could be established to run the `postmap` commands at regular intervals, thereby reducing the risk of stale data impacting mail delivery.

Attention must be given to scheduling and synchronization issues when multiple administrators perform concurrent updates to the configuration files. Version control systems, such as Git, can help track changes and provide rollback capabilities. Maintaining an audit trail of configuration updates not only improves operational transparency but also facilitates compliance with organizational security standards.

The overall efficiency of virtual hosting in Postfix rests on the proper integration of its components. Domain definitions, mailbox mappings, and alias rewrites must work in unison to deliver email securely and efficiently. Each component must be meticulously configured and tested, ensuring that the system scales to accommodate growth in domain numbers and email traffic. This level of detail is critical to preventing vulnerabilities and ensuring that the email service remains resilient under varying load conditions.

In environments where virtual domain hosting is combined with other advanced configurations—such as sender-dependent relays and transport maps—the interplay between these components becomes more complex. Administrators must carefully plan and document their configurations to enable seamless integration between different Postfix modules. A well-organized configuration not only simplifies troubleshooting but also supports future enhancements to the email server infrastructure without incurring significant downtime or performance degradation.

4.2. Configuring Sender-Dependent Relays

Sender-dependent relay configurations in Postfix allow administrators to tailor the relay host used for outbound mail based on the sender's email address. This configuration is particularly valuable in environments where different senders require distinct outbound routing behaviors. For example, a service provider hosting multiple domains may need to relay emails for some users through specific SMTP servers that support unique authentication mechanisms or specialized content filtering, while other users continue to use the default route. The following details explain the configuration process, analyze the underlying parameters, and introduce practical examples to solidify understanding.

The primary parameter enabling sender-dependent relay functionality is `sender_dependent_relayhost_maps`. By assigning different relay hosts to specific sender addresses or domains, Postfix directs outbound emails through alternative channels, thus providing granular routing control. An exemplary configuration in the `main.cf` file might include:

```
sender_dependent_relayhost_maps = hash:/etc/postfix/sender_relay
```

The file referenced here, `/etc/postfix/sender_relay`, contains mappings that determine which relay server to use based on the envelope sender. A sample content of this file may be structured as follows:

```
user1@example.com    [relay1.example.com]:587
@example.org         [relay2.example.org]:587
```

In the above configuration, emails sent from `user1@example.com` are relayed through `relay1.example.com` on port 587, while any sender from the domain `example.org` is assigned to `relay2.example.org` using the same port. The usage of the prefix @ in the second mapping acts as a wildcard for all senders within the specified domain, streamlining the configuration process where multiple users within the same

106

domain share outbound routing policies.

After editing the mapping file, it is necessary to compile it into a format that Postfix can quickly access. This is accomplished using the postmap utility:

```
postmap /etc/postfix/sender_relay
```

When implementing sender-dependent relay configurations, it is important to consider authentication. Different relay servers may require unique credentials based on the sender identity. To address this, Postfix allows the use of sender-dependent SASL authentication by setting the smtp_sender_dependent_authentication parameter to yes and specifying the smtp_sasl_password_maps file. A typical configuration might appear as:

```
sender_dependent_relayhost_maps = hash:/etc/postfix/sender_relay
smtp_sender_dependent_authentication = yes
smtp_sasl_password_maps = hash:/etc/postfix/sasl_passwd
```

The /etc/postfix/sasl_passwd file then maps relay hosts to the corresponding authentication credentials:

```
[relay1.example.com]:587    user1:password1
[relay2.example.org]:587    user2:password2
```

Following any modifications to the authentication file, it must also be processed with postmap:

```
postmap /etc/postfix/sasl_passwd
```

These settings ensure that when an outbound email is processed, Postfix consults sender_dependent_relayhost_maps to determine the appropriate relay host, and then utilizes the credentials provided in smtp_sasl_password_maps for authentication against that relay server. This dual-level configuration segregates routing decisions from authentication, thereby enhancing both security and flexibility.

Configurations of sender-dependent relays must be carefully positioned within the broader Postfix environment to avoid conflicts. The default relay host, managed by the `relayhost` parameter, acts as a fallback unless a specific sender mapping is detected. Consequently, the `relayhost` directive should remain configured for general use, while sender-dependent mappings create exceptions where required. A typical configuration might therefore look like:

```
relayhost = [default.relay.example.com]:25
sender_dependent_relayhost_maps = hash:/etc/postfix/sender_relay
```

An important aspect to consider is the order of processing. When an email is sent, Postfix first determines the sender identity and then checks the sender-dependent relay host maps. If no specific mapping exists for that sender, it falls back to the globally defined `relayhost`. This behavior ensures that only designated senders will utilize alternative routing pathways.

The application of sender-dependent relay configurations is most notable in organizations that operate multiple sender profiles and need to adhere to different outbound policies. For instance, corporate affiliates, marketing teams, and automated services hosted on the same server can be routed through distinct external SMTP servers that specialize in handling volume, filtering, or policy enforcement. By diversifying relay hosts based on the sender, administrators can ensure that each email adheres to the specific requirements of its origin, such as compliance with spam regulations or content filtering criteria.

Troubleshooting sender-dependent relay configurations requires thorough testing and diagnostic checks. An effective method to verify mapping correctness is by using the `postmap -q` command. For example, querying the mapping for a specific sender can reveal the relay host being used:

```
postmap -q user1@example.com hash:/etc/postfix/sender_relay
```

The output of this command should match the expected relay host defined in the configuration file. If the mapping is incorrect or missing, it may result in emails being relayed through the default host, potentially violating intended routing policies. Similarly, verifying SASL authentication details with queries against the sasl_passwd map can prevent authentication failures that might lead to undelivered messages.

Considerations for security are paramount when employing sender-dependent relays. The use of multiple relay hosts introduces potential vulnerabilities if the mapping files or authentication credentials are not properly secured. Files such as /etc/postfix/sender_relay and /etc/postfix/sasl_passwd must have appropriate file permissions to prevent unauthorized modifications. Best practices include setting restrictive file permissions (e.g., chmod 600) and employing access control lists (ACLs) where applicable.

Advanced scenarios may require a more dynamic approach to sender-dependent relay configuration. In certain environments, the mapping of senders to relay hosts might be sourced from an external database rather than static text files. Integrating with relational databases such as MySQL or LDAP can provide more robust scalability for managing a large number of sender mappings. In such cases, the configuration syntax in main.cf would adjust accordingly. For example, using a MySQL backend could entail:

```
sender_dependent_relayhost_maps = mysql:/etc/postfix/mysql-
    sender_relay.cf
```

The corresponding MySQL configuration file /etc/postfix/mysql-sender_relay.cf would specify the details required to connect to the database, including the query to retrieve the relay host for a given sender. This approach centralizes configuration management and facilitates real-time updates without the need for manual file alterations and regeneration of static maps.

A crucial design aspect is the interplay between sender-dependent relay configurations and the overall email delivery path. In environments where multiple routing policies coexist, administrators must ensure that sender-dependent settings do not conflict with other mechanisms such as transport maps or address rewriting. Coordination among these components is essential to maintain an unambiguous routing strategy. One must document the configuration parameters and the hierarchy in which Postfix processes them, ensuring that sender-dependent relay maps remain the definitive source for outbound routing decisions based on sender identity.

Performance aspects of sender-dependent relay configurations are also worthy of attention. In deployments with a high volume of outbound mail, the lookup operations for sender mappings can become a performance bottleneck if not optimized. Employing efficient database backends or well-indexed hash maps can mitigate this risk. Administrators should monitor Postfix's performance metrics and adjust their configurations accordingly, ensuring that the additional processing overhead does not adversely affect email throughput.

Auditing and logging are instrumental in maintaining the integrity of sender-dependent relay configurations. Postfix's logging system records detailed information about mail processing, including the relay host selected for each email. Regular analysis of these logs can uncover deviations from intended behavior, such as misrouted emails or authentication errors. Utilizing log analysis tools can help correlate routing decisions with sender identities, thereby facilitating prompt correction of configuration errors.

Maintaining sender-dependent relay configurations necessitates periodic reviews to accommodate changes in organizational policies or external relay server configurations. Scheduled audits, combined with automated scripts that verify map file integrity, can preempt many common issues. Version control for configuration files is also advisable; tracking changes via systems like Git ensures that previous configurations can be restored if needed, thus preserving operational continuity.

Careful planning and testing are indispensable when implementing sender-dependent relays. Prior to deploying configuration changes in production, administrators should simulate the effects in a controlled environment or staging system. This approach minimizes the risk of inadvertent misconfigurations that could interrupt email services. Comprehensive testing includes verifying that each sender's emails are relayed through the intended server and that authentication credentials are properly applied. Continuous monitoring during the initial deployment phase assists in identifying issues promptly.

Clearly, the flexibility imparted by sender-dependent relay configurations significantly enhances Postfix's utility in multifaceted email environments. By leveraging this feature, organizations can assign precise outbound routing based on sender identities, thereby enforcing tailored policies for diverse sender groups. The approach streamlines operations while adhering to security and compliance requirements, making it a critical component in modern email server management.

4.3. Using Transport Maps

Transport maps provide a flexible method for defining custom routing rules for mail delivery in Postfix. They allow administrators to override standard routing mechanisms by explicitly specifying how emails destined for particular addresses or domains should be handled. This capability is especially useful in hosting environments and complex network scenarios where mail delivery must follow specialized paths. Transport maps extend the modular flexibility of Postfix, enabling granular control over delivery by decoupling routing decisions from mailbox or alias configurations.

The transport mapping mechanism in Postfix is activated using the transport_maps parameter in the main.cf file. A typical configuration entry appears as follows:

```
transport_maps = hash:/etc/postfix/transport
```

In the configuration above, the file /etc/postfix/transport contains a set of rules that associate recipient addresses or domains with specific transport definitions. Each entry in this file directs Postfix to route the email through a designated channel, which might involve relaying through an external SMTP server, utilizing a different delivery method, or even processing mail with content filters.

A typical transport table might contain entries similar to:

```
example.net              smtp:[mail.example.net]:587
subdomain.example.com    error:mail for subdomains not accepted
special.example.org      lmtp:unix:/var/run/dovecot/lmtp
```

In the first entry, the domain example.net is associated with an SMTP transport definition, directing messages to mail.example.net on port 587. The square brackets around the relay host indicate that MX lookups should be bypassed, and Postfix will connect directly to the specified server. The second entry demonstrates how transport maps can be used to reject email for a particular subdomain by returning an explicit error message. In the third example, mail destined for special.example.org is sent via LMTP, using a UNIX socket for local delivery through a content delivery service such as Dovecot.

Transport maps are processed in a manner similar to other lookup tables within Postfix. After updating the /etc/postfix/transport file, the changes must be compiled using the postmap command:

```
postmap /etc/postfix/transport
```

This command converts the human-readable text file into a hash table that Postfix can query efficiently during mail delivery. It ensures that the transport rules are available for rapid lookup as each message is processed.

One notable advantage of transport maps lies in their ability to fine-tune mail routing without interfering with other aspects of mail processing. For instance, virtual domain hosting, sender-dependent relay configurations, and address rewriting rules operate independently from transport maps. This separation of concerns allows each component to be maintained and debugged individually. When transport maps are in use, Postfix first consults them to determine whether a custom delivery path has been specified. If a match is found, the mail is routed according to the defined instructions; if not, Postfix falls back to the default routing behavior specified by the global `relayhost` parameter or local delivery rules.

It is also possible to define transport rules for individual email addresses, not just entire domains or subdomains. This level of granularity is useful when certain users require distinct handling. Consider the following transport table entries:

```
user1@example.com      smtp:[smtp-relay1.example.com]:25
user2@example.com      smtp:[smtp-relay2.example.com]:25
```

Each mapping above forces mail for a specific user to be relayed through a designated server, potentially with different relay policies, authentication credentials, or network routes. These settings ensure that delivery policies are enforced at the individual sender level, providing administrators with precise control over outbound and routing behavior.

Transport maps can be leveraged to redirect mail across organizations or across network boundaries. For instance, organizations may choose to forward for archiving or filtering purposes. A configuration may direct outbound emails toward a specialized content scanning service before reaching the final destination. An example of this type of configuration might be:

```
archive.example.com    smtp:[scanner.internal.example.com]:2525
```

In this scenario, any emails destined for archive.example.com are rerouted to an internal scanning service operating on port 2525. Such configurations are particularly useful when email traffic must pass through multiple layers of security or compliance checks. The explicit nature of transport mappings reduces ambiguity and reinforces policy enforcement.

The implementation of transport maps interacts with other Postfix features in a coherent manner. For example, while sender-dependent relays determine the outbound gateway based on the sender's address, transport maps are concerned with the final hop on the delivery path. Postfix evaluates transport maps after all preliminary routing decisions have been made, offering a final opportunity to override default delivery mechanisms. This layered approach supports complex delivery scenarios, where multiple routing policies may need to be applied simultaneously. Administrators must ensure that these configurations do not conflict, and maintaining comprehensive documentation is advisable for environments with overlapping rules.

Although the transport map configuration appears to be straightforward, understanding its limitations is equally important. Transport maps operate on a simple lookup basis without dynamic content evaluation. As a result, they may not be suitable for highly dynamic environments where routing decisions are influenced by real-time factors such as system load or current network conditions. In such cases, combining transport maps with external policy servers or content filters might be necessary to achieve the desired behavior. Integrating these elements requires careful planning, as the sequence of processing events in Postfix can affect overall performance and message flow.

Security considerations regarding transport maps are also significant.

Since the transport lookup can include directives that override default DNS lookup behaviors, misconfigurations may inadvertently expose the mail system to malicious redirection. It is essential to validate all entries in the transport map file and ensure that proper access control is enforced on the mapping files and related resources. Setting strict permissions and performing routine audits of the configuration help mitigate risks associated with incorrect or unauthorized modifications.

In practice, testing and validation form integral parts of deploying transport maps. Running targeted queries using the `postmap -q` command can confirm that specific email addresses or domains are correctly mapped to their corresponding transports. For example:

```
postmap -q user1@example.com hash:/etc/postfix/transport
```

This command outputs the transport rule applied to `user1@example.com`. Consistency between expected outcomes and actual responses is crucial for ensuring that the custom routing rules behave as intended. Additionally, monitoring Postfix log files during testing can provide insight into how effectively messages are routed through the specified paths. Log entries typically include the transport mechanism chosen, allowing administrators to correlate email flow with the defined transport maps.

The use of transport maps also facilitates the implementation of fallback mechanisms. If a particular delivery route fails, Postfix may revert to a secondary route or generate an error message if the delivery cannot be accomplished. This redundancy is vital in multi-tiered email environments where reliability and uptime are of paramount importance. Administrators can design transport maps to prioritize primary delivery paths and add secondary entries as backups. The ability to control this behavior enhances the resilience of email delivery, ensuring continuous operation despite transient network issues or server outages.

115

Operational maintenance of transport maps involves periodic updates and reviews. As organizations evolve, changes to network infrastructure, relay server configurations, or email security policies may necessitate adjustments to the transport map. Utilizing version control systems to track changes in the configuration files aids in maintaining consistency and provides a mechanism for rollback in the event of errors. Automated scripts or configuration management tools can further streamline the updating process by regenerating transport maps in response to changes in the environment.

Administrators should also consider performance impacts when deploying extensive transport maps. In scenarios with a large number of transport entries, the lookup process might impose additional overhead on email processing. To address this, it is prudent to use efficient file formats and indexing mechanisms. For example, when using large-scale deployments, a database-backed lookup (such as DNS or MySQL) might be more appropriate than static hash maps. While the fundamental principles remain the same, the scalability of the mapping mechanism can significantly influence server performance and deliverability.

Transport maps, when used correctly, offer a powerful tool for tailoring email delivery paths to meet specific business or technical requirements. By explicitly defining routes for particular addresses or domains, administrators can enforce complex delivery policies while maintaining clear separation between routing logic and other mail processing functions. Such clarity simplifies troubleshooting and ensures that any deviations in mail delivery can be rapidly identified and corrected. The structured approach provided by transport maps not only improves operational efficiency but also enhances the security and reliability of the email infrastructure.

The integration of transport maps into the broader Postfix configuration represents an advanced technique that builds on the foundational concepts of virtual domain hosting and sender-dependent relays. By combining these features, a robust email routing environment is achieved, where each message is dynamically directed according to precisely defined rules. The capacity to tailor delivery pathways, apply custom transport mechanisms, and integrate with external authentication and filtering systems underscores the flexibility of Postfix as an email server solution. This configurability is particularly advantageous in scenarios that demand adherence to strict policy requirements and rapid adaptation to evolving network architectures.

4.4. Implementing Address Rewriting

Address rewriting in Postfix provides the necessary mechanism to modify email addresses in both outgoing and incoming messages. This functionality is essential when there is a need to standardize, mask, or otherwise transform addresses to comply with internal policies, external expectations, or security requirements. By configuring address rewriting, administrators gain fine-grained control over how sender and recipient addresses appear, thus ensuring consistency across various mail flows.

One of the primary tools for implementing address rewriting in Postfix is the set of canonical maps. The canonical_maps parameter allows both sender and recipient addresses to be transformed in a uniform way as messages traverse the mail system. In the main.cf file, the configuration can be specified as follows:

```
canonical_maps = hash:/etc/postfix/canonical
```

The file /etc/postfix/canonical contains mapping rules that replace one address with another. A typical entry might be:

```
olduser@example.com    newuser@newdomain.com
```

117

In this example, any instance of `olduser@example.com` will be rewritten as `newuser@newdomain.com`. If the mapping file is modified, the `postmap` utility must be executed to regenerate the database:

```
postmap /etc/postfix/canonical
```

While `canonical_maps` apply to both sender and recipient addresses, there are circumstances where different rewriting rules are needed for outgoing versus incoming messages. For sender-specific rewrites, the `sender_canonical_maps` parameter can be used:

```
sender_canonical_maps = hash:/etc/postfix/sender_canonical
```

A sample `/etc/postfix/sender_canonical` file might include:

```
user@localdomain.local    user@example.com
@localdomain.local        @example.com
```

In this configuration, all emails sent from hosts within `localdomain.local` are rewritten to use the organizational domain `example.com`. The first line rewrites a specific address, while the second line applies domain-wide. Similarly, `recipient_canonical_maps` can be used to modify recipient addresses if necessary.

Another variant of address rewriting is provided by generic maps. The `smtp_generic_maps` parameter is often applied to outgoing mail when messages leave the Postfix system. Generic maps are primarily used to remove local naming conventions from sender addresses. Configuring generic maps may appear as:

```
smtp_generic_maps = hash:/etc/postfix/generic
```

A typical file `/etc/postfix/generic` might include entries such as:

```
user              user@example.com
info@localhost    info@mycompany.com
```

When mail is sent through Postfix, these rules ensure that internal names are replaced with externally acceptable addresses. Like canonical maps, the generic map file must be compiled using `postmap` after modification:

```
postmap /etc/postfix/generic
```

Address rewriting also plays a crucial role in masquerading. The `masquerade_domains` parameter simplifies addresses by removing subdomains from the displayed sender address. For example, a configuration line in `main.cf` may state:

```
masquerade_domains = example.com, sub.example.com
```

This setting causes the hostname portion of addresses to be rewritten so that users outside the local network see only the primary domain. Another related parameter is `append_dot_mydomain`, which controls whether a dot is appended to unqualified addresses. Such parameters are particularly useful when deploying policies intended to standardize outgoing mail headers and comply with external identity requirements.

In environments where multiple rewriting rules coexist, it is critical to understand the order of precedence. Postfix applies rewriting rules in a specific sequence, first consulting `sender_canonical_maps` and `recipient_canonical_maps`, followed by more general canonical rules. Generic maps are applied later in the processing chain, ensuring that any transformations applied to locally submitted mail are compatible with what external systems expect. This layered approach minimizes conflicts and ensures consistency throughout the entire mail delivery path.

Additional customization may involve rewriting not only envelope addresses but also header addresses. Postfix does not rewrite message headers by default when canonical mapping is used. To modify header addresses, one must ensure that the `canonical_envelope_sender` and `canonical_header_sender` options are set appropriately. For instance, to rewrite both the envelope and header addresses from `user@localdomain` to `user@example.com`, the following configuration can be applied:

```
canonical_envelope_sender = user@localdomain
canonical_header_sender = user@localdomain
```

These directives force the rewriting of header fields in addition to the envelope sender, ensuring that the change is visible in the email headers and for subsequent processing by receiving systems.

The flexibility provided by address rewriting in Postfix is particularly beneficial in scenarios where email address normalization is required due to mergers, rebranding, or coexistence of legacy and modern naming conventions. For instance, an organization that has recently adopted a new domain name may use rewriting rules to ensure all outbound emails reflect the new identity without demanding an immediate overhaul of the internal mail system. Similarly, a service provider hosting multiple domains can employ address rewriting to standardize sender addresses, preserving consistency while still supporting multiple identities.

Developer testing and continuous validation of rewriting rules is an integral part of configuration management. Administrators are encouraged to simulate address rewriting behavior using the postmap -q command. A common command to test a canonical map might be:

```
postmap -q user@localdomain hash:/etc/postfix/sender_canonical
```

The output should accurately reflect the desired rewritten address. System logs, typically found in /var/log/mail.log, also provide runtime evidence of rewriting actions. By examining log entries, administrators can determine if addresses in the headers and envelopes are being modified as intended.

Address rewriting configurations must be approached with careful planning and thorough documentation. Changes applied to rewriting rules can have widespread effects on mail deliverability and authenticity. In environments with multiple rewriting rules, it is advisable to maintain a clear, hierarchical mapping of configuration files. This practice facilitates troubleshooting and minimizes the risk of unintended side effects, such as address collisions or the inadvertent exposure of internal hostnames. Version control systems, such as Git, can be utilized to manage changes to rewriting configuration files, allowing rollback and collaboration among administrators.

Security considerations are also paramount. Improper rewriting of addresses may lead to issues such as spoofing vulnerabilities or unintended routing loops. Therefore, every rewriting rule should be validated against security policies to ensure that only authorized modifications are employed. File permissions on rewriting configuration files should be set restrictively (e.g., using chmod 600) to prevent unauthorized changes. Furthermore, detailed auditing of rewriting actions aids in the early detection of misconfigurations that might expose sensitive internal information.

Interoperability with other Postfix modules, such as virtual domain hosting and sender-dependent relay configurations, is a critical aspect of a comprehensive mail server setup. Address rewriting is designed to work in concert with these modules, ensuring that transformations applied to addresses are consistent regardless of the underlying mail routing logic. For example, a message routed via a sender-dependent relay may have its sender address transformed by a generic map to meet external domain policies. Similarly, messages destined for virtual mailboxes may be modified to adhere to standardized naming conventions. To maintain this coherence, administrators must continuously verify that changes in one component do not conflict with another.

Advanced implementations of address rewriting may involve conditional rewrites based on context, such as the presence of particular header fields or the use of specific protocols. While Postfix provides a standard set of tools for address rewriting, complex scenarios may necessitate the integration of external policy services. These services can inspect messages in real time and apply rewriting rules dynamically, further enhancing the flexibility of email processing. Such integrations, however, require careful orchestration to maintain performance and consistency across the system.

By employing address rewriting, administrators can refine how mail addresses appear both internally and externally, thereby managing the public identity of an organization while seamlessly supporting internal administrative needs. The robust rewriting capabilities within Postfix not only serve to enforce consistency but also contribute to an overall secure, reliable, and policy-compliant mail delivery environment.

4.5. Integration with LDAP and MySQL

Integrating Postfix with LDAP and MySQL databases enables advanced mail routing and recipient validation by providing dynamic, centralized storage for configuration data. This approach is particularly useful in environments with high user variability and complex mail routing requirements, where static text files and hash maps can become cumbersome to maintain. The integration process leverages the inherent scalability and query capabilities of databases, allowing administrators to perform real-time lookups for virtual domains, alias mappings, and recipient validations. By interfacing with LDAP or MySQL, Postfix can efficiently manage user credentials and routing policies, ensuring that mail delivery adheres to current organizational standards.

The configuration in Postfix is achieved by defining database-specific lookup tables in the main.cf file. Instead of referencing static files, administrators specify configuration files that contain directives for connecting to the desired database and performing specific queries. For example, to use LDAP for retrieving virtual mailbox domains, one would include a directive similar to the following in `main.cf`:

```
virtual_mailbox_domains = ldap:/etc/postfix/
    ldap_virtual_mailbox_domains.cf
```

Similarly, for MySQL integration, a directive might be:

```
virtual_mailbox_domains = mysql:/etc/postfix/
    mysql_virtual_mailbox_domains.cf
```

Each configuration file encapsulates the parameters required to connect to the database, such as host, port, binding credentials, query templates, and search base. These files must be secured appropriately, with file permissions set to prevent unauthorized access.

A typical LDAP configuration file (`/etc/postfix/ldap_virtual_mailbox_domains.cf`) may contain entries like:

```
server_host = ldap.example.com
search_base = dc=example,dc=com
query_filter = (mailDomain=%s)
result_attribute = mailDomain
bind = yes
bind_dn = cn=postfix,dc=example,dc=com
bind_pw = secretpassword
```

In this configuration, the `query_filter` parameter specifies the search criteria that Postfix uses to match a given domain. The placeholder %s is substituted with the domain name being looked up. The result of the query determines whether the domain is under Postfix's control. The use of LDAP provides a flexible schema that can accommodate nested organizational units and group-based restrictions, enhancing recipient validation processes.

When employing MySQL for similar functionality, the configuration file (`/etc/postfix/mysql_virtual_mailbox_domains.cf`) would contain analogous parameters. An example configuration is:

```
user = postfix_user
password = mysqlpassword
```

```
hosts = mysql.example.com
dbname = maildb
query = SELECT domain FROM virtual_domains WHERE domain = '%s'
```

In this case, the query directive is executed against the MySQL database. The query returns the domain name if a valid entry is found in the virtual_domains table. The use of SQL allows for more complex validation rules and can integrate with other organizational data, such as user status and departmental affiliations. This flexibility is particularly useful in large-scale deployments where mail server configurations are dynamically updated.

Advanced mail routing capabilities come into play when additional mappings, such as alias maps and mailbox maps, are also retrieved from LDAP or MySQL databases. For instance, instead of maintaining a static file for virtual alias mapping, the following directive may be included in main.cf:

```
virtual_alias_maps = ldap:/etc/postfix/ldap_virtual_aliases.cf
```

An example LDAP configuration for virtual aliases might look like:

```
server_host = ldap.example.com
search_base = dc=example,dc=com
query_filter = (&(objectClass=mailAlias)(mail=%s))
result_attribute = destination
bind = yes
bind_dn = cn=postfix,dc=example,dc=com
bind_pw = secretpassword
```

This configuration searches for entries of the mailAlias object class, returning the destination address where mail should be forwarded. The structure of the LDAP directory, including inheritance and group membership, can be leveraged to implement complex aliasing schemes. For MySQL setups, a corresponding configuration file for virtual aliases (/etc/postfix/mysql_virtual_aliases.cf) might include:

```
user = postfix_user
password = mysqlpassword
hosts = mysql.example.com
```

```
dbname = maildb
query = SELECT destination FROM virtual_aliases WHERE alias = '%s'
```

Use of SQL queries in this context allows for normalized data structures, reducing redundancy and ensuring consistent updates across multiple virtual alias definitions.

Integration with databases also extends to recipient validation, where Postfix consults external data sources to determine the legitimacy of an email address. This can prevent unauthorized mail from being accepted by verifying recipient details against a controlled database. The configuration for recipient validation using LDAP might be:

```
local_recipient_maps = ldap:/etc/postfix/ldap_recipients.cf
```

A sample LDAP configuration file for recipient validation is:

```
server_host = ldap.example.com
search_base = dc=example,dc=com
query_filter = (mail=%s)
result_attribute = mail
bind = yes
bind_dn = cn=postfix,dc=example,dc=com
bind_pw = secretpassword
```

This query ensures that only addresses that exist in the LDAP directory are accepted, reducing the likelihood of accepting invalid or spoofed recipients. For MySQL, a similar configuration for recipient validation is defined as:

```
local_recipient_maps = mysql:/etc/postfix/mysql_recipients.cf
```

With the corresponding MySQL configuration file:

```
user = postfix_user
password = mysqlpassword
hosts = mysql.example.com
dbname = maildb
query = SELECT email FROM users WHERE email = '%s'
```

Using databases for recipient validation leverages structured data management systems to enforce accurate mail delivery policies. This integration reduces administrative overhead by permitting frequent data updates without the need to restart the Postfix service or regenerate static maps.

Security considerations are paramount when integrating with LDAP and MySQL. Connection strings and authentication credentials must be protected by setting file permissions restrictively (for example, chmod 600 on configuration files). Secure connections using TLS or SSL are recommended to encrypt traffic between Postfix and the external databases. LDAP configurations can include parameters such as tls_enable = yes and tls_verify = yes to enforce secure communication. Similarly, MySQL connections may be secured by specifying SSL parameters within the configuration file. Failure to secure these connections can expose sensitive data and potentially compromise the mail system.

Performance tuning is another essential aspect of database integration. Frequent queries to external databases may introduce latency, particularly in high-volume mail environments. Caching mechanisms should be considered to mitigate this risk. Postfix does not implement caching at the protocol level for LDAP or MySQL lookups; therefore, administrators may need to implement external caching solutions or optimize database indices and queries to improve performance. Monitoring the query performance using tools provided by the database vendor, such as MySQL's slow query log or LDAP monitoring utilities, can help in fine-tuning the system for optimal response times.

The integration process requires meticulous testing to ensure that lookup tables behave as expected. Administrators can simulate database queries using command-line tools such as ldapsearch for LDAP and the MySQL client for SQL queries. For instance, testing an LDAP query might involve:

```
ldapsearch -x -H ldap://ldap.example.com -b "dc=example,dc=com" "(
```

```
mail=user@example.com)"
```

Similarly, a MySQL query test might be executed as follows:

```
mysql -u postfix_user -p -h mysql.example.com maildb -e "SELECT email
    FROM users WHERE email = 'user@example.com';"
```

These tests verify both connectivity and query accuracy, ensuring that Postfix's lookup tables will return the correct results during normal mail processing.

Operational maintenance of database integration involves careful documentation and regular updates. As organizational needs evolve, the schema within LDAP directories or MySQL databases may change. Administrators must ensure that the Postfix query parameters remain in sync with the latest data structure. Version control systems for configuration files can assist in tracking changes, and scheduled audits of database connectivity and performance can preempt potential issues.

Integration with LDAP and MySQL not only facilitates dynamic recipient validation and routing but also enhances flexibility when used in conjunction with other Postfix features such as virtual domain hosting, address rewriting, and transport maps. This modular integration ensures that mail routing policies are consistently applied across various components of the mail system. It simplifies administrative tasks by centralizing critical data in modern database management systems, enabling scalable and resilient mail server setups.

Overall, the database integration approach represents a significant advancement over static file-based configurations. The ability to perform real-time queries, enforce dynamic validation rules, and adapt to changes without service interruptions highlights the robustness of this method. Administrative efficiency is increased, and the overall reliability of the mail system is bolstered through improved data integrity and streamlined configuration management.

4.6. Policy Services and Restrictions

Policy services and restrictions in Postfix provide additional layers of control over email processing, enabling administrators to enforce security, compliance, and routing policies beyond the basic configuration. These mechanisms allow for real-time decision-making during SMTP transactions and are essential in environments with complex trust relationships or high volumes of traffic. Policy services can reject, defer, or modify a message before it is delivered, while restrictions applied within Postfix help mitigate spam, unauthorized relay attempts, and other malicious activities.

The primary means of invoking policy decisions in Postfix is via the SMTPD protocol. By using the `check_policy_service` directive within the `smtpd_recipient_restrictions` or other relevant configuration parameters, Postfix delegates policy decisions to an external policy daemon. For example, one might configure Postfix to consult an external policy server as follows:

```
smtpd_recipient_restrictions =
    permit_mynetworks,
    permit_sasl_authenticated,
    reject_unauth_destination,
    check_policy_service inet:127.0.0.1:10031
```

In this configuration, after basic checks, Postfix sends policy queries to an external service running on port 10031. The external policy service examines various aspects of the SMTP transaction such as sender reputation, recipient status, and message content. Based on the policy algorithm implemented by the service, it returns an action such as DUNNO (no opinion), REJECT, or DEFER_IF_REJECT to modify the handling of the message.

The separation of policy evaluation from the core mail processing engine allows organizations to update or modify security rules without modifying the main Postfix configuration. This is accomplished by deploying policy daemons that listen on a specified port or UNIX socket and respond to Postfix queries. A common approach is to use a simple policy daemon script written in Python or Perl. An example using Python and the `twisted` framework might resemble:

```python
#!/usr/bin/env python
from twisted.internet import protocol, reactor
from twisted.protocols import basic

class PolicyProtocol(basic.LineReceiver):
    delimiter = b'\n'

    def lineReceived(self, line):
        # Parse the key/value pairs in the received line.
        query = dict(item.split('=') for item in line.split(b' '))
        # Implement custom logic for policy decision.
        if query.get(b'request') == b'RCPT':
            sender = query.get(b'sender', b'')
            recipient = query.get(b'recipient', b'')
            # Reject if the recipient domain is not allowed for the
    sender.
            if b'@unauthorized.com' in recipient:
                response = "action=REJECT Invalid recipient address"
            else:
                response = "action=DUNNO"
        else:
            response = "action=DUNNO"
        self.transport.write(response.encode() + b'\n')
        self.transport.loseConnection()

class PolicyFactory(protocol.Factory):
    def buildProtocol(self, addr):
        return PolicyProtocol()

reactor.listenTCP(10031, PolicyFactory())
reactor.run()
```

In this example, a policy service listens on TCP port 10031, processing each line received from Postfix. The script inspects key parameters such as the sender and recipient addresses, then returns a policy decision that Postfix uses to decide whether to permit or reject an SMTP transaction. While this is a basic implementation, more advanced policy daemons can query external databases, integrate with reputation services, or perform heuristic analyses on message content.

In addition to using external policy services, Postfix provides built-in restrictions that can be configured directly in the main.cf file. For instance, restrictions such as reject_unauth_destination and reject_non_FQDN_sender help enforce adherence to mail routing policies. These built-in parameters are part of the SMTPD restriction classes that define what is acceptable during a mail session. An example configuration is shown below:

```
smtpd_sender_restrictions =
    reject_non_fqdn_sender,
    reject_unknown_sender_domain,
    permit_sasl_authenticated

smtpd_client_restrictions =
    reject_rbl_client zen.spamhaus.org,
    permit_mynetworks
```

This configuration ensures that only senders with fully qualified domain names are accepted, that the sender's domain is known, and that client IP addresses are checked against a real-time blacklist (RBL) provided by Spamhaus. These restrictions combine with external policy services to create multiple layers of filtering.

Integrating policy services and restrictions enhances email security by providing real-time defenses against spam and unauthorized email traffic. For example, organizations often implement bracketed restrictions that first allow trusted networks and authenticated users to bypass certain checks, while unauthenticated traffic is subject to stringent policy evaluations. The hierarchy of restrictions is critical; decisions made at earlier stages (such as rejecting non-existent domains) reduce the load on more complex policy evaluations later in the process.

Another aspect of policy implementations is content filtering. Postfix can hand off emails to separate content filter daemons, such as

Amavisd-new, before completing the mail delivery process. Although these filters are not part of the native Postfix policy interface, they interact closely with the overall mail processing pipeline. Headers can be scanned and, if certain patterns are detected that violate policy or indicate potential threats (such as phishing attempts), the message can be discarded or flagged for quarantine. A simple configuration to integrate a content filter may involve:

```
content_filter = scan:[127.0.0.1]:10025
```

In this scenario, Postfix forwards messages to a scanning service listening on port 10025. The scanning service, in turn, can return verdicts that result in modifications to the message or its routing. The use of content filtering as part of the broader policy architecture further emphasizes the need for flexible and modular policy implementations.

Policy services are also used to implement rate limiting and connection control. By employing dynamic policy services, Postfix can enforce limits on the number of messages accepted from a single client over a defined time interval. This is particularly useful in mitigating the effects of compromised systems or automated spam campaigns. For instance, a policy service could examine the number of connections from a given IP address and issue a DEFER action if the limit is exceeded. Such rate limiting is often implemented in conjunction with firewall rules and intrusion detection systems to form a comprehensive defense strategy.

In environments where multiple policy decisions need to be aggregated, administrators may consider a layered approach. At the connection level, restrictions such as reject_unauth_destination serve as a first barrier to unauthorized relays. At the transaction level, external policy services can dynamically evaluate each email based on sender reputation, recipient validation, and even the content of the message. Later in the process, content filters and rate limiting ensure that even if some spam slips past the earlier checks, additional measures exist to capture and mitigate threats. This layered strategy is essential for complex, high-security environments where the cost of spam or malicious emails is high.

Logging and auditing are critical components when deploying policy services and restrictions. Detailed logs allow administrators to analyze the decisions made by both built-in restrictions and external policy daemons. The Postfix log entries typically include information about which restrictions were triggered and the corresponding actions taken. Regular review of these logs helps identify trends, potential misconfigurations, and new threat patterns. For instance, if a particular external policy service consistently rejects legitimate emails, it may signal the need for policy adjustments or a reevaluation of the trusted sources used in the decision algorithm.

Updating and maintaining policy services requires careful coordination with changes in overall mail infrastructure. As organizational needs evolve or new threats emerge, administrators must update policy daemons, firewall rules, and Postfix configuration parameters. Keeping a detailed change log and using version control for configuration files are practices that ensure stability and traceability. Testing changes in a staging environment before deploying them to production minimizes the risk of unintended disruptions.

While Postfix's built-in restrictions provide a robust starting point, the flexibility offered by external policy services allows for customization that suits the unique requirements of an organization. For example, a media company might implement policies that perform content-based routing, directing emails containing large attachments to a separate processing queue. Likewise, a financial institution might implement additional encryption and validation rules for emails containing sensitive information. These advanced policies are managed through external daemons that can interact with other systems, such as databases or even artificial intelligence modules designed to detect fraud.

The configuration of policy services and restrictions is not static; it must adapt to evolving security landscapes and the operational needs of the organization. Administrators are encouraged to document the rationale behind each policy decision and continuously monitor the effectiveness of the restrictions in place. Fine-tuning may involve iterative adjustments to thresholds, modification of policy scripts, and collaboration with security teams to align email processing with broader organizational policies.

Through careful implementation of policy services and restrictions, Postfix becomes a highly adaptable and secure mail system that can meet the demands of modern email environments. The advanced control over email processing afforded by these mechanisms enables administrators to create a resilient system that not only delivers messages efficiently but also safeguards against a wide range of email-borne threats.

Chapter 5

Security and Encryption Practices

This chapter addresses vital security measures for Postfix, including configuring TLS for encrypted SMTP connections and implementing SASL authentication. It covers the setup of SPF, DKIM, and DMARC to combat email spoofing. Additionally, integration with firewalls, SELinux, anti-spam tools, and greylisting/blacklisting ensures a comprehensive defense strategy, safeguarding your email server against unauthorized access and enhancing overall mail security.

5.1. Securing SMTP Connections with TLS

Transport Layer Security (TLS) is essential for maintaining the confidentiality and integrity of the data exchanged over SMTP connections. By encrypting the data stream between mail servers, TLS minimizes the risk of interception and man-in-the-middle attacks. In Postfix, configuring TLS involves specifying a set of parameters that point to certificate files, define supported protocols, and establish session caching behaviors. These configurations interact directly with previous security settings, such as firewall and SELinux parameters, ensuring that encryption practices operate within a comprehensive security framework.

Postfix relies on X.509 certificates to enable TLS. The certificate file contains the public key and identifying information about the server, while the private key file must be rigorously protected as it is used to establish the secure link. When preparing these files, it is advisable to either use certificates signed by a recognized certificate authority (CA) or, during testing and limited deployments, generate self-signed certificates. The trade-off involves balancing ease of setup against trust requirements across external systems. Providing a well-defined certificate chain further improves the trust model by linking the server certificate to a root CA certificate.

The core of the TLS configuration in Postfix is managed in the `main.cf` file. The following configuration excerpt illustrates common parameters for enabling TLS for incoming SMTP connections:

```
# Path to the public certificate file
smtpd_tls_cert_file = /etc/ssl/certs/postfix.pem
# Path to the server's private key file
smtpd_tls_key_file = /etc/ssl/private/postfix.key
# Enable TLS for incoming connections by setting this parameter to '
    yes'
smtpd_use_tls = yes
# Specify the list of CA certificates used to verify client
    certificates, if applicable
smtpd_tls_CAfile = /etc/ssl/certs/ca-certificates.crt

# Enable session caching for performance
smtpd_tls_session_cache_database = btree:${data_directory}/
    smtpd_scache
smtp_tls_session_cache_database = btree:${data_directory}/smtp_scache
```

Each parameter plays a specific role in the encryption process. The `smtpd_tls_cert_file` and `smtpd_tls_key_file` entries indicate the appropriate certificate and private key for the server, whereas `smtpd_use_tls` must be enabled to activate TLS mechanics. The `smtpd_tls_CAfile` parameter is particularly useful when handling client certificates or verifying peer certificates from external connections. For systems where certificate revocation is a concern, incorporating Online Certificate Status Protocol (OCSP) checks or certificate revocation lists (CRLs) further strengthens the authentication process by ensuring that only valid certificates are accepted.

A vital component of TLS configuration involves the management of supported protocols and cipher suites. Specifying these contributes to defining the security posture by disallowing outdated or vulnerable versions of TLS. In Postfix, such configurations may be appended to `main.cf` as follows:

```
# Enforce minimum TLS version and define allowed protocols to avoid
    deprecated options.
smtpd_tls_protocols = !SSLv2, !SSLv3, !TLSv1, !TLSv1.1
smtp_tls_protocols = !SSLv2, !SSLv3, !TLSv1, !TLSv1.1

# Optionally tighten cipher suite preferences to allow only robust
    algorithms.
smtpd_tls_mandatory_ciphers = high
smtp_tls_mandatory_ciphers = high
```

By explicitly disabling SSLv2, SSLv3, TLSv1, and TLSv1.1, the configuration steers the server away from protocols known to have weaknesses. The use of a strong cipher suite minimizes vulnerabilities to cryptographic attacks such as BEAST or POODLE. Adjusting these parameters is particularly important in environments with strict regulatory requirements, where only the most secure algorithms may be permitted.

Another layer of TLS configuration involves adjusting the security level at which TLS is enforced. The parameter `smtpd_tls_security_level` determines if TLS is optional or mandatory for incoming communications. Setting the level to may allows encryption where available, while setting it to encrypt mandates that connections use TLS. In many deployments, a conditional approach is advisable to balance security with compatibility:

```
# Enable opportunistic TLS for incoming connections
smtpd_tls_security_level = may

# Enforce encryption for outgoing connections to other secure mail
    servers
smtp_tls_security_level = encrypt
```

The choice between opportunistic and enforced TLS is informed by the operational context of the mail server. Opportunistic TLS ensures that connections capable of supporting TLS will use it, thereby maximizing compatibility while enhancing security. Conversely, requiring encryption for outgoing connections guarantees that sensitive information is transmitted securely between trusted servers, but may lead to connectivity issues if remote servers do not support TLS.

Session caching is another critical aspect of TLS performance and security. By caching session parameters, Postfix reduces the computational overhead associated with the TLS handshake process, thereby improving overall throughput. The cache databases referenced in the configuration play a significant role in this context. Proper management of the cache leverages disk-based storage to persist session information, which must be monitored for growth and performance bottlenecks. Administrators should ensure that the designated data directory has appropriate access controls in place to protect cached session data from unauthorized access.

Client authentication under TLS may also be integrated to provide an extra layer of security. When mutual TLS is desired, the server can request that clients provide valid certificates. This configuration involves additional parameters, such as smtpd_tls_verify_client_cert, that instruct Postfix to require certificate validation. Incorporating this tactic substantially increases the cost of unauthorized access; only clients with approved certificates can establish communication. While this setup is more complex, it is particularly useful in environments where security requirements are elevated, such as corporate or governmental networks.

To verify successful TLS operation, administrators can inspect log entries generated by Postfix. The log detail can be increased using the smtp_tls_loglevel parameter in order to capture detailed troubleshooting information. The output logs, viewed via system log tools, reveal handshake processes, certificate chain verifications, and potential negotiation failures:

```
# Increase log verbosity for TLS negotiations (set to 1 in production
   )
smtp_tls_loglevel = 1
smtpd_tls_loglevel = 1
```

The following output represents a typical log snippet during successful TLS negotiation:

```
Jul 21 12:34:56 server postfix/smtpd[1234]:
   TLS connection established from mail.example.com[192.0.2.1]: TLSv1.2 with c
ipher ECDHE-RSA-AES256-GCM-SHA384 (256/256 bits)
```

This logging detail confirms that the correct protocol version and cipher suite have been engaged. Such output is used not only for troubleshooting but also for routinely verifying that TLS remains active and secure.

It is important to consider both operational and compliance strategies when configuring TLS in Postfix. Administrators must maintain an updated certificate, monitor for the timely revocation or renewal of certificates, and adhere to industry standards such as those defined by the Internet Engineering Task Force (IETF) and relevant security frameworks. Additionally, ensuring that system libraries and Postfix itself are updated to support the most secure encryption protocols is fundamental to preserving the security posture of the email server.

When testing changes to TLS configurations, performing controlled experiments in a staging environment is recommended. This process allows for regression testing and ensures that envelope and header data are processed correctly when TLS is enabled. The following checklist is useful before deploying TLS configuration changes in a production environment: confirm certificate validity, test client connections under various security levels, verify that session caching is functioning, and monitor log files for anomalies during the handshake process.

The configuration and maintenance of TLS in Postfix require continuous attention. As vulnerabilities are discovered and standards evolve, administrators must review and update the TLS-related settings periodically. This iterative process of monitoring, testing, and updating ensures that encrypted communications persist as a robust defense against emerging threats. The integrated approach, combining well-maintained certificates, strictly enforced protocol settings, rigorous cipher suite standards, and detailed logging, forms a cohesive strategy that solidifies the reliability and security of SMTP communications.

The detailed configurations described leverage Postfix's extensive capabilities to implement a scalable and secure email infrastructure. This focus on TLS not only benefits direct SMTP connections but also serves as an essential layer within an overall security model that includes SASL authentication, SPF, DKIM, and anti-spam solutions. Effective TLS configuration is indispensable for organizations requiring secure and reliable email services.

5.2. Implementing SASL Authentication

Simple Authentication and Security Layer (SASL) plays a pivotal role in verifying the identity of users who attempt to send email through your Postfix server. By delegating the authentication process to a SASL mechanism, Postfix is able to prevent unauthorized relay and ensure that only legitimate users gain access to mail services. This section builds upon the previously discussed security configurations, such as TLS, and explains the integration of SASL as an essential layer in email security.

Postfix does not handle SASL authentication internally; instead, it integrates with external authentication daemons, typically Cyrus SASL or Dovecot's authentication library. To integrate SASL with Postfix, the administrator must carefully configure both the Postfix main configuration file (main.cf) and the SASL daemon configuration. This integration allows for secure verification of user credentials during the SMTP session, typically on the submission port but also applicable to other ports if necessary.

The starting point in the configuration process is to ensure that Postfix is compiled with SASL support and that the SASL libraries are available on the system. For a system using Cyrus SASL, configuration files are located in /etc/sasl2/ and the main file for Postfix is commonly named smtp.conf or smtpd.conf. The service provider must specify the appropriate mechanisms (e.g., PLAIN, LOGIN, CRAM-MD5) in these files. The following is an example content of the /etc/sasl2/smtpd.conf file:

```
pwcheck_method: saslauthd
mech_list: PLAIN LOGIN
log_level: 7
```

The pwcheck_method directive indicates that the authentication daemon, typically saslauthd, is used to verify credentials. The mech_list parameter establishes the permitted authentication mechanisms. In production environments, additional mechanisms like CRAM-MD5 may be considered, although they introduce specific requirements for shared secrets and challenge-response protocols.

On the Postfix side, the `main.cf` file must be edited to include SASL settings that instruct Postfix to use the external SASL daemon. The following excerpt illustrates a basic configuration:

```
# Enable SASL authentication for incoming SMTP mail on submission
    port
smtpd_sasl_auth_enable = yes
smtpd_sasl_security_options = noanonymous
smtpd_sasl_local_domain = $myhostname
smtpd_sasl_authenticated_header = yes

# For outgoing mail connections with SASL authentication
smtp_sasl_auth_enable = yes
smtp_sasl_password_maps = hash:/etc/postfix/sasl_passwd
smtp_sasl_security_options = noanonymous
```

The parameter `smtpd_sasl_auth_enable` activates SASL for incoming connections, ensuring that users must be authenticated before their email is accepted. The option `noanonymous` disables anonymous login methods, fortifying the authentication process. When Postfix acts as a client for outgoing mail (e.g., relaying emails via another mail server), similar parameters are configured in the `smtp_sasl_*` settings.

The file `/etc/postfix/sasl_passwd` is critical for authenticating outgoing connections. This file stores user credentials in a key-value format used when Postfix needs to authenticate to a remote server. An example entry might look as follows:

```
smtp.example.com    username:password
```

After creating or modifying the `sasl_passwd` file, it is necessary to convert it into a format readable by Postfix using the `postmap` command:

```
postmap /etc/postfix/sasl_passwd
```

142

This step generates a hash file that Postfix uses, ensuring that plaintext credentials are not directly read during normal operation. It is important to restrict file permissions on both sasl_passwd and its corresponding hash file to prevent unauthorized access.

SASL authentication for incoming email is commonly used in conjunction with submission port usage. The service configuration for the submission port in /etc/postfix/master.cf must be updated to indicate that SASL authentication is required. An updated configuration might appear as follows:

```
submission inet n        -       n       -        -       smtpd
  -o syslog_name=postfix/submission
  -o smtpd_tls_security_level=encrypt
  -o smtpd_sasl_auth_enable=yes
  -o smtpd_relay_restrictions=permit_sasl_authenticated,reject
```

This configuration ensures that users connecting to the submission port must complete the TLS handshake prior to authentication and are only allowed to relay messages once they have provided valid credentials. The smtpd_relay_restrictions parameter works in tandem with SASL by permitting relays only when authentication has succeeded, thereby minimizing the risk of unauthorized use.

A common diagnostic challenge when implementing SASL is verifying that the authentication process functions as expected. Increasing the verbosity of logging for SASL can provide insights into failed or successful authentications. Postfix logs and the SASL daemon logs are usually consulted when troubleshooting. For example, enabling detailed logging in the SASL configuration might involve modifying settings in the smtpd.conf file or consulting system logs stored in /var/log/mail.log or a similar location. A typical log entry for a successful authentication session could be as follows:

```
Jul 21 13:45:02 server saslauthd[456]: ruser=unknown, tuser=username, mech=PL
AIN, rip=192.0.2.10, lip=192.0.2.1, execid=1234, sasl_method=PLAIN, service=s
mtp
```

143

This entry confirms that the SASL daemon has correctly processed the authentication request and logged pertinent details such as the mechanism used and the client IP address.

Security considerations during SASL configuration are paramount. Preventing brute-force attacks requires monitoring authentication attempts and potentially integrating rate-limiting measures. It is advisable to implement logging and alerting mechanisms within the overall server monitoring strategy. Further, ensuring that the SASL daemon is itself properly secured is critical. Running the authentication daemon under a dedicated, non-privileged user account and implementing strict access controls to its configuration and socket files contribute to a reduced attack surface.

Another aspect of implementing SASL involves careful selection of the authentication mechanism. While PLAIN and LOGIN are widely supported, their inherent vulnerability under plaintext transmission necessitates their use only in conjunction with TLS encryption. The enforcement of TLS on submission ports further mitigates the risks of employing these simple authentication mechanisms. When operating in a controlled environment where encryption is guaranteed, these mechanisms are acceptable due to their simplicity and broad compatibility.

For environments with heightened security requirements, deploying challenge-response mechanisms such as CRAM-MD5 introduces an additional layer of protection. The CRAM-MD5 mechanism requires both the client and server to share a secret, and the server transmits a challenge to which the client must respond with a hash response. Though more secure, this mechanism demands greater configuration effort, including the careful management of shared secrets. The following is an example line from a configuration file when opting for CRAM-MD5:

```
mech_list: PLAIN LOGIN CRAM-MD5
```

The inclusion of CRAM-MD5 in the mech_list ensures that clients capable of supporting this mechanism may choose it for enhanced security. However, interoperability considerations should be assessed, as not all mail clients support CRAM-MD5 uniformly.

In addition to configuring server parameters, administrators should ensure that the underlying authentication daemon, such as saslauthd, is robustly configured. Typical saslauthd options are specified in its start-up configuration, for instance:

```
# Start saslauthd with options to use PAM for authentication and
    define the socket path
/usr/sbin/saslauthd -a pam -m /var/run/saslauthd
```

The selection of PAM (Pluggable Authentication Modules) allows for integration with the system's native authentication mechanisms, which can include LDAP, Kerberos, or local user accounts. This configuration ensures that password policies and account lockout protocols defined system-wide are enforced when users attempt to authenticate via Postfix.

It is also essential to consider the implications of deploying SASL in a heterogeneous network environment. Compatibility issues between various client implementations and the selected authentication mechanisms can lead to unexpected behavior. Thorough testing in a staging environment, coupled with rigorous log monitoring, facilitates the identification and resolution of these issues prior to deployment in a production setting.

Administrators must remain vigilant by applying patches and updates to the SASL libraries, authentication daemons, and Postfix itself. Security advisories from software maintainers provide crucial guidance on mitigating vulnerabilities in authentication systems. Regular audits of the authentication logs help in detecting anomalies that may indicate attempted breaches or misconfigurations.

Integrating SASL with Postfix ultimately contributes to a layered security model. The combination of transport encryption via TLS and the assurance provided by SASL authentication significantly elevates the security level of email communications. This multifaceted approach ensures that not only are the contents of messages secured in transit, but the identities of participating entities are also validated and authenticated, reducing the likelihood of impersonation or unauthorized relay.

The comprehensive configuration presented herein for SASL authentication demonstrates careful attention to operational security, usability, and compatibility. By aligning SASL settings with the previously established TLS configurations, Postfix administrators can establish a secure email service that robustly authenticates users while maintaining encryption integrity. This alignment of security measures optimizes the overall integrity of the mail system and supports the goal of safeguarding sensitive communications against potential threats.

5.3. Configuring SPF, DKIM, and DMARC

Preventing email spoofing requires a multi-layered approach that combines domain-based policies with cryptographic verification methods. In this section, we detail how to deploy Sender Policy Framework (SPF), DomainKeys Identified Mail (DKIM), and Domain-based Message Authentication, Reporting, and Conformance (DMARC) to strengthen the trust and authenticity of email communications. Building on the encryption and authentication mechanisms discussed previously, these protocols work collectively to ensure that email messages are accepted only when they are verified as coming from authorized sources.

SPF provides a method for specifying which mail servers are permitted to send email on behalf of a domain. By publishing SPF records in the domain's DNS zone, administrators can instruct recipient servers to verify that incoming messages originate from IP addresses listed in these records. An SPF record is implemented as a TXT record in DNS. A typical SPF record might have the following form:

```
v=spf1 ip4:192.0.2.0/24 ip4:203.0.113.5 -all
```

In this example, the record indicates that only mail servers within the specified IP ranges are allowed to send email for the domain, and any message originating from an unauthorized IP address should be rejected. The use of "-all" at the end of the record enforces a strict policy. Alternative qualifiers such as " all" can be used for a more relaxed test mode that marks messages as suspicious rather than outright rejecting them.

DKIM adds another layer of security by enabling a cryptographic signature to be embedded in the header of each email. The signature is generated using a private key held by the sending domain and later verified using the corresponding public key published in DNS. This process ensures that the email contents have not been altered in transit and confirms the authenticity of the sender. The implementation of DKIM involves multiple steps: generating a key pair, signing outgoing messages, and publishing the public key in DNS.

A DKIM public key is added as a TXT record under a selector subdomain. For instance, if the selector is "default" and the domain is "example.com", the public key DNS record would be created for the subdomain "default._domainkey.example.com". An example DNS record for DKIM is as follows:

```
default._domainkey.example.com IN TXT "v=DKIM1; k=rsa; p=
    MIGfMA0GCSqGSIb3DQEBAQUAA4GNADCBiQKBgQC3..."
```

The private key generated should be securely stored and used by the mail transfer agent (MTA) during the email signing process. DKIM signing is typically managed through third-party tools or integrated solutions such as OpenDKIM, which interfaces directly with Postfix. The following snippet from an OpenDKIM configuration illustrates standard settings used to designate key locations and domain information:

```
# OpenDKIM configuration snippet
Domain          example.com
KeyFile         /etc/opendkim/keys/example.com/default.private
Selector        default
Socket          inet:12345@localhost
```

DMARC extends the trust framework by providing guidance on handling email that fails SPF or DKIM checks. DMARC policies are published as DNS TXT records and signal to recipient servers how to process unauthenticated email, whether to quarantine it, or to reject it outright. An example DMARC record could be written as follows:

```
v=DMARC1; p=reject; rua=mailto:dmarc-feedback@example.com; ruf=mailto
    :dmarc-errors@example.com; pct=100; aspf=s; adkim=s
```

In this configuration, the policy specifies that recipients should reject emails that fail DMARC evaluation. The tags `rua` and `ruf` designate reporting addresses that collect aggregate and forensic data, providing administrators with actionable insights regarding mail flow and potential abuse. The qualifiers `aspf` and `adkim` enforce strict alignment for SPF and DKIM, ensuring that both the envelope sender and the domain used in the DKIM signature match exactly the domain published in the DMARC record.

Coordinating SPF, DKIM, and DMARC requires careful synchronization of DNS records and mail server settings. For proper DMARC enforcement, it is imperative that the underlying SPF and DKIM configurations function correctly. An operational pipeline can be validated through simulated email traffic, where tools such as `dig` and `opendkim-testkey` are used to verify DNS entries and key functions.

For example, validating the SPF record might involve:

```
dig TXT example.com
```

This command retrieves the TXT records associated with the domain, enabling verification of the SPF record's syntax and content. Likewise, verifying the DKIM key can be conducted using:

```
opendkim-testkey -d example.com -s default -vvv
```

This command validates the key for the `default` selector, providing detailed output that indicates whether the public key is correctly published in DNS and the private key is properly loaded by the signing daemon.

Once the SPF, DKIM, and DMARC records are in place, it is essential to monitor their performance. DMARC reporting facilitates insight into how recipient servers execute these policies, presenting data on compliance, traffic volumes, and potential spoofing attempts. Administrators can process these reports using dedicated DMARC analysis tools to refine policy settings continuously. Fine-tuning the DMARC policy might include moving from a "none" policy, where actions are only monitored, to "quarantine" or "reject" policies as reliability is established.

The deployment of these protocols should also consider the impact on legitimate email traffic. It is common to initially configure DMARC with a policy of p=none to merely collect data without affecting message delivery. This reporting phase is critical for understanding how external email servers interpret SPF and DKIM validations. The gradual transition from monitoring to enforcement enables organizations to adjust their policies, ensuring that trusted marketing or transactional emails are not inadvertently blocked if misconfigurations occur.

A thorough configuration process also involves periodic reviews and updates. In particular, DNS records for SPF, DKIM, and DMARC must be maintained to reflect changes in mail server infrastructure. For example, when adding additional IP addresses or switching cloud providers, the SPF record must be updated to incorporate the new sending sources. Similarly, if DKIM keys need rotation due to key expiration or compromise, a new key pair must be generated, and corresponding DNS records updated accordingly.

It is prudent to maintain detailed documentation regarding the DNS records used for these protocols. This includes noting the selectors used for DKIM, the domains targeted by DMARC policies, and any exceptions or subdomains that have separate handling. Keeping a versioned record of these changes assists in troubleshooting and ensures coherent policy enforcement across the mail ecosystem.

The integration of SPF, DKIM, and DMARC not only improves email deliverability but also reduces the risk of domain spoofing and phishing attacks. By verifying that emails originate from verified servers and that messages have remained unchanged in transit, recipient servers build higher confidence in the legitimacy of the message. Additionally, detailed DMARC reports empower administrators to track unauthorized use of their domains and respond to incidents promptly.

Administrators should also be aware of potential limitations with these systems. For instance, forwarding emails can sometimes break SPF checks, and care must be taken to either adjust the SPF record with mechanisms such as `include` directives or rely more heavily on DKIM validation. This interplay between the protocols underscores the importance of a coherent configuration that addresses real-world email routing and delivery scenarios.

Command-line tools and software packages available for monitoring and testing these implementations provide valuable feedback. Automated scripts can be developed to periodically query DNS and simulate email sending, verifying that the public keys are correct and that mail servers properly apply DMARC policies. An example of such a testing script might include the use of the `nslookup` tool:

```
nslookup -type=TXT _dmarc.example.com
```

This command returns the DMARC configuration for the domain, offering an easy method for verifying that policy updates have propagated correctly. Additionally, integrating such checks with existing monitoring infrastructure ensures that any misconfiguration is detected rapidly, reducing the window during which spoofed emails might be accepted.

Deploying these mechanisms requires adherence to best practices and a detailed review of vendor and community-provided guidelines. Each component—SPF, DKIM, and DMARC—has associated documentation on deployment, troubleshooting, and performance optimization. By following these guidelines and continuously calibrating the settings with operational feedback, administrators can ensure that the email infrastructure remains resilient against evolving threats.

Deploying SPF, DKIM, and DMARC in tandem establishes a robust defense against email spoofing. The detailed configuration processes described herein integrate seamlessly with other server security measures such as TLS and SASL. In achieving a high degree of accuracy in specifying authorized sending sources, cryptographically signing email content, and enforcing sending policies, the resulting infrastructure significantly mitigates the risk of email abuse. This tightly coupled security framework not only supports improved deliverability and trust among email recipients but also fortifies the overall posture of the communication system.

5.4. Using Postfix with Firewall and SELinux

Integrating Postfix with a hardened firewall and configuring Security-Enhanced Linux (SELinux) provides additional layers of security that mitigate unauthorized access and minimize the risk of exploitation. This section details methods to secure Postfix services by applying precise firewall rules to restrict network access and by leveraging SELinux policies to enforce mandatory access controls on mail processes.

Postfix, as a network-facing application, is subject to a variety of network-level threats. Employing a firewall to limit incoming and out-going traffic to and from Postfix not only reduces the attack surface but also provides an initial barrier against port scanning and brute-force attacks. Administrators can utilize various firewall solutions, such as iptables, nftables, or firewalld, depending on the system requirements and distribution. A common strategy is to restrict access on the default SMTP (port 25), SMTPS (port 465), and submission (port 587) ports to trusted networks or specific IP address ranges.

For instance, using `iptables` to limit connections to the SMTP port may involve a set of rules similar to the following:

```
# Accept incoming SMTP traffic from trusted networks
iptables -A INPUT -p tcp -s 192.0.2.0/24 --dport 25 -j ACCEPT
iptables -A INPUT -p tcp -s 203.0.113.0/24 --dport 25 -j ACCEPT

# Drop other incoming SMTP traffic
iptables -A INPUT -p tcp --dport 25 -j DROP

# Allow loopback connections
iptables -A INPUT -i lo -j ACCEPT
```

These rules permit SMTP connections only from specific subnets while rejecting unauthorized traffic. An equivalent configuration can be managed using `firewalld` by creating a custom service definition or by adding rich rules. A sample configuration with `firewall-cmd` com-mands might be:

```
# Add trusted IP ranges to a custom firewall zone
firewall-cmd --permanent --new-zone=trusted_mail
firewall-cmd --permanent --zone=trusted_mail --add-source
    =192.0.2.0/24
firewall-cmd --permanent --zone=trusted_mail --add-port=25/tcp
firewall-cmd --permanent --zone=trusted_mail --add-port=587/tcp

# Reload firewall settings
firewall-cmd --reload
```

In environments where dynamic IP addresses are in use or where external services must relay mail, administrators may need additional flexibility. This can be achieved by incorporating stateful firewall rules that track established connections, ensuring that only legitimate sessions are permitted to continue communication while new attempts are evaluated against existing security policies.

Beyond network filtering, SELinux provides robust mechanisms to enforce access controls that are independent of traditional discretionary access control (DAC) systems. Configuring SELinux for Postfix involves ensuring that all processes, files, and network ports have their correct contexts assigned. SELinux policies are designed to confine Postfix operations and prevent privilege escalation even if an attacker compromises one element of the system.

SELinux operates using predefined type enforcement rules that label processes and files. The Postfix executable and its configuration files must have the appropriate SELinux context. For example, the main Postfix binaries and spool directories are typically associated with the postfix_t type. Checking the SELinux context of a critical Postfix file is performed with the ls -Z command:

```
ls -Z /usr/sbin/postfix
```

A typical output would indicate a domain such as system_u:object_r:postfix_exec_t:s0 for the executable, ensuring that it operates under the restrictions intended by SELinux. If contexts are found to differ from expected values, the utility restorecon can be used to reapply the default contexts:

```
restorecon -Rv /etc/postfix /var/spool/postfix
```

SELinux policies for Postfix can be fine-tuned using booleans, which provide administrators with a modular approach to modify security constraints at runtime without rewriting the entire policy. For instance, when Postfix is configured to send emails via a remote SMTP server or when integration with external authentication services is required, a boolean may need to be adjusted to permit these operations. To view the current status of mail-related booleans, the command `getsebool -a | grep postfix` is useful:

```
getsebool -a | grep postfix
```

Should administrators need to enable Postfix networking beyond its default set of operations, they might set a boolean value as follows:

```
setsebool -P postfix_local_write_mail_spool 1
```

The `-P` flag ensures that the change persists across reboots. Similarly, integrating Postfix with certain Dovecot configurations or SASL authentication may require toggling additional booleans to expand allowed interactions while retaining strict access controls.

When configuring SELinux, conflicts are sometimes identified through audit logs. These logs, located in `/var/log/audit/audit.log` or accessed via the `ausearch` command, record denials that require administrative intervention. A typical denial may indicate that Postfix attempted to access a resource with an incorrect context. For example:

```
type=AVC msg=audit(1609459200.123:456): avc:  denied  { write } for  pid=1234
 comm="postfix" name="maildrop" dev="sda1" ino=56789 scontext=system_u:system
_r:postfix_t:s0 tcontext=system_u:object_r:mail_spool_t:s0 tclass=dir
```

In such cases, the `audit2allow` tool can help generate a custom policy module to permit the legitimate access while preserving overall SELinux security. An example process for generating and applying a custom policy module is as follows:

```
# Generate a policy module from the audit logs
ausearch -c 'postfix' --raw | audit2allow -M postfix_local_policy

# Install the module
semodule -i postfix_local_policy.pp
```

This mechanism ensures that any necessary permissions are granted in a controlled manner, reducing the risk of overly broad adjustments that could compromise the security model.

It is also pertinent to combine firewall and SELinux configurations effectively. When the firewall restricts network access at the packet level, SELinux continues to enforce process-level controls. This dual approach ensures that even if an attacker bypasses one line of defense, subsequent layers provide robust barriers. Administrators must coordinate the rules between these systems so that they do not inadvertently conflict. For example, while firewall rules may allow traffic on a specific port, SELinux must also permit the Postfix daemon to bind to that port. Verifying this binding is accomplished with the `semanage port -l | grep smtp` command:

```
semanage port -l | grep smtp
```

This will list the port assignments and their associated SELinux types. To add a new port, the following command demonstrates the process:

```
semanage port -a -t smtp_port_t -p tcp 587
```

In scenarios where mail submission is facilitated through nonstandard ports, ensuring that SELinux policy recognizes and permits access to these ports is essential for maintaining services without triggering security denials.

An additional layer of protection is achieved by monitoring the effects of firewall and SELinux integration. Automated scripts and monitoring tools can be configured to audit the rules periodically, checking for deviations in SELinux contexts or misconfigurations in firewall settings. Tools such as `fail2ban` may be integrated with Postfix to detect unusual authentication attempts and subsequently modify firewall entries dynamically. A simple configuration snippet for `fail2ban` might include:

```
[postfix]
enabled = true
```

```
port    = smtp,ssmtp,submission
filter  = postfix
logpath = /var/log/mail.log
maxretry = 3
```

Combining such tools enhances overall security by rapidly detecting and mitigating potential intrusions, while SELinux policies continue to enforce strict process restrictions.

Integrating Postfix with a firewall and SELinux is an exercise in balancing operational flexibility with security rigidity. Both systems require careful configuration and continuous maintenance to ensure that legitimate email traffic is not inadvertently disrupted while blocking unauthorized access. Maintaining documentation for firewall rules and SELinux policies, including backup copies of configuration files and a log of changes applied, is essential for troubleshooting and auditing purposes. This documentation supports adherence to best practices and compliance with institutional security policies.

Incorporating these practices not only hardens the Postfix service but also aligns with a defense-in-depth strategy, ensuring that each network communication step and process execution is verified and contained. Combining network-layer filtering with mandatory access controls provides resilience against both external and internal threats. The strategies and examples provided in this section underscore the importance of a holistic approach to electronic mail security, wherein multiple, overlapping security mechanisms collectively safeguard against the evolving landscape of cyber threats.

5.5. Mitigating Spam with Anti-Spam Tools

Mitigating unsolicited email is essential for maintaining both server performance and user satisfaction. Anti-spam tools integrate with Postfix to inspect incoming messages, score their likelihood of being spam, and take appropriate actions based on predefined thresholds. This section details the implementation and configuration of anti-spam solutions to enhance Postfix's filtering capabilities by leveraging systems such as SpamAssassin, along with supporting tools that include Bayesian filtering, DNS block list lookups, and supplementary services like Razor and Pyzor.

SpamAssassin is one of the most widely deployed anti-spam solutions in the email ecosystem. It employs a combination of heuristic rules, Bayesian statistical techniques, and external network tests (for example, DNS-based blacklists) to generate a spam score for each message. When a message's score exceeds a specified threshold, it can be tagged, quarantined, or rejected based on policy decisions. Its flexibility allows administrators to tune scoring thresholds and incorporate custom rules that reflect the threat landscape specific to their environment.

To integrate SpamAssassin with Postfix, one common configuration involves setting up SpamAssassin as a content filter. In this model, Postfix passes incoming messages to the spam filter via a dedicated content filter service. The filtered messages are subsequently re-injected into the Postfix pipeline for further processing or delivery. A typical integration can be achieved by adding a content filter directive in the main.cf file as shown below:

```
# Configure Postfix to use SpamAssassin as a content filter
content_filter = spamassassin:dummy
```

Following this, a service must be defined in the master.cf file to redirect email traffic through SpamAssassin. A common approach uses the pipe delivery method combined with the SpamAssassin client spamc:

```
spamassassin unix -    n    n    -    -    pipe
   flags=Rq user=spamd argv=/usr/bin/spamc -f -e
   /usr/sbin/sendmail -oi -f ${sender} ${recipient}
```

In this configuration, Postfix calls spamc, which forwards the message to the SpamAssassin daemon for filtering. The sendmail command is then used to re-inject the message into Postfix after processing. Key flags used in the configuration include -f to maintain the original sender's identity and -e to ensure that errors in spam processing do not cause message loss.

In addition to setting up the content filter, administrators must fine-tune SpamAssassin's configuration to suit local requirements. Critical parameters include the score threshold above which a message is considered spam, as well as settings for enabling Bayesian analysis and external rule sets. The following snippet illustrates sample configuration options typically placed in the local.cf file in SpamAssassin's configuration directory:

```
# Set the score threshold for classifying messages as spam
required_score 5.0

# Enable safe report mode to append analysis results rather than
    altering message content
report_safe 0

# Activate Bayesian filtering with automatic learning from incoming
    messages
use_bayes 1
bayes_auto_learn 1

# Integrate with additional rule sets and collaborative filtering
    tools
use_razor2 1
use_pyzor 1
```

These options ensure that the anti-spam filtering mechanism remains adaptive over time. The bayes_auto_learn option allows SpamAssassin to automatically update its learning database based on the messages processed. Additionally, integration with collaborative filtering tools such as Razor and Pyzor extends the detection capabilities by incorporating community-driven intelligence regarding spam characteristics.

SpamAssassin also supports custom rule definitions that can be tailored to local spam trends. Administrators may create custom rules that examine various headers, message body patterns, or even embedded URLs. For example, a custom rule might be defined to flag messages with suspicious subject lines:

```
body    LOCAL_RULE_1  /Free\s+Offer/i
score   LOCAL_RULE_1  2.5
describe LOCAL_RULE_1  Suspicious subject phrase detected
```

Rules like these can be added to a user-defined rules file, enabling administrators to address spam patterns that are unique to their environment. It is important to test new rules in a staging environment before deploying them into production to minimize false positives that might inadvertently affect legitimate communications.

Detailed logging and monitoring of the anti-spam filter's performance are integral to the overall email security strategy. SpamAssassin logs can be integrated with system logging facilities to capture scoring information and actions taken on each message. Administrators should periodically review these logs to identify recurring issues or to adjust thresholds and rule weights as needed. A typical log entry from SpamAssassin might resemble the following:

```
Aug 18 15:23:45 server spamd[2345]: spamd: result: 7.2, required: 5.0, tests:
BAYES_99, SPF_FAIL, RCVD_IN_DNSWL_LOW;
```

This output indicates that the message exceeded the spam threshold and lists the tests that contributed to the final score, helping administrators refine the configuration.

Postfix can also be configured to work in tandem with additional anti-spam tools that perform pre-filtering, such as postscreen. Postscreen is a built-in feature of Postfix that performs early checks on incoming SMTP connections, reducing the volume of unwanted connections before messages are handed off to the full Postfix processing engine. By verifying the legitimacy of connecting clients using techniques such as connection pruning and protocol anomaly detection, postscreen effectively reduces the workload on SpamAssassin and other comprehensive filters.

Configuration of postscreen in `main.cf` may include parameters such as:

```
# Enable postscreen to perform early spam and abuse checks
postscreen_enable = yes
postscreen_dnsbl_sites = zen.spamhaus.org, bl.spamcop.net
postscreen_greet_action = enforce
```

In this configuration, postscreen checks connecting clients against well-known DNS-based block lists (DNSBLs) before accepting the connection. Messages from IP addresses listed in these DNSBLs can be delayed or rejected, thereby reducing the spam load on subsequent filtering stages.

Complementary to postscreen and SpamAssassin, ad hoc anti-spam measures such as header rewriting and spam tagging also bolster overall protection. Once SpamAssassin assigns a spam score, administrators may choose to modify the email headers to include tags that indicate the spam status. Custom header modifications can be configured through SpamAssassin directives:

```
# Append a custom header to flag spam
add_header all Spam-Flag _YESNOCONFIRMED_
add_header all Spam-Score %{score} (threshold=%{required_score})
```

These headers not only provide visual feedback to end users and mail administrators but also enable downstream systems to automate further actions (for example, moving messages to a designated spam folder).

Integrating these anti-spam measures with a learning and feedback loop further refines the email filtering process. Administrators can configure systems to automatically feed confirmed spam or false positives back into SpamAssassin for ongoing learning. This iterative process improves the accuracy of Bayesian filters and helps adjust scoring algorithms to better reflect the current threat landscape. Manual training of the spam filter may be accomplished through command-line utilities or by configuring user interfaces that allow end users to mark messages as spam or non-spam. Such training can be periodically executed using commands like:

```
sa-learn --spam /path/to/spam/folder
sa-learn --ham /path/to/ham/folder
```

Regular use of these commands ensures that the Bayesian classifier maintains a high level of accuracy, minimizing the potential for misclassification.

Effective anti-spam implementations require periodic reviews and updates. Spam trends evolve constantly, and the rule sets and external services leveraged by SpamAssassin must be kept current. Automated updates of rule sets can be enabled through tools provided by SpamAssassin, while community-provided feeds offer supplementary protections. Administrators are encouraged to subscribe to relevant mailing lists and security advisories, ensuring that the spam-filtering system remains robust against emerging threats.

It is essential to consider the performance implications of deploying comprehensive anti-spam solutions. Running SpamAssassin on high volumes of email may introduce processing delays during peak times. In such scenarios, load balancing via additional filtering servers or leveraging cloud-based anti-spam services can distribute the processing load effectively. Consolidating postscreen, SpamAssassin, and any additional filtering layers into an integrated architecture that addresses both spam detection and throughput will enhance the overall stability of the email service.

Coordinated integration, thorough testing, and attentive tuning of these anti-spam tools complement the previously discussed security configurations such as TLS and SASL. With a layered approach to email protection, Postfix installations benefit from a robust environment that reduces unwanted email while ensuring that legitimate messages are delivered promptly. The careful interplay of content filtering, early connection screening, and adaptive learning forms a comprehensive defense against spam, thereby supporting the operational integrity and reputation of the mail system.

5.6. Setting Up Greylisting and Blacklisting

Greylisting and blacklisting are effective techniques employed to reduce unwanted email traffic. Both methods aim to block potentially malicious or unsolicited messages by imposing temporary or permanent restrictions on email traffic based on sender characteristics. Greylisting temporarily rejects emails from unknown senders, while blacklisting permanently blocks senders identified as sources of spam. These mechanisms complement the encryption, authentication, and anti-spam strategies discussed previously, providing an additional layer of defense against unwanted email.

Greylisting operates by rejecting all inbound email from a sender–client combination that the mail server does not recognize. The underlying assumption is that legitimate mail servers will retry delivery after a short delay in accordance with SMTP standards, while many spam servers either do not attempt a retry or have significantly delayed retry intervals. Upon receiving an email from an unrecognized sender, Postfix issues a temporary rejection code. When a compliant server retries after the specified time window, the sender's information is added to a temporary whitelist and subsequent messages are accepted. This method results in a delay in email delivery from new senders but significantly reduces spam volume.

One popular tool for implementing greylisting with Postfix is `postgrey`.

Installation on many Linux distributions can be performed via the package manager. For example, on a Debian-based system, one might execute:

```
apt-get install postgrey
```

After installation, `postgrey` is typically integrated with Postfix by adding a content filter or by adjusting the master service configuration. A sample configuration modification in `/etc/postfix/master.cf` may look as follows:

```
# Greylisting service using postgrey
smtp      inet  n       -        n        -        -        smtpd
  -o content_filter=postgrey:dummy

postgrey unix  -        n        n        -        -        spawn
    user=postgrey argv=/usr/sbin/postgrey --inet=10023 --delay=300
```

In this configuration, Postfix redirects incoming SMTP traffic to the greylisting service running on a non-standard port (in this example, port 10023). The `--delay=300` option specifies that temporary rejections will be issued for a period of 300 seconds. This delay window is selected based on the expected behavior of reputable mail servers that will automatically retry transmission after several minutes. Tuning the delay parameter allows administrators to balance the trade-off between spam reduction and the impact on email delivery latency.

Greylisting implementations often maintain a temporary database of accepted sender–client pairs. This database can be stored in memory or on disk; the choice of storage has implications on both performance and resource usage. File-based storage may require periodic cleanup of expired entries to ensure the database remains efficient. Administrators should monitor the greylisting logs to fine-tune these aspects, ensuring that legitimate traffic is not adversely affected by overly aggressive time limits.

Blacklisting, by contrast, is a more permanent filtering mechanism that identifies and blocks traffic from sources known to send spam. Black-lists may contain IP addresses, domain names, or sender IDs that have a documented history of sending unsolicited email. These lists can be locally maintained or sourced from reputable third-party providers such as Spamhaus, SpamCop, and others. When an incoming email matches an entry in the blacklist, it is either rejected outright or sub-jected to further scrutiny.

For local blacklisting in Postfix, administrators can use hash files that map sender addresses or IP ranges to a rejection status. A common im-plementation involves creating a text file containing entries that define the blacklisted entities. An example of a `blacklist_sender` file might include:

```
spammer@example.com     REJECT
123.123.123.123         REJECT
bad-domain.com          REJECT
```

After populating the file with the desired entries, the administrator must convert it into a hash table that Postfix can query using the `postmap` command:

```
postmap /etc/postfix/blacklist_sender
```

The main Postfix configuration file, `main.cf`, is then updated to refer-ence the blacklist file. For example:

```
smtpd_sender_restrictions =
    check_sender_access hash:/etc/postfix/blacklist_sender,
    permit_mynetworks,
    reject_unauth_destination
```

This configuration checks the sender's address against the locally main-tained blacklist. If a match is found, the message is rejected accord-ing to the policy specified. The ordering of restrictions is critical; lo-cal rules should follow checks that permit internal communications but should take precedence over generic relay restrictions to ensure that spam is blocked before progressing through the mail processing pipeline.

Beyond local blacklisting, integration with external DNS-based black-lists (DNSBLs) enhances Postfix's capability to recognize and block traffic from known spam sources. DNSBLs function by providing a real-time lookup service that maps IP addresses to reputational scores. Postfix can query these lists as part of its restriction configuration. An example setting in main.cf might be:

```
smtpd_client_restrictions =
    permit_mynetworks,
    reject_rbl_client zen.spamhaus.org,
    reject_rbl_client bl.spamcop.net
```

In this configuration, any client IP address that appears in the DNS-BLs maintained by Spamhaus or SpamCop is rejected during the SMTP handshake. Utilizing DNSBLs requires careful monitoring, as over-reliance may lead to false positives. It is important to periodically review the reputational status of the DNSBL providers and adjust configurations as necessary.

For both greylisting and blacklisting, comprehensive logging and report analysis are essential to ensuring that legitimate email is not inadvertently delayed or dropped. Postfix and its associated tools generate logs that capture the reasons for temporary rejections or permanent blocks. An administrator could use system tools like grep and tail to extract relevant log entries. For example:

```
tail -f /var/log/mail.log | grep 'postgrey'
```

This command filters logs in real time for entries generated by postgrey, allowing administrators to assess the behavior of greylisting and determine if any adjustments are needed to the delay or retry parameters.

One aspect to consider when setting up greylisting is its potential impact on legitimate senders. While most compliant mail servers will

165

retry delivery automatically, some may experience delays that are noticeable to users. Administrators may mitigate this by implementing an allowlist (whitelist) for trusted senders or IP ranges. Whitelisting can be implemented in `postgrey` by maintaining a separate file of trusted entities. A sample whitelist file could appear as follows:

```
trusted-sender@example.com      OK
192.0.2.10                      OK
```

After modifying the whitelist, a similar `postmap` operation may be required, and the greylisting service must be reloaded or restarted to apply the changes.

Blacklisting policies must also be dynamic. Spam sources evolve, and blacklists must be updated regularly to remain effective. Automation plays a key role in this process, such as using scheduled scripts (via cron) to update local blacklists from reputable DNSBL providers. An example cron job to update a blacklist daily might be:

```
0 3 * * * /usr/local/bin/update_blacklist.sh
```

The `update_blacklist.sh` script could download updated lists, merge them with the locally maintained file, and then regenerate the hash file via `postmap`. Such automation ensures that the system remains current without requiring frequent manual intervention.

A combined approach that uses both greylisting and blacklisting can yield significant benefits. Greylisting provides a low-overhead mechanism to delay communication from unknown senders, while blacklisting definitively blocks senders identified as malicious. Implementing both techniques provides complementary layers of filtering that are effective against different spammer behaviors. Furthermore, these techniques work in tandem with other anti-spam tools such as SpamAssassin and postscreen, creating a comprehensive system that inspects emails at multiple layers before delivery.

Evaluation and fine-tuning of greylisting and blacklisting rules form an ongoing maintenance task. Administrators should regularly review logs, analyze false positive rates, and adjust parameters to ensure the balance between security and usability. Monitoring tools and dashboards can be deployed to provide at-a-glance status updates on greylisting and blacklisting performance. These tools may visualize retry statistics, temporary rejection rates, and the frequency of blacklisted entries, thereby offering insight into potential adjustments needed in greylisting delay periods or blacklist thresholds.

Implementing these systems within an overall robust email security architecture ensures that Postfix continues to provide a high-quality service. The combined use of greylisting and blacklisting elevates the capability to filter spam before it reaches user mailboxes, reducing the likelihood of spam-related attacks, phishing attempts, and resource depletion due to excessive processing. By carefully configuring these mechanisms, monitoring performance, and automating updates, administrators can maintain a resilient mail system that adapts to new threats and evolving email traffic patterns.

This multifaceted approach, which integrates both temporary and permanent blocking measures, is central to modern email defense strategies. Fine-grained control over greylisting parameters and dynamic, automated blacklisting of known offenders helps ensure that legitimate email flows with minimal disruption while unwanted traffic is effectively curtailed. The techniques and examples provided in this section build upon previous security enhancements such as TLS, SASL, and anti-spam filtering, culminating in a secure, resilient, and efficient email infrastructure.

Chapter 6

Managing Users and Mailboxes

This chapter provides guidance on managing users and mailboxes in Postfix, including creating local users and configuring virtual mailboxes. It covers the use of aliases and forwarding for efficient mail routing and the integration of mailbox quotas to control storage usage. Additionally, it explains how to manage mailing lists and utilize external authentication sources like LDAP for scalable and streamlined user management.

6.1. Creating and Managing Local Users

Managing local user accounts on a Postfix email server involves creating system user accounts, configuring mailbox settings, and ensuring that Postfix correctly interacts with these accounts. Local users can either be genuine system users or dedicated mail accounts designed solely for handling emails. In environments where system-level authentication is preferred, local users correspond directly to user accounts in the operating system. Postfix leverages these accounts to deliver email directly to mail spools within designated directories, commonly under /var/mail or /home/username/Maildir.

When setting up a local user intended for email reception, it is essential to decide on the mailbox format. Postfix supports both *mbox* and *Maildir* formats. The *mbox* format stores all emails in a single file per user, while the *Maildir* format uses a directory structure that holds individual email files. The choice between these formats often depends on performance requirements and administrative preferences. In many modern installations, *Maildir* is preferred because it facilitates easier management of large volumes of messages and reduces the risk of file corruption.

To create a new local user, system administrators typically use the useradd or adduser commands available on Linux distributions. These commands not only establish a new user account but also create a home directory which can be configured to serve as the mail storage location. A sample command to create a user with a dedicated home directory might be:

```
useradd -m -s /bin/bash exampleuser
```

In this example, the -m flag ensures that a home directory is created, and the shell is set to /bin/bash using the -s option. After creating the account, it is necessary to configure the mailbox environment. For a Maildir format mailbox, the user's home directory should contain a Maildir directory. The following command creates this structure for the new user:

```
mkdir -p /home/exampleuser/Maildir/{cur,new,tmp}
chown -R exampleuser:exampleuser /home/exampleuser/Maildir
```

Postfix must be informed of the chosen mailbox format. This is typically done by adjusting the home_mailbox or mail_spool_directory parameter in the Postfix configuration file (/etc/postfix/main.cf). For example, if the system uses the mbox format by default, but a specific user requires a Maildir mailbox, a transport mapping may be configured to override the default. The following configuration snippet illustrates how a virtual alias map might be used to redirect mail to the correct location:

```
home_mailbox = Maildir/
```

This directive directs Postfix to deliver mail into the Maildir subdirectory of the user's home directory. In scenarios where multiple mailbox formats coexist, the configuration may require more granular control using transport maps or user-specific configurations.

A common task in local user management is modifying user settings after account creation, such as changing mailbox quotas and updating user passwords. Quotas can be managed either through system-level quota tools or integrated into Postfix via external scripts or policies. One standard approach involves using utilities like edquota to set storage limits on the user's home directory. This ensures that excessive email growth does not result in full disk capacity, potentially disrupting mail delivery for all users.

Password management is equally critical. Security best practices dictate periodic password changes and the use of strong passwords. System administrators can enforce these policies using tools such as passwd:

```
passwd exampleuser
```

The passwd command initiates an interactive session where the new password is securely entered by the administrator or user. Output from this command in a typical session appears as:

```
Changing password for user exampleuser.
```

```
New password:
Retype new password:
passwd: all authentication tokens updated successfully.
```

Integrating these user management practices with Postfix requires careful synchronization between system configurations and email delivery parameters. The user's home directory, shell, and mailbox configuration must be consistent. In Postfix, certain directives in main.cf control this interaction. For example, the mailbox_command parameter can be modified to use a custom delivery agent depending on the mailbox format or additional processing requirements. A sample configuration might be:

```
mailbox_command = /usr/lib/dovecot/deliver
```

Here, Postfix hands off incoming mail to the Dovecot Local Delivery Agent (LDA), which is responsible for placing emails in the user's mailbox. This kind of integration is particularly useful when additional processing like spam filtering or message indexing is performed by the LDA.

Furthermore, administrators may need to audit and monitor the management of local users to ensure the health and security of the email system. Regular auditing can involve verifying the consistency of home directories, checking file permissions, and reviewing changes to the Postfix configuration. Using system tools like ls -l and log checking utilities aids in this process. For example:

```
ls -l /home/exampleuser/Maildir
```

This command lists the contents of the Maildir, providing insight into whether the directory and its files have proper ownership and permissions. Misconfigured permissions may result in undelivered mail or security vulnerabilities.

In addition to hand-crafting configurations and commands,

172

automated scripts can streamline the process of local user management. A bash script that combines user creation, Maildir setup, and permission assignment reduces manual intervention and minimizes errors. An example script is provided below:

```bash
#!/bin/bash
# Create a new local user and set up Maildir for Postfix

if [ "$#" -ne 1 ]; then
    echo "Usage: $0 username"
    exit 1
fi

USERNAME=$1

# Create user and home directory
useradd -m -s /bin/bash "$USERNAME"
if [ $? -ne 0 ]; then
    echo "Error creating user $USERNAME."
    exit 1
fi

# Set up Maildir structure
MAILDIR="/home/$USERNAME/Maildir"
mkdir -p "$MAILDIR"/{cur,new,tmp}
chown -R "$USERNAME":"$USERNAME" "$MAILDIR"
echo "User $USERNAME created with Maildir at $MAILDIR."
```

Running this script with a valid username automates several steps. An execution might look like this:

```
$ sudo ./create_mailuser.sh exampleuser
User exampleuser created with Maildir at /home/exampleuser/Maildir.
```

This script encapsulates best practices by checking for errors and ensuring proper ownership throughout the process.

Effective management of local users also involves handling account removal and associated cleanup tasks. When a local user is removed, it is critical to ensure that their mail spool is addressed appropriately. If their mailbox is not archived or purged properly, residual data may lead to disk usage anomalies or potential security issues. The removal process should thus combine system-level user deletion with cleanup steps for mailbox directories. A command to remove a user and their home directory is:

```
userdel -r exampleuser
```

The -r flag ensures that the home directory and associated files are removed. If Postfix was configured to use a centralized location for mail storage rather than user home directories, corresponding adjustments must be made to the cleanup scripts and file management policies.

Another point of consideration in managing local users is the synchronization between Postfix and any additional mail-related services such as spam filters, antivirus engines, or backup systems. These services often need access to mailbox files and directories. Therefore, coordinating file permissions, group memberships, and access control policies is necessary to ensure that all components function harmoniously without compromising security. Advanced administrators may employ system audit tools to monitor changes in these directories and adjust configurations in response to identified anomalies.

Robust user management also entails ensuring redundancy and reliability in the face of hardware or software failures. Local user accounts form the backbone of authentication for email delivery. As such, backup strategies that encompass both user account data and mailbox contents are integral to maintaining service continuity. Backup mechanisms may range from simple file system snapshots to more advanced replication techniques, ensuring that user data is recoverable.

Postfix, in conjunction with other system services, provides administrators with the tools necessary to create, modify, and remove local user accounts reliably. Each change in the user management schema should be considered in the context of the overall email service architecture. Consistency in configuration between Postfix and system-level settings is paramount to avoid disruptions in service.

Understanding and implementing these practices in a coordinated manner ensures that local users are managed effectively on a Postfix email server.

6.2. Configuring Virtual Mailboxes

Configuring virtual mailboxes in Postfix enables email handling without the need for corresponding system user accounts. This method separates mailbox management from system-level authentication and account creation, offering improved scalability and flexibility. Virtual mailboxes typically rely on external databases or flat files to store mapping information, directing emails to designated directories under a common virtual user or a dedicated mail storage area.

In a typical setup, Postfix distinguishes between local and virtual domains. Virtual domains are defined in the Postfix configuration through the parameter `virtual_mailbox_domains`. This directive lists domains for which Postfix will use virtual mailbox mappings rather than system users. For example, a configuration in `/etc/postfix/main.cf` might include:

```
virtual_mailbox_domains = example.com, example.org
```

Mapping email addresses to corresponding mailbox directories is achieved using the `virtual_mailbox_maps` parameter. This parameter can reference a hash table, a MySQL database, or other lookup mechanisms. A common approach is to use a hash map stored in a flat file. An excerpt demonstrating this configuration is:

```
virtual_mailbox_maps = hash:/etc/postfix/vmailbox
```

The file `/etc/postfix/vmailbox` contains entries that map individual email addresses to their mailbox paths. A typical entry appears as follows:

175

```
user1@example.com     example.com/user1/
user2@example.com     example.com/user2/
```

After editing the file, it is necessary to compile it into a format that Postfix can query effectively using the `postmap` command:

```
postmap /etc/postfix/vmailbox
```

This command produces a corresponding `/etc/postfix/vmailbox.db` file that Postfix accesses during mail delivery operations.

The delivery mechanism itself is defined by the `virtual_transport` directive in `main.cf`. In configurations that use Dovecot's Local Delivery Agent (LDA) or LMTP, this parameter directs mail accordingly. For instance:

```
virtual_transport = lmtp:unix:private/dovecot-lmtp
```

This setting instructs Postfix to hand off emails to the Dovecot LDA via LMTP, ensuring that messages are delivered to the appropriate virtual mailbox as defined in the mapping table. The use of LMTP bypasses the constraints of system user authentication, providing a streamlined delivery process.

Virtual mailbox configurations often require careful attention to file system permissions and directory layouts. A dedicated virtual mailbox directory is generally created to house all mail data. An administrator might designate a directory such as `/var/vmail` as the root for all virtual mailboxes. Within this directory, subdirectories are created for each domain and user. The following shell commands illustrate the creation of such a directory structure:

```
mkdir -p /var/vmail/example.com/user1
mkdir -p /var/vmail/example.com/user2
chown -R vmail:vmail /var/vmail
```

Here, a dedicated system user (commonly named `vmail`) is used to own the mailbox directories, ensuring that Postfix and the associated de-

176

livery agent have the necessary permissions to write email files. The configuration file `main.cf` should reflect this directory structure by incorporating the virtual mailbox base:

```
virtual_mailbox_base = /var/vmail
```

A virtual mailbox mapping entry then becomes relative to this base. For instance, the entry for `user1@example.com` remains `example.com/user1/`, and Postfix constructs the full mailbox path by prefixing it with the base directory.

Another critical aspect of configuring virtual mailboxes is managing recipient verification. To prevent unauthorized delivery attempts, Postfix uses the `virtual_mailbox_domains` and `virtual_mailbox_maps` parameters to validate incoming email addresses at the RCPT TO stage. This mechanism ensures that only addresses defined in the mapping table are accepted for virtual domains. The integration of these checks is automatic once the corresponding directives in `main.cf` are correctly set.

Virtual mailbox configurations can also incorporate aliasing features. The parameter `virtual_alias_maps` provides a facility to redirect messages from one virtual address to another, or even to a different domain. A typical alias mapping file might look like:

```
info@example.com     user1@example.com
support@example.org user2@example.com
```

After creating this `/etc/postfix/virtual` file, it should be compiled using:

```
postmap /etc/postfix/virtual
```

The final file configuration in `main.cf` would then include:

```
virtual_alias_maps = hash:/etc/postfix/virtual
```

This configuration allows administrators to maintain a flexible email routing strategy without having to create corresponding system user accounts.

A further advantage of virtual mailbox systems is the ability to integrate with external authentication databases. Postfix can be configured to query MySQL, PostgreSQL, or LDAP directories for user and mailbox information, thereby streamlining administration in environments with a large number of virtual users. The configuration typically requires additional directives within main.cf as well as the creation of query files. An example MySQL query file for retrieving mailbox paths might contain:

```
query = SELECT maildir FROM virtual_users WHERE email='%s'
```

The corresponding virtual_mailbox_maps directive in main.cf would reference this query using the mysql: syntax:

```
virtual_mailbox_maps = mysql:/etc/postfix/mysql-virtual-mailbox-maps.
    cf
```

The configuration file /etc/postfix/mysql-virtual-mailbox-maps.cf must include the necessary connection details, such as the database server, user credentials, and SQL query. This approach centralizes user management and is especially useful in large-scale deployments.

An important consideration in virtual mailbox management is the maintenance of mailbox quotas. Quotas restrict the maximum amount of disk space used by each mailbox, thereby preventing any single user from consuming disproportionate resources. Quota management might be handled by dovecot or other mailbox management software integrated with Postfix. Configuration involves setting parameters in the associated configuration files of the delivery agent. For example, Dovecot's quota configuration file might include:

```
plugin {
  quota = maildir:User quota
  quota_rule = *:bytes=0:104857600
}
```

This rule sets a quota of 100 MB for each user. Coordination between Postfix and the delivery agent is critical, ensuring that quota checks are enforced upon every mail delivery.

Managing virtual mailboxes also includes regular auditing and monitoring of the mailbox directories. System administrators should routinely verify that mailbox paths remain consistent with the mappings defined in the configuration files. Diagnostic commands help check for possible discrepancies. For example:

```
find /var/vmail -type f -name cur -exec ls -l {} \;
```

This command lists current email files within subdirectories, assisting in confirming that mail files are being stored appropriately. Logs generated by Postfix, often found in /var/log/maillog or /var/log/mail.log, offer valuable insight into the operation of the virtual delivery process. Analyzing these logs may reveal delivery failures or configuration mismatches, prompting corrective action.

For administrators working with automated deployment or configuration management systems, scripting the setup of virtual mailboxes can minimize errors and ensure consistency. A sample bash script to initialize a virtual mailbox directory structure is provided below:

```
#!/bin/bash
# Initialize virtual mailbox directory for a given domain and user

if [ "$#" -ne 2 ]; then
    echo "Usage: $0 domain username"
    exit 1
fi

DOMAIN=$1
USER=$2
MAILDIR="/var/vmail/$DOMAIN/$USER"

mkdir -p "$MAILDIR"/{cur,new,tmp}
chown -R vmail:vmail "$MAILDIR"
echo "Virtual mailbox for $USER@$DOMAIN initialized at $MAILDIR."
```

179

Executing this script with appropriate arguments creates the necessary directories with proper permissions. An example run of the script might yield:

```
$ sudo ./init_vmail.sh example.com user1
Virtual mailbox for user1@example.com initialized at /var/vmail/example.com/u
ser1.
```

This automation supports rapid deployment in environments with numerous virtual mailboxes.

Ensuring the security of virtual mailbox configurations involves several practices. Maintaining strict file permissions on directories containing mailbox data is paramount. The dedicated vmail user and group should own all virtual mailbox directories, and care must be taken that no sensitive data is exposed to unauthorized users. Additionally, periodic audits should verify that configuration files, lookup tables, and databases used for virtual mailbox mapping are secure and consistent.

The benefit of virtual mailboxes is their flexibility in hosting multiple domains and users within a single mail server framework while minimizing system-level footprint. By decoupling mail storage from system user accounts, administrators can implement scalable solutions that cater to environments ranging from small businesses to large service providers. Through precise configuration of virtual_mailbox_domains, virtual_mailbox_maps, and related parameters, Postfix is able to efficiently route and deliver messages even when local system accounts are not present.

The configuration of virtual mailboxes represents a critical component of modern email server management. With careful planning and integration of database-driven lookup tables, file-based mappings, and automated directory management, administrators can achieve reliable, secure, and scalable email delivery.

6.3. Utilizing Aliases and Forwarding

Implementing mail aliases and forwarding in Postfix enhances the flexibility of email routing by allowing messages addressed to one recipient to be delivered to one or more alternative destinations. This mechanism provides administrators with a means to consolidate multiple addresses, distribute incoming mail among several recipients, or forward messages to external addresses without altering the core system user or virtual mailbox configurations introduced previously.

The foundation of alias management in Postfix is the mapping of one email address to one or more alternate email addresses. In many deployments, this functionality is achieved using the alias_maps parameter in the Postfix main configuration file (main.cf). A typical configuration might include:

```
alias_maps = hash:/etc/aliases
```

The file /etc/aliases contains mappings in which a canonical email address is associated with a list of recipients. An example entry in the /etc/aliases file is:

```
postmaster: root, admin@example.com
support: tech1@example.com, tech2@example.com
```

After modifying the alias file, it is necessary to generate a binary database file using the newaliases command. This step compiles the plain text file into a format optimized for fast lookups by Postfix:

```
newaliases
```

In this configuration, any mail addressed to postmaster is delivered to both the root account and the email address admin@example.com. Similarly, emails sent to support are distributed to multiple technical staff accounts. It is important that the alias database remains synchronized with the text file to ensure reliable delivery.

181

Forwarding is a related concept that redirects mail from one address to another. In many cases, forwarding is managed at the user level through files such as .forward located in user home directories. When a user configures a .forward file, every message delivered to that mailbox is automatically redirected to the addresses listed in the file. A simple .forward file may contain a single email address:

```
otheruser@example.com
```

Or multiple addresses, separated by commas:

```
friend1@example.com, friend2@example.com
```

During mail processing in Postfix, if a destination mailbox contains a .forward file, the mail delivery agent reads the file and re-injects the mail into the delivery process with the new recipient addresses. This facility offers a straightforward method to manage mail forwarding per individual user without the need for changes in the central configuration, though it should be administered with attention to security and proper file permissions.

For system-wide forwarding rules that go beyond individual user configurations, administrators may also leverage virtual aliasing through the virtual_alias_maps parameter in main.cf. This parameter works similarly to the alias mapping for local addresses but is intended for virtual domains. A typical configuration is as follows:

```
virtual_alias_maps = hash:/etc/postfix/virtual
```

Within the /etc/postfix/virtual file, entries can define simple one-to-one forwarding or one-to-many distribution. An example configuration entry is:

```
sales@example.com          marketing@example.com, ceo@example.com
info@example.com           customer.support@example.com
```

After making changes, the file is compiled with:

```
postmap /etc/postfix/virtual
```

This configuration informs Postfix that any email delivered to sales@example.com must be forwarded to both the marketing and CEO addresses. Similarly, mail for info@example.com is rerouted to the customer support team's address. The forwarding mechanism in this context is transparent to the original sender, ensuring that the alias or virtual forwarding rule does not modify header information such as the sender's address.

The design of alias and forwarding systems in Postfix benefits from thoughtful planning, particularly in environments where email routing rules must balance simplicity with the need to adjust delivery paths dynamically. When configuring these systems, administrators must consider resolution order. Postfix typically processes the alias maps first before applying virtual alias maps. In scenarios where both local aliases and virtual aliases may apply, ensuring that mapping tables do not conflict is critical, as overlapping definitions can lead to unpredictable routing behavior. Clear documentation and cautious planning of alias rules contribute to maintaining an orderly mail routing system.

The concept of forwarding can be extended by employing more complex delivery rules using Postfix's built-in regular expression tables. Such flexibility is advantageous when email forwarding needs to depend on patterns within the recipient addresses. For example, administrators can set up a file that rewrites parts of an address to match a particular naming convention or redirect entire groups of addresses to a new domain. An excerpt using the regexp syntax in main.cf is:

```
virtual_alias_maps = regexp:/etc/postfix/virtual_regexp
```

In the /etc/postfix/virtual_regexp file, a rule might be written as:

```
/^sales-(.*)@old-domain\.com$/    sales-$1@new-domain.com
```

This regular expression captures any email sent to addresses starting with `sales-` at the old domain and reassigns them to a corresponding address at the new domain. The use of regular expressions can facilitate bulk changes and provide an additional layer of flexibility compared to traditional hash maps.

When forwarding emails externally, it is imperative to evaluate the security implications, such as protecting against mail loops and unauthorized message dissemination. A forward loop can occur if an alias or forwarding rule inadvertently references another forwarding rule that circles back to the original address. Postfix has built-in loop detection mechanisms that track the number of hops or re-injections a message undergoes. Configuring an appropriate limit with the `max_use` parameter in the alias or forwarding context can minimize the risk of infinite loops. Administrators should test forwarding configurations with a set of dummy addresses and use Postfix log files to verify that messages are classified correctly and delivered without unnecessary repetition.

The delivery behavior of forwarded messages can also be influenced by envelope settings and header rewrites. In some cases, forwarded emails retain the original sender and timestamps, while in other scenarios, administrators might choose to modify the email headers to indicate that a message was forwarded. This may involve employing Postfix's header checks to add or alter header fields. For example, an entry in the header checks file `/etc/postfix/header_checks` could be used to annotate forwarded messages:

```
if /^Received:/
  PREPEND X-Forwarded-By: Postfix Mail Gateway
endif
```

This rule prepends a custom header to all messages that contain a `Received` header, helping downstream systems understand that a message has been processed by a forwarding mechanism. After editing the header checks file, the configuration must be activated by reloading Postfix. Effective header manipulation allows for more transparent tracking of message origins and routing modifications, aiding in debugging and compliance with organizational policies.

Appropriate logging and monitoring of mail alias and forwarding activities are essential in maintaining a robust email infrastructure. Postfix log files, typically found in directories such as /var/log/mail.log or /var/log/maillog, provide insights into the alias resolution and forwarding process. Administrators can filter the logs for alias or forwarding events to identify potential misconfigurations, for example:

```
grep "alias" /var/log/mail.log
```

Such analyses enable proactive detection of issues, such as unresolved addresses or unintended forwarding loops, and assist in verifying that configuration changes have been successfully implemented.

Automation can significantly ease the management of aliases and forwarding configurations. For large-scale deployments with frequent updates, configuration management systems can automate the update of alias maps and the associated Postfix commands. An example of an automation script using a shell script is provided below:

```bash
#!/bin/bash
# Update alias file and rebuild database

ALIAS_FILE="/etc/aliases"
VIRTUAL_FILE="/etc/postfix/virtual"

if [ -f "$ALIAS_FILE" ]; then
    newaliases
    echo "Local alias database updated."
else
    echo "Alias file not found: $ALIAS_FILE" >&2
    exit 1
fi

if [ -f "$VIRTUAL_FILE" ]; then
    postmap "$VIRTUAL_FILE"
    echo "Virtual alias database updated."
else
    echo "Virtual alias file not found: $VIRTUAL_FILE" >&2
fi
```

Execution of this script ensures that both local and virtual alias configurations remain current, thereby reducing manual intervention and the risk of operator error. Such automation contributes to the stability and maintainability of the mail server.

In environments where forwarding must interact with both local and virtual domains, it is essential to establish clear policies that define which addresses are eligible for forwarding and under what conditions. This may include restrictions based on the sender's domain, message content analysis, or security considerations. Organizations that employ forwarding extensively should also consider the implications on archival and spam filtering mechanisms. For instance, messages that are forwarded might be reprocessed by spam filters, and duplicate filtering settings should be adjusted to account for re-injected mail.

The integration of aliasing and forwarding with external authentication sources and directory services further enhances centralized control. In such cases, alias information may be stored in a relational database or LDAP directory, and Postfix will query these sources during the recipient verification phase. Configuring Postfix to use a MySQL-based alias map may involve a configuration snippet such as:

```
alias_maps = mysql:/etc/postfix/mysql-alias-maps.cf
```

The file /etc/postfix/mysql-alias-maps.cf includes connection parameters and a SQL query that retrieves alias mappings. This approach centralizes alias management and allows dynamic updates to email routing rules without the need to manually edit flat files. Centralized alias storage is particularly advantageous in multi-domain environments where consistency and quick propagation of changes are required.

The practical implementation of mail aliases and forwarding in Postfix exemplifies the balance between operational efficiency and flexibility. By leveraging both local alias maps and virtual alias maps, administrators can design robust email delivery systems that accommodate a variety of routing requirements. The integration of these mechanisms with automated scripts, regular monitoring, and external authentication sources ensures that the email infrastructure adapts to evolving organizational needs without sacrificing performance or reliability.

Through diligent configuration and regular maintenance, mail aliases and forwarding become essential tools that help reconcile disparate email addresses under cohesive policies and routing strategies. The careful use of mapping tables, file permissions, logging, and automation supports a high degree of control over how messages are delivered and processed, providing a scalable solution suited for both small installations and large-scale deployments.

6.4. Integrating Mailbox Quotas

Managing mailbox quotas is essential for maintaining the integrity of an email server by preventing individual mailboxes from consuming disproportionate amounts of disk space. By setting storage limits per mailbox, administrators can ensure that available resources are distributed equitably and that no single user can affect the performance or stability of the entire server through excessive email storage.

Administrators can implement mailbox quotas using a variety of approaches. In a Postfix environment integrated with a delivery agent such as Dovecot, mailbox quotas are typically enforced at the delivery level. Dovecot offers robust quota management facilities that work with both the mbox and Maildir formats. The configuration of quotas in Dovecot usually involves setting parameters in dedicated configuration files, which may include directives to define quota rules and corresponding storage thresholds.

A common configuration approach involves using a plugin configu-

ration file for Dovecot quotas. For example, in a setup utilizing the
Maildir format, administrators may create or modify a configuration
file (e.g., /etc/dovecot/conf.d/90-quota.conf) to include quota settings. An example snippet from such a file is provided below:

```
plugin {
  quota = maildir:User quota
  quota_rule = *:storage=0:104857600
  quota_rule2 = Trash:storage=0:52428800
}
```

In this configuration, the universal quota rule
*:storage=0:104857600 sets a maximum quota of 100 MB for
all folders by default, while a secondary rule, quota_rule2, may apply
a lower quota to specific folders such as Trash. The first part of the
rule, a wildcard, indicates that the quota applies to all mailboxes
unless overridden by more specific rules.

In addition to Dovecot, Postfix itself does not enforce mailbox quotas
directly. Instead, the actual quota management is integrated into
the mailbox delivery agent. Therefore, the cooperation between
Postfix and Dovecot is critical. Postfix routes mail to Dovecot via
the Local Delivery Agent (LDA) or LMTP. The configuration in
/etc/postfix/main.cf should include an appropriate delivery
method so that quota enforcement takes effect. A typical directive
may appear as follows:

```
virtual_transport = lmtp:unix:private/dovecot-lmtp
```

This configuration ensures that messages delivered to virtual mailboxes are processed by Dovecot, which then applies the defined quota
rules before final storage. The integration between Postfix and quota-
aware delivery systems allows administrators to maintain fine-grained
control over resource usage even as the number of mailboxes increases.

Apart from Dovecot, some systems may leverage file system quotas
at the operating system level. In such environments, administrators

can use native file system quota management tools to limit the disk usage of the directories where mailbox data is stored. Tools such as edquota, quota, and repquota offer mechanisms for setting per-user quotas on systems where mailbox directories correspond to individual system users. For example, to set a disk quota for a user, one might use:

```
edquota -u exampleuser
```

This command opens a text editor with the current quota settings for the user exampleuser. Administrators can then modify soft and hard limits for blocks and inodes, ensuring that mail storage does not exceed predetermined thresholds. While file system quotas provide an alternative method to control resource usage, they are typically less flexible than application-level quotas provided by tools like Dovecot, as they do not directly integrate with mail delivery logic.

Integrating mailbox quotas requires careful planning of directory structures and ownership. In configurations where virtual mailboxes are stored under a dedicated directory (for instance, /var/vmail), the file system must be optimized to support efficient quota checks. Permissions are usually set such that a dedicated user (commonly vmail) owns all mailbox directories. The quota system, whether it is part of the operating system or implemented through Dovecot, must correspond to this structure. An administrator might ensure proper permissions with commands such as:

```
chown -R vmail:vmail /var/vmail
```

Ensuring that the directory structure remains intact and that correct ownership is maintained across all mailbox directories is vital; any deviation may result in misapplied quota limits or access problems during mail delivery.

For administrators handling a large number of mailboxes, automated tools or scripts can simplify the management of quota configurations.

A sample bash script might be deployed to ensure that new mailboxes are created with the appropriate directory structure and that default quota files are copied into place. An example script is provided below:

```
#!/bin/bash
# Script to initialize a new virtual mailbox with default quota
    configuration

if [ "$#" -ne 2 ]; then
    echo "Usage: $0 domain username"
    exit 1
fi

DOMAIN=$1
USER=$2
MAILDIR="/var/vmail/$DOMAIN/$USER"
QUOTA_TEMPLATE="/etc/dovecot/quota_template"

mkdir -p "$MAILDIR"/{cur,new,tmp}
chown -R vmail:vmail "$MAILDIR"

# Optionally copy a default quota configuration if needed
if [ -f "$QUOTA_TEMPLATE" ]; then
    cp "$QUOTA_TEMPLATE" "$MAILDIR/.quota"
    chown vmail:vmail "$MAILDIR/.quota"
fi

echo "Virtual mailbox for $USER@$DOMAIN has been initialized with
    quota settings."
```

This script creates the necessary directory structure for a new virtual mailbox under /var/vmail, assigns appropriate ownership, and copies a default quota configuration file into the mailbox directory. Automation scripts like this one reduce manual configuration errors and streamline the deployment process, particularly in environments with hundreds or thousands of mailboxes.

Furthermore, managing mailbox quotas involves routine monitoring and diagnostics to ensure quotas are enforced correctly. Log files serve as an invaluable resource for verifying that the quota system is functioning as intended. Both Postfix and Dovecot log files, typically found in directories such as /var/log/mail.log and

`/var/log/dovecot.log`, provide insights into delivery attempts that may have failed because of exceeded quotas. Analyzing these logs with tools such as `grep` or more sophisticated log monitoring solutions helps administrators detect and address issues promptly. For instance, an administrator might use the following command to check for quota-related errors:

```
grep -i "quota" /var/log/dovecot.log
```

Regular log review not only aids in troubleshooting but also in forecasting trends in mailbox usage, thereby informing future quota adjustments to accommodate changing user behavior.

In some configurations, administrators may grant users the ability to check their current quota usage via client tools or web-based dashboards that query Dovecot's quota status. Providing end users with transparent access to their quota information can be facilitated by integrating quota query functionality into the mail delivery interface or through custom scripts that report on disk usage. This proactive feedback helps users manage their mailbox sizes and reduces the likelihood of deliveries failing due to quota overruns.

The evolution of mailbox quota management techniques reflects a trend toward more dynamic and user-friendly administration. In large-scale environments, administrators may utilize centralized configuration management systems that push quota policies to all mail servers in a cluster. Such systems can dynamically adjust quotas based on factors like usage trends, departmental requirements, or changes in available storage resources. Integration with monitoring solutions like Nagios or Zabbix provides real-time alerts when quotas approach critical thresholds, thereby allowing preemptive action before a mailbox becomes unresponsive due to exceeded limits.

It is also important to consider the implications of quota policies on mail retention and backup strategies. Strict quotas may necessitate complementary measures such as archiving or automated email purging to maintain overall system performance. When designing a mailbox quota scheme, administrators must balance the need for generous user storage against the risk of resource depletion. Strategies such as incremental quotas, where users can request temporary increases, or softer quota enforcement policies that generate warnings rather than outright rejections can provide flexibility, thereby blending user convenience with system safeguards.

Interoperability between various email components also demands that quota information is propagated accurately throughout the system. For example, if a user's mailbox is accessed through multiple devices or across different email clients, quota updates must be synchronized to avoid discrepancies between reported usage and actual consumption. Leveraging protocols that support quota reporting, such as IMAP's QUOTA extension, ensures that all client interactions reflect current quota statuses. This synchronization enhances user satisfaction by providing accurate feedback on available space regardless of the access point.

Detailed planning, rigorous configuration, and ongoing monitoring are crucial components in successfully integrating mailbox quotas into an existing Postfix and Dovecot environment. Whether using Dovecot's native quota plugins or system-level file quotas, maintaining consistency between configuration files, directory structures, and user policies demands a comprehensive approach that spans initial setup, automation, and regular audits. Such diligence ensures that mailbox quotas contribute to the overall stability and efficiency of the mail server, ultimately protecting system resources against misuse and ensuring a consistently high quality of service.

6.5. Managing Mailing Lists

Managing mailing lists involves the creation and administration of group email addresses that streamline communication for multiple recipients. This feature is vital for organizations that rely on bulk mailing for updates, newsletters, or collaborative discussions. Within a Postfix environment, mailing lists can be configured either through native list management tools or by integrating specialized mailing list software. The techniques discussed in this section build upon the principles of local user and virtual mailbox management, emphasizing routing, filtering, and delivery control for group communications.

One popular method for managing mailing lists in a Postfix setup is to use programs like `mailman` or `majordomo`. These dedicated tools offer comprehensive interfaces to subscribe and unsubscribe users, moderate incoming messages, and archive discussion threads. When integrated with Postfix, these programs handle the routing of emails to list members by reading configuration files and interacting with external databases. As an example, integrating a mailing list managed by `mailman` requires ensuring that Postfix correctly hands off emails to the list management process. A typical configuration in `/etc/postfix/main.cf` might include a transport map such as:

```
mailbox_transport = lmtp:unix:private/dovecot-lmtp
virtual_transport = lmtp:unix:private/dovecot-lmtp
```

This configuration delegates incoming mail to the designated transport agent, which can then apply more refined processing such as list membership checks. For environments where a lightweight approach is preferred, administrators can manage mailing lists using Postfix's virtual alias maps. In this method, a dedicated mapping assigns a mailing list address to a series of individual recipients. An entry in the virtual alias file might appear as follows:

```
list@example.com    user1@example.com, user2@example.com,
```

```
user3@example.com
```

After processing the virtual alias map, Postfix expands the mailing list address into individual recipient addresses, delivering a copy of each email to every member of the list. To compile the configuration, the following command is used:

```
postmap /etc/postfix/virtual
```

In advanced setups, regular expressions or dynamic alias mapping can be employed to manage lists that automatically include all users within a specific domain or matching a given pattern. A configuration using regular expressions might be referenced in the main.cf file as:

```
virtual_alias_maps = regexp:/etc/postfix/virtual_regexp
```

An example entry in /etc/postfix/virtual_regexp could be constructed to match a set of addresses and forward them to a designated mailing list. For instance:

```
/^all-users@domain\.com$/   user1@domain.com, user2@domain.com,
    user3@domain.com
```

Such configurations provide dynamic control over list composition and simplify the routine management of large groups. Administrative control over mailing lists involves several key tasks: subscription management, moderation settings, and maintenance of mailing list archives. Many mailing list solutions provide a web-based interface or command-line tools for adding and removing subscribers. When using software such as mailman, a subscription might be added or removed by executing commands that interface directly with the mailing list database. For example, the command to add a new member using mailman might be:

```
bin/add_members -r new_members.txt listname
```

In the above example, the file new_members.txt contains a list of email addresses to be added to the mailing list named listname. This capacity to automate membership management proves especially useful in environments with dynamic teams or frequently changing communication groups.

Moderation is another important facet of mailing list management and is critical when controlling bulk mail to ensure that spam or inappropriate content does not overwhelm the subscriber base. Moderation settings may include requiring pre-approval of all messages before distribution or filtering content based on specific rules. In systems like mailman, moderators can be designated during the setup process. Corresponding configuration files and interfaces allow each moderator to review pending posts and approve, modify, or reject them as needed. For instance, configuring moderation settings might involve modifying a file such as mm_cfg.py in the mailing list's directory, setting parameters such as:

```
DEFAULT_TO_DISTRIBUTE_NON_DIGEST=True
MODERATE_ACTION_REJECT=True
```

These parameters instruct the mailing list software to reject posts that do not meet moderation guidelines and to distribute messages immediately once approved.

Archiving mailing list messages is often necessary for maintaining records of communications and for legal or compliance purposes. Mailing list software typically supports automatic archiving of both public and private lists. Administrators may configure archiving settings by specifying parameters in the configuration file. In mailman, for example, archiving is controlled by settings that determine the retention period and the format of archived messages. An archive configuration may include settings like:

```
ARCHIVE_PUBLIC=True
ARCHIVE_PRIVATE=True
ARCHIVE_PERIOD=90  # days
```

With these settings, messages are stored in the archive for a specified period (in this case, 90 days) before being purged or moved to long-term storage. This approach helps in managing disk space while ensuring that historical communications remain accessible when necessary.

For a more customized mailing list experience, some administrators choose to implement mailing list functionality via scripting and custom Postfix filters. A common strategy is to create a dedicated transport that calls a script upon receiving mail for a particular list. The script parses the email and distributes it to multiple recipients based on a configuration file. An example of a simple bash script for this purpose is provided below:

```
#!/bin/bash
# Simple mailing list distributor

LISTFILE="/etc/postfix/mailing_list.txt"

if [ ! -f "$LISTFILE" ]; then
    echo "Mailing list file not found."
    exit 1
fi

RECIPIENTS=$(cat "$LISTFILE" | tr '\n' ',')
echo "Forwarding message to: $RECIPIENTS"

# Forward the mail to all recipients
/usr/sbin/sendmail $RECIPIENTS
```

This script reads a list of email addresses from /etc/postfix/mailing_list.txt and uses the sendmail command to forward the incoming email to all addresses. The mailing list file contains one address per line and can be managed manually or through an automated process. A corresponding entry in the Postfix transport map might be defined as:

```
list@example.com    local:mailinglist
```

After updating the transport map, the map should be compiled using the postmap command:

```
postmap /etc/postfix/transport
```

This integration of a custom script with Postfix provides a flexible solution for handling special mailing list requirements without the overhead of more comprehensive list management systems.

A critical aspect of running mailing lists is ensuring that delivery is both efficient and secure. Bulk mailings can generate significant load, which necessitates strategies for load balancing and rate limiting. Postfix includes several parameters that allow administrators to manage outgoing mail rates, preventing a single list from consuming excessive system resources. Parameters such as default_destination_recipient_limit and smtp_destination_rate_delay can be tuned to spread the delivery load over time. An excerpt from main.cf addressing this might include:

```
default_destination_recipient_limit = 50
smtp_destination_rate_delay = 1s
```

These settings limit the number of recipients per SMTP connection and introduce a slight delay between deliveries, thereby mitigating the risk of overwhelming remote servers or triggering spam filters.

The scalability of mailing lists also depends on monitoring and feedback mechanisms. Postfix log files capture detailed information about mail transactions, which administrators can analyze to detect performance bottlenecks or delivery failures. Employing log analysis tools or scripts that filter for list addresses can help identify issues, for example:

```
grep "list@example.com" /var/log/mail.log
```

Such monitoring enables proactive adjustments to the mailing list configuration, whether it involves changing delivery limits, modifying membership rules, or refining filtering criteria.

Documentation and maintenance of mailing list policies are integral to sustaining an efficient communication environment. Administrators are advised to regularly review membership, moderation settings, and archive policies to address evolving organizational needs. Additionally, clear guidelines should be established for subscribers regarding acceptable use, posting frequency, and message formatting. Maintaining a well-documented process reduces administrative overhead and ensures consistency across different mailing lists.

By integrating these techniques with the broader Postfix environment, administrators can create mailing lists that are both robust and flexible. The combination of virtual alias maps, dedicated mailing list software, and custom scripting allows for tailored solutions that meet specific organizational requirements. Regular monitoring, load management, and policy updates ensure that mailing lists remain a reliable tool for group communication, capable of scaling to support both internal discussions and bulk mailings to large subscriber bases.

6.6.   Using External Authentication Sources

In large-scale email systems, managing user accounts solely through system-level and flat-file configurations can become cumbersome and difficult to scale. To address this limitation, Postfix can be configured to authenticate and look up user data using external sources such as LDAP or MySQL. This approach centralizes control over user information, enabling more seamless administration across multiple servers and domains, and is essential for organizations that require dynamic and scalable email infrastructures.

The integration of external authentication sources primarily involves configuring Postfix to query databases or directory services during the mail routing process. For instance, Postfix can utilize external maps to retrieve details such as mailbox locations, alias mappings, and virtual domain configurations. These mappings are specified in `main.cf` by referencing external query files, allowing Postfix to defer user verification and additional routing logic to centralized external systems.

A common method to implement an external authentication source is by using MySQL. In a MySQL-based setup, virtual user information (including email addresses and mailbox paths) is stored in a relational database. Postfix then consults this database when an email is received. To achieve this, administrators need to set up a dedicated configuration file that contains the database connection parameters and the SQL query used to retrieve the required data. A typical configuration file that defines a virtual mailbox map might look like the following:

```
/etc/postfix/mysql-virtual-mailbox-maps.cf
user = mailuser
password = mailpass
hosts = localhost
dbname = postfix
query = SELECT maildir FROM virtual_users WHERE email='%s'
```

This file instructs Postfix to connect to a MySQL server on `localhost` using the provided credentials. The SQL query retrieves the mailbox directory associated with a given email address, where `'%s'` represents a placeholder that Postfix replaces with the recipient address during lookup. To enable this external mapping, the `main.cf` file should include a directive similar to:

```
virtual_mailbox_maps = mysql:/etc/postfix/mysql-virtual-mailbox-maps.
    cf
```

This configuration allows Postfix to dynamically resolve mailbox paths from the MySQL database, thereby decoupling user management from static system files. The use of external data sources like MySQL also enables the consolidation of user information across various services, promoting consistency and simplifying administration.

Another powerful external authentication source is LDAP, which is widely used for centralized directory services. LDAP provides a hierarchical view of user data and is particularly beneficial in environments with complex organizational structures. To integrate LDAP with Postfix, administrators must create an LDAP query configuration file that specifies details about the LDAP server, search base, and filters to locate the required user information. A sample configuration file for LDAP-based virtual mailbox mapping might be structured as follows:

```
/etc/postfix/ldap-virtual-mailbox-maps.cf
server_host = ldap.example.com
search_base = ou=users,dc=example,dc=com
query_filter = (mail=%s)
result_attribute = mailDirectory
bind = yes
bind_dn = cn=admin,dc=example,dc=com
bind_pw = secret
```

In this example configuration, `server_host` specifies the LDAP server's address. The `search_base` defines the starting point in the LDAP directory from which searches are conducted, while the `query_filter` is used to locate an entry with a matching email address. The `result_attribute` indicates the LDAP attribute that contains the mailbox directory information. Binding to the LDAP directory using `bind_dn` and `bind_pw` ensures that the queries have sufficient permissions to access the directory data. To enable LDAP-based lookup within Postfix, the `main.cf` file must include the following directive:

```
virtual_mailbox_maps = ldap:/etc/postfix/ldap-virtual-mailbox-maps.cf
```

This approach allows Postfix to query the LDAP directory for each incoming email, ensuring that the latest user information is applied during the mail delivery process. The advantage of using LDAP is the centralization of user data in a single directory service, which may also be used by other systems for authentication and authorization.

In both MySQL and LDAP integrations, it is critical to consider the security aspects of connecting to external data sources. Secure handling of authentication credentials and encryption of data in transit (e.g., using TLS) are essential practices. For LDAP, administrators should configure the connection to use `ldaps://` or StartTLS if supported by the directory server. For example, modifying the LDAP configuration to use a secure connection might look like:

```
server_host = ldaps://ldap.example.com
```

Similarly, ensuring that the MySQL connection is secured, possibly by restricting database access to designated hosts and using encrypted connections, is crucial for maintaining overall system security.

Integration of external authentication sources not only improves scalability but also simplifies the management of large email deployments. By centralizing user information in an external database or directory service, administrators can apply consistent policies across multiple machines and domains. This centralization facilitates automated provisioning and deprovisioning of user accounts. For example, when a user is added or removed in the central database, those changes are automatically reflected in the Postfix delivery process, eliminating the need for manual updates to configuration files on each individual mail server.

The performance of external authentication sources can directly affect mail delivery times, so performance monitoring and optimization are important aspects of configuration. MySQL databases can be tuned for read performance by indexing columns that are frequently queried, such as the email address in the virtual user table. Similarly, LDAP directories can be optimized by properly structuring the directory tree and applying search filters that reduce the search scope. Administrators should also consider the caching mechanism in Postfix, which can store query results to mitigate the impact of high query volumes on the external sources. Testing and benchmarking these external systems under load is recommended to ensure that they do not become bottlenecks.

To further illustrate the integration process, consider an environment where both MySQL and LDAP are used to manage different types of user accounts. For example, an organization might maintain local system users in LDAP and virtual users in MySQL. Configuring Postfix to consult both sources requires a careful arrangement of lookup maps. One strategy involves defining separate mapping configurations for different domains or user types. In main.cf, multiple maps can be specified using comma-separated values:

```
virtual_mailbox_maps = mysql:/etc/postfix/mysql-virtual-mailbox-maps.
    cf, ldap:/etc/postfix/ldap-virtual-mailbox-maps.cf
```

In this configuration, Postfix will attempt to resolve a mailbox address by first querying the MySQL source; if the address is not found, it will proceed to query the LDAP directory. This layered approach ensures that all user types are covered without requiring redundant entries in a single database.

Another consideration when using external authentication sources is the management of configuration changes. Since external sources often contain dynamic data, administrators must update the Postfix configuration or query files when schema changes occur or when migrating to a new data source. Using version control systems to manage these configuration files helps ensure consistency and facilitates rollback if needed. Additionally, integrating configuration management tools such as Ansible or Puppet can automate the deployment and updating of these configurations across multiple servers.

Testing the configuration thoroughly before deployment is essential. Administrators can use the postmap command to verify the external map entries. For example, to test a MySQL query, the following command can be executed:

```
postmap -q user@example.com mysql:/etc/postfix/mysql-virtual-mailbox-
    maps.cf
```

This command queries the MySQL map for the specified email address and outputs the corresponding mailbox directory. A similar approach applies when verifying LDAP configurations by replacing the map type in the command. Viewing sample outputs in a controlled test environment helps validate that the queries are configured correctly and that the external sources return expected results.

Using external authentication sources like LDAP and MySQL with Postfix significantly enhances the scalability and manageability of email systems. The integration of these sources allows for dynamic user management, centralized control over email routing data, and streamlined administrative workflows. By leveraging dedicated query configuration files, secure database connections, and caching strategies, Postfix can efficiently delegate user authentication and mailbox resolution tasks to external systems. The resulting configuration supports a robust email environment that can adapt to the needs of growing organizations, while maintaining high performance and security standards across the entire mail delivery infrastructure.

Chapter 7

Monitoring and Logging

This chapter explores effective monitoring and logging techniques for Postfix servers. It examines log analysis and configuration, queue monitoring, and integration with system monitoring tools. By understanding and adjusting log levels, you can gain valuable insights into server operations, while customized monitoring scripts offer tailored oversight. These strategies ensure proactive management and timely identification of potential issues, enhancing system reliability and performance.

7.1. Understanding Postfix Logging

Postfix logging constitutes a critical component in the administration of email servers, providing an essential mechanism for recording operational events and diagnosing issues. In its interaction with system logging facilities, Postfix utilizes the syslog service to capture informa-tion about various processes, including the SMTP daemon, queue man-agement, and the system's error handling routines. This integration al-lows administrators to track both routine operations and exceptional events within a unified logging framework, thereby facilitating efficient troubleshooting and system monitoring.

The logging mechanism of Postfix operates at several levels of granular-ity. Each component, such as the `master`, `smtp`, and `local` processes, emits messages that are handled by the syslog daemon according to predefined configuration rules. Log entries are tagged with specific fa-cility and severity levels, making it possible to filter messages based on urgency and source. For example, routine status updates and success-ful message deliveries are typically logged at the `info` level, whereas message delivery failures and authentication issues might be recorded at the `warning` or `error` levels. This differentiation enables administra-tors to focus on critical issues without being overwhelmed by verbose logs detailing normal operations.

The types of logs generated by Postfix include connection logs, message delivery logs, and error logs. Connection logs record the establishment, maintenance, and termination of network connections, which are vital for tracing communication patterns and identifying potential security threats such as unauthorized access or spamming activities. Message delivery logs provide detailed records of the email routing process, in-cluding steps from queuing to final reception or rejection. Errors, on the other hand, encapsulate not only failed delivery attempts but also configuration issues and internal faults within the Postfix suite. By de-lineating logs in this way, the system allows for a targeted approach to diagnosing specific types of operational anomalies.

A practical approach to working with Postfix logs begins with under-standing the default configuration. Postfix typically writes log mes-sages to files such as `/var/log/mail.log` on many Linux distributions.

206

An administrator can inspect these logs using command-line tools such as `tail`, `grep`, or more sophisticated log analysis programs. A simple command to monitor the mail log file is provided in the following example:

```
tail -f /var/log/mail.log
```

This command displays new log entries in real time as they are written, thus offering immediate feedback on server activity. By combining such monitoring with filtering mechanisms—using commands like `grep`—administrators can isolate log messages related to specific processes or error codes. The versatility of these tools, when used in conjunction with Postfix's logging capabilities, forms the backbone of effective operational oversight.

The significance of Postfix logging extends beyond simple record-keeping. Detailed logs allow for post-event analysis, which is paramount when diagnosing system failures or performance bottlenecks. For instance, by tracing the log entries that lead up to a queue overflow or a delivery timeout, administrators gain insight into the sequence of events that culminated in the failure. This historical perspective not only aids in understanding immediate issues but also helps in identifying recurring patterns that can inform preventive maintenance and long-term performance tuning.

Custom configurations of logging parameters can yield further benefits. Administrators might choose to adjust the verbosity of logs, a process which generally involves editing the main configuration file—commonly `/etc/postfix/main.cf`. By setting parameters that govern the level of detail in the logs, such as changing the log level filters or altering the destination for log output, a tailored logging environment can be achieved. For example, modifying the `debug_peer_list` parameter can help capture detailed communications with specific hosts, an approach that is useful when troubleshooting connectivity issues with remote mail servers. A configuration snippet demonstrating such a customization might appear as shown below:

```
debug_peer_level = 3
debug_peer_list = [hostname.example.com]
```

In this example, the debug level is increased for communications with a defined host, thus expanding the detail of log messages generated for that specific connection. Such targeted adjustments are valuable in complex environments, where a single misconfiguration or transient network issue can result in widespread email delivery problems. The ability to focus logging efforts on particular areas of interest simplifies the diagnostic process and minimizes unnecessary log volume.

Postfix logging also plays a crucial role in enhancing server security. By monitoring log entries that report on authentication events, connection attempts, and delivery failures, administrators can detect potential indicators of malicious activity. Automated log analysis tools, which parse through syslog entries and extract patterns indicative of attacks—such as repeated failed login attempts or unusually high connection rates from a single source—can be integrated into a broader security strategy. These alerts may be further processed by external monitoring systems that trigger notifications or automated countermeasures. Recognizing and acting on such log-derived signals is vital for maintaining not only the operational effectiveness of the email server but also its overall security posture.

The evaluation of log data is not restricted to manual inspection. A number of open-source and commercial tools are available to carry out sophisticated analyses of Postfix logs. These tools can aggregate logs from multiple sources, correlate events over time, and even apply statistical models to predict and detect anomalies. By employing such applications, administrators benefit from a comprehensive overview that extends beyond individual log entries to reveal systemic trends. Integration with system monitoring solutions provides a holistic perspective on server performance, underscoring the role of logging data as a key input for predictive maintenance and operational optimization.

A methodical analysis of the logging information also helps in identifying configuration errors that might otherwise remain undetected until they significantly disrupt operations. For example, repeated indications of a parameter mismatch or misrouting of network packets can be uncovered by a systematic review of the logs. When these entries are correlated with known system behavior under various load conditions, it becomes possible to fine-tune the parameters defined within the Postfix configuration files. This iterative refinement process ensures that the logging setup remains appropriate to the evolving requirements of the system, balancing the need for comprehensive diagnostic data against the risk of overwhelming administrators with excessive information.

Understanding Postfix logging and its integration with syslog is fundamental for effective server management. The capabilities of the logging system empower administrators with information that is pertinent to both day-to-day operations and long-term strategic planning. By systematically capturing and analyzing the spectrum of log messages—from routine notifications to critical errors—the logging system not only reflects the state of the server but also serves as a diagnostic archive that supports ongoing system enhancement. The effective use of logging information reinforces operational reliability and ensures that potential issues can be swiftly identified and addressed, preserving the overall integrity of the email server infrastructure.

7.2. Analyzing Log Files

Postfix logs generate a diverse array of valuable data that, when properly analyzed, can offer deep insights into the functioning of a mail server. The process of analyzing log files involves isolating relevant events, identifying patterns, and correlating these observations with system performance or configuration parameters. The techniques employed range from simple command-line utilities to complex automated parsing solutions. The methodology presented here builds upon previous sections that detail the structure and mechanics of Postfix logging.

The initial step in log analysis is the extraction of pertinent data. System administrators often rely on grep, awk, and sed to filter and search for specific keywords, error codes, or patterns within vast log files. For instance, one might need to identify all entries related to a specific error or isolate transactions handled by the SMTP service. Consider the following command-line example that filters log entries containing the word warning:

```
grep "warning" /var/log/mail.log
```

This simple yet effective command returns all log lines marked with a warning severity, which can then be analyzed further. When dealing with larger logs or needing more sophisticated filtering, combining utilities in a pipeline can be advantageous. For example, one might extract a time range of interest and display the count of each message type:

```
grep "Nov 05" /var/log/mail.log | awk '{print $5}' | sort | uniq -c
```

In this command, the log file is filtered to include only entries for a specific date, and then the fifth field (which can often denote the process or log level) is extracted and counted. Such manipulations aid in pinpointing frequent issues or unusual activity over a given period.

A more in-depth analysis requires parsing complex log entries. Tools like awk can be extended to break down each log entry into its constituent elements (date, time, process name, and message content), facilitating granular statistical analysis. A sample awk script may look like this:

```
awk '{
```

```
    split($0, parts, " ");
    date = parts[1] " " parts[2] " " parts[3];
    process = parts[5];
    print date, process, $0;
}' /var/log/mail.log
```

This script segments each log line into a formatted date and the process responsible for the log entry, thereby assisting in grouping and time-based trend analysis. By aggregating these details over multiple days or weeks, administrators are able to detect anomalies such as irregular spikes in error messages or unexpected changes in process behavior.

Beyond manual inspection, automated log parsers have been developed to simplify the analysis of Postfix log files. These tools parse logs into structured records which can be stored in databases and queried using SQL-like syntax. An example of such a parser might be pflogsumm, which aggregates and summarizes mail log data. Running pflogsumm on a log file produces a comprehensive report:

```
pflogsumm /var/log/mail.log
```

The output of pflogsumm typically includes statistics such as the number of processed messages, failed deliveries, and common transmission errors. Such information is invaluable in understanding the overall health of the mail system and can direct the administrator's focus to problematic configurations or operational bottlenecks.

When analyzing log files, the identification of correlation patterns is crucial for troubleshooting. Multiple log entries, often across different timestamps, may collectively indicate a systemic issue. For example, a series of messages such as connection rejections followed by delivery failures can suggest problems with a specific client or misconfiguration in the authentication process. By correlating events surrounding queue build-up with entries that show connection timeouts, the underlying causes may be identified, such as network latency or conflicting service configurations.

211

Statistical tools and visualization techniques further enhance log file analysis. Data from logs can be imported into environments such as R or Python to perform statistical analysis or generate time-series graphs that help illustrate trends. A straightforward example using Python involves reading a log file and plotting the frequency of different types of events over time. A snippet of Python code that performs this task may resemble the following:

```python
import matplotlib.pyplot as plt
from collections import Counter
import re

# Read log file
with open('/var/log/mail.log', 'r') as log_file:
    log_entries = log_file.readlines()

# Extract dates from log entries
date_pattern = re.compile(r'^\w+\s+\d+')
dates = [date_pattern.match(entry).group() for entry in log_entries
        if date_pattern.match(entry)]
date_counts = Counter(dates)

# Plot frequency of log entries per day
dates = list(date_counts.keys())
counts = list(date_counts.values())

plt.figure(figsize=(8, 4))
plt.bar(dates, counts, color='skyblue')
plt.xlabel('Date')
plt.ylabel('Number of Log Entries')
plt.title('Daily Frequency of Postfix Log Entries')
plt.xticks(rotation=45)
plt.tight_layout()
plt.show()
```

In this example, the script utilizes regular expressions to extract date information from each log entry, counts occurrences using a Counter object, and generates a bar chart illustrating daily log entry frequencies. Visual representations such as these can quickly reveal periods of heightened activity or unusual patterns that warrant further investigation.

212

Performance optimization in Postfix can also benefit from the analytical approach to log files. Slow mail deliveries or queue congestion often correlate with specific log patterns that reveal timing issues or resource constraints. Timestamps in the logs, alongside process identifiers, can reveal delays at various stages of mail processing—from initial reception to final delivery. By computing the differences between these timestamps, administrators can quantify processing delays. If delays are detected consistently at a particular stage, it indicates a possible configuration bottleneck or an overloaded component.

Furthermore, log analysis contributes to capacity planning. Trends observed in the volume of processed messages over time can inform decisions related to hardware upgrades or configuration changes aimed at scaling the mail server. Analyzing logs to determine the peak activity hours, average delivery times, and frequency of retry events provides a clear picture of performance under load. These insights are crucial when modifying service parameters or planning future deployments to ensure that the system can accommodate anticipated growth without degradation in service quality.

A robust log analysis framework must also consider error handling and the resolution of recurring issues. Postfix logs will often contain similar error messages triggered by intermittent network problems or transient misconfigurations. Grouping these errors by error code or message fragment and calculating their frequency allows administrators to prioritize the most pressing issues. A command-line example that categorizes error messages might be:

```
grep "error" /var/log/mail.log | awk -F": " '{print $2}' | sort |
    uniq -c | sort -nr
```

This command first filters log lines containing the word error, extracts the specific error message, and then counts and sorts the message occurrences. The resulting output helps in identifying which errors recur most frequently, aiding in systematic troubleshooting and remediation.

Advanced log analysis might also involve the use of machine learning techniques to predict and preemptively address potential failures. By training algorithms on historical log data, it is possible to develop models that flag unusual patterns or predict system outages. The implementation of such models requires structuring log data into a format that can be ingested by machine learning frameworks. Processing pipelines might include transforming timestamped log entries into feature vectors that represent the frequency and temporal distribution of events. Once a model is trained, it can be integrated into an alerting system that notifies administrators when the probability of an impending issue surpasses a predetermined threshold.

Automated log analysis is a key element in proactive system management. Integration with real-time monitoring systems ensures that alerts are generated almost instantly when anomalies are detected. These systems parse the same log files and, through pattern matching and statistical inference, alert administrators to unusual events, such as a surge in queue wait times or unexpected connection refusals. The combination of manual analysis and automated monitoring provides a comprehensive solution that leverages both human intuition and algorithmic precision.

Effective analysis of Postfix log files thus serves as a dual-purpose tool: it aids in the immediate diagnosis of problems while also providing valuable historical data that can drive long-term performance optimizations. By extracting specific data points, correlating events over time, and employing both manual and automated methods, administrators can maintain a nuanced understanding of system performance. The resulting insights facilitate timely interventions and informed decision-making that enhance service reliability and performance.

Understanding and applying these analytical techniques in the context of Postfix logs empowers system administrators to mitigate issues before they evolve into significant problems. The continuous cycle of monitoring, analysis, and refinement of log-based insights forms the backbone of proactive email server management, ensuring that performance is optimized and operational integrity is maintained across varying conditions.

7.3. Configuring Log Levels

The ability to adjust log levels in Postfix is vital for managing the volume and granularity of information recorded during server operations. Postfix, by design, integrates closely with the system's syslog facility to generate log messages at varying levels of detail. The configuration of these log levels determines the balance between sufficient diagnostic information and the minimization of extraneous data that can obscure operational issues. Fine-tuning these levels allows administrators to focus on critical events during troubleshooting while maintaining a lean logging process during regular operations.

Postfix does not directly implement a dedicated log level control within its own internal architecture but relies on syslog's configuration along with selective Postfix parameters to adjust the verbose logging behavior of its different components. The default configuration typically logs standard operational information such as connections, deliveries, and failures at an info level, while more detailed diagnostic messages are logged at debug levels. Modifying these parameters is accomplished through the /etc/postfix/main.cf file, where various directives can be set to influence the nature and amount of log output.

One common configuration directive is the debug_peer_level. This parameter increases the verbosity level for communications with specific remote peers. By default, Postfix logs a balanced amount of detail;

215

however, when troubleshooting problematic interactions with a particular mail host, it is often necessary to elevate the debug level. For example, setting the debug_peer_level to a higher value allows an administrator to capture more detailed information relevant to that peer. A typical configuration snippet is presented below:

```
debug_peer_level = 3
debug_peer_list = hostname.example.com
```

In this configuration, the debug level is explicitly increased for the peer identified in debug_peer_list. The value, typically ranging from 0 (minimal output) to higher integers denoting progressively more verbose output, assists in capturing the exact sequence of events during a communication session. Administrators can thus isolate issues related to connection establishment, message transmission, or authentication failures, aided by detailed contextual information.

Another aspect of configuring log levels involves managing the overall verbosity of Postfix logging. Postfix itself generates logs at various severity levels: debug, info, notice, warning, and error. The syslog daemon governs how these messages are recorded, typically via its configuration file (for instance /etc/rsyslog.conf or similar). Adjusting the syslog configuration to filter messages from the mail facility allows administrators to control the extent to which debugging information is stored. For instance, a syslog configuration line that emphasizes error reporting for mail-related logs might be as follows:

```
mail.err                        /var/log/mail.err
```

In contrast, a more inclusive configuration that captures messages up to the info level might specify:

```
mail.info                       /var/log/mail.info
```

By carefully structuring these directives, a balance is achieved between having comprehensive logs for diagnostic purposes and overloading the log files with redundant or non-critical information. It is crucial

216

during periods of troubleshooting to temporarily elevate logging detail and then revert to lower levels to preserve system performance and conserve disk space.

A practical method for verifying the active log level settings in Postfix is to utilize the postconf command-line utility. This tool prints the effective configuration settings as they are applied by Postfix. Executing the following command displays the relevant parameters:

```
postconf -n | grep -E 'debug_peer_level|debug_peer_list'
```

This command quickly confirms whether the customized settings are active, ensuring that any modifications to main.cf are correctly loaded after a configuration reload. Correct configuration is essential in environments that demand high reliability and prompt issue resolution.

In certain scenarios, it is beneficial to introduce conditional logging. For example, when experiencing intermittent issues, system administrators might opt to increase log verbosity only during peak hours or under specific conditions. While Postfix does not directly provide conditional logging based on time or system load, external scripting solutions can enable dynamic adjustments. A shell script can periodically modify the Postfix configuration and signal a reload to apply new logging levels. A sample script is presented below:

```
#!/bin/bash
# Check current system load and adjust Postfix log level accordingly

LOAD=$(uptime | awk -F'load average:' '{ print $2 }' | cut -d',' -f1
    | xargs)
THRESHOLD=1.5

if (( $(echo "$LOAD > $THRESHOLD" | bc -l) )); then
    postconf -e "debug_peer_level = 3"
    echo "High load detected: increased logging verbosity" >> /var/
    log/postfix_dynamic.log
else
    postconf -e "debug_peer_level = 0"
    echo "Normal load: reduced logging verbosity" >> /var/log/
    postfix_dynamic.log
```

```
fi
postfix reload
```

This script dynamically adjusts the `debug_peer_level` based on the system load, using `bc` for floating-point comparisons and logging changes to a dedicated log file. Such dynamic adjustments ensure that during periods of stress, sufficient detail is available for diagnosis, while under normal conditions, a streamlined log ensures efficient resource utilization.

Optimizing log levels is not solely a matter of increasing verbosity; often, the challenge is to minimize noise while retaining critical connectivity and error information. Administrators must carefully consider the implications of prolonged high-level debug logging in production. Elevated logging generates larger log files, which can lead to performance degradation both in terms of disk I/O and the time required to sift through voluminous logs when analyzing issues. This risk is particularly acute on systems with limited resources. Therefore, it is advisable to approach changes in log level settings with moderation and to monitor the impact on system performance.

It is prudent, then, to maintain a repository of best practices for log level configuration adjustments within the operational documentation. This practice ensures that temporary changes made during troubleshooting do not inadvertently become permanent fixtures in the configuration. Additionally, scheduled reviews of log file sizes and content can trigger policy updates that dynamically adjust logging levels during periods of heavy system use.

The significance of configuring log levels extends into the realm of automated monitoring and alert systems. Many monitoring tools rely on predefined thresholds and patterns within log files to trigger alerts. If the log level is set too low, critical events might be missed; if set excessively high, extraneous details may obscure the actionable insights needed by the monitoring tools. The threshold values used in these tools must, therefore, correlate with the Postfix log level configuration. In cases where log files are integrated with Security Information and Event Management (SIEM) systems, precise log level configuration ensures that performance metrics and error events are accurately reported and analyzed.

Furthermore, adjusting log levels can also assist in tracing down timing and efficiency issues, which are often precursors to broader operational problems. For example, a high debug level may reveal delays between different stages of message processing, allowing the detection of latency issues that are not evident at the info level. Detailed timestamps and process identifiers within the debug logs can be analyzed to pinpoint stages where message throughput slows down. Such insights are actionable; administrators can then examine network performance, disk I/O, and CPU usage metrics to isolate and address the underlying cause of the delays.

In summary, the configuration of log levels in Postfix is a multi-faceted process that requires balancing between detailed diagnostic information and the operational need for efficient logging. Through a combination of Postfix configuration directives, syslog integration, dynamic adjustments via scripting, and careful monitoring of system performance, administrators can achieve a finely tuned logging setup. A well-configured logging regime thus provides a robust foundation for proactive maintenance, immediate problem resolution, and long-term performance optimization.

7.4. Monitoring Mail Queues

Effective monitoring and management of mail queues is essential for maintaining the performance and reliability of a Postfix mail server. The mail queue holds messages that are pending delivery and serves as an indicator of overall system health. Postfix utilizes several directories to manage different states of messages, such as the active, deferred, and hold queues. By continuously monitoring these queues, administrators can detect bottlenecks, resolve issues, and ensure that email processing remains efficient. This section discusses key concepts, relevant tools, and practical techniques to monitor and manage the mail queues in a Postfix environment.

Postfix organizes mail queues into several distinct states. The `active` queue contains messages that are currently being processed for immediate delivery. The `deferred` queue contains messages that have experienced temporary delivery failures and are scheduled for later attempts. The `hold` queue holds messages manually held for administrative review, while the `corrupt` queue captures messages that could not be processed correctly. Monitoring these directories can reveal patterns, such as unexpected build-ups in the deferred queue that might indicate network issues or misconfigurations impacting message delivery.

A basic tool for inspecting the mail queue is the `mailq` command, which provides an overview of queued messages, including their sizes, sender and recipient addresses, and current status. Running this command typically yields output similar to the following:

```
mailq
```

This command lists messages by their queue ID, along with additional metadata. For administrators requiring greater detail or a sortable format, the `postqueue -p` command generates a more comprehensive listing, which can be processed further using standard text processing utilities like `grep` or `awk`.

The following example demonstrates how to filter the output for deferred messages, which often require closer inspection:

```
postqueue -p | grep "deferred"
```

By identifying messages stuck in the deferred queue, administrators can further interrogate individual cases to determine underlying causes such as transient network errors or misconfigured remote servers. In such situations, it is helpful to extract additional details of a specific mail item using its queue ID. For example, retrieving information about a particular message can be achieved with the `postcat` command:

```
postcat -q <queue-id>
```

The output from `postcat` includes complete details of the email, including headers and body, which can be scrutinized for abnormal routing details or attachment issues.

Monitoring tools can also be integrated into automated scripts that periodically assess the state of the mail queues. A common approach involves checking the number of messages in each queue directory and triggering alerts if thresholds are exceeded. The following shell script demonstrates how to count the number of messages in the deferred queue and log a warning if the count exceeds a specified limit:

```
#!/bin/bash
# Set the threshold for deferred messages
THRESHOLD=50
# Count the number of messages in the deferred queue using the
    postqueue command
DEFERRED_COUNT=$(postqueue -p | grep -c "deferred")

if [ "$DEFERRED_COUNT" -gt "$THRESHOLD" ]; then
    echo "$(date): Warning - Deferred queue contains $DEFERRED_COUNT
    messages." >> /var/log/postfix_queue_monitor.log
fi
```

This script, when scheduled via cron, provides real-time monitoring and logging of mail queue conditions, which is useful for early detection of issues impacting email throughput.

Performance optimization is often directly linked to effective queue monitoring. A build-up of messages may be symptomatic of delays caused by external factors, such as connectivity issues with remote mail servers or misconfigured DNS settings. By correlating queue monitoring outputs with log files from previous sections, administrators can obtain a holistic view of the mail delivery process. For instance, a sudden increase in deferred messages may coincide with repeated DNS lookup failures reported in the logs, leading administrators to investigate potential network problems or service interruptions.

In addition to monitoring queue sizes, administrators can proactively manage mail queues by flushing them. The `postqueue -f` command forces an immediate re-attempt of delivery for all deferred messages. This operation can be beneficial after resolving transient issues or updating configuration settings that previously impeded delivery. For example:

```
postqueue -f
```

Executing this command instructs Postfix to reprocess its queued messages, thus minimizing latency once underlying problems have been addressed. However, caution must be exercised when flushing the queues, as an uncoordinated flush during peak load periods might exacerbate resource contention issues.

For more controlled queue management, the `postsuper` utility provides advanced administrative functions. This tool can be used to delete, hold, or requeue messages based on their queue IDs. For example, if an administrator identifies a corrupted message or one that is spam-like, it may be appropriate to remove it from the queue. The following command demonstrates the deletion of a message from the mail queue:

```
postsuper -d <queue-id>
```

Likewise, to temporarily prevent a problematic message from being processed further, it can be placed on hold:

```
postsuper -h <queue-id>
```

Such targeted interventions allow administrators to isolate problematic messages, conduct further forensic analysis, and ensure that the portion of the mail system unaffected by these irregularities continues to operate smoothly.

Another aspect of monitoring includes scheduled regular reviews of the queue status. Administrators often integrate mail queue statistics into broader system performance dashboards. Tools like Munin, Nagios, or Zabbix can be configured to parse mail queue information and graph queue depth over time. By delivering this data in real time, monitoring solutions help in identifying trends, such as a gradual increase in the deferred queue size that may precede larger systemic issues. This proactive monitoring is particularly useful in environments with a high volume of email traffic, where delayed delivery can have significant operational implications.

Implementing log rotation and archiving mechanisms for mail queue logs is another consideration. Given that frequent monitoring can generate large volumes of data, managing historical records is necessary to prevent disk space issues. Standard log rotation utilities like logrotate can be configured to handle these logs efficiently, ensuring that current analytics remain accessible while older records are archived for long-term performance and capacity analyses.

In some environments, customized scripts can further extract and analyze specific metrics from mail queues. For instance, a script designed to generate a daily report may analyze the number of messages processed, the percentage of deferred versus active messages, and the average age of messages in the deferred queue. The report output can guide system administrators in adjusting service parameters, such as reconfiguring retry intervals or modifying resource allocations for the mail transfer agent. The following example illustrates how a script might summarize key metrics:

```
#!/bin/bash
# Generate a report of mail queue metrics
TOTAL_MESSAGES=$(postqueue -p | grep -c "^[A-F0-9]")
DEFERRED_MESSAGES=$(postqueue -p | grep -c "deferred")
ACTIVE_MESSAGES=$((TOTAL_MESSAGES - DEFERRED_MESSAGES))

echo "Mail Queue Report - $(date)"
echo "--------------------------"
echo "Total messages: $TOTAL_MESSAGES"
echo "Active messages: $ACTIVE_MESSAGES"
echo "Deferred messages: $DEFERRED_MESSAGES"
```

The report can be expanded to include additional metrics such as message age, average delivery retries, and error codes associated with failed deliveries. Such detailed metrics are valuable for both operational troubleshooting and strategic capacity planning.

It is essential to interpret mail queue metrics in the context of overall email system performance. Continuous monitoring not only informs administrators about current conditions but also serves as historical data for trend analysis. Refinements in queue management practices typically arise from long-term observations, such as recurring spikes in deferred message counts during specific times of day or during periods of increased load. By integrating this data with system logs and external monitoring tools, administrators can implement policies that optimize email processing parameters and minimize latency.

Utilizing Postfix's built-in tools, along with supplemental scripting and monitoring systems, provides a comprehensive framework for the dynamic management of mail queues. Through careful observation, proactive queue flushing, and targeted message interventions, administrators can ensure that the mail system functions efficiently even under heavy load or in the face of transient errors. This disciplined approach to mail queue monitoring not only aids in identifying immediate delivery problems but also supports broader strategies for maintaining system performance and reliability over time.

7.5. Integrating with System Monitoring Tools

Incorporating system monitoring tools into the management of Postfix operations transforms raw logging data and queue metrics into actionable insights, enhancing the overall operational reliability of the email server. By integrating with tools capable of real-time tracking and alerting, administrators can rapidly detect anomalies and initiate corrective measures. This section elaborates on various approaches and best practices for connecting Postfix with monitoring systems, outlining configuration details, scripting techniques, and example configurations that illustrate effective integration.

Postfix generates a wealth of data through its logging and queue management mechanisms. When combined with system monitoring tools such as Nagios, Zabbix, Prometheus, or custom scripts, this data forms the backbone for an automated alerting system. The first step in this integration is ensuring that Postfix logs are structured in a manner that external tools can parse readily. Postfix typically logs messages to files located in /var/log/mail.log, which are subsequently processed by syslog daemons and forwarded to monitoring systems. Many monitoring systems are configured to watch these log files directly or rely on syslog to relay events.

A common integration method involves utilizing log analysis scripts that filter and interpret Postfix log data. Administrators can schedule these scripts to run at regular intervals or configure them to push real-time data to a monitoring dashboard. A straightforward example using grep and awk extracts key events from the log and outputs them in a simplified format:

```
#!/bin/bash
# Script: postfix_alert.sh
# Extract errors and warnings from the Postfix log for monitoring
    purposes
LOGFILE="/var/log/mail.log"
ALERT_FILE="/var/log/postfix_alerts.log"
```

225

```
grep -E "warning|error" $LOGFILE | awk '{print $1, $2, $3, $5, $6}' >
    $ALERT_FILE
```

This script highlights occurrences of errors and warnings, capturing the timestamp, process identifier, and relevant message fragments. The output file, postfix_alerts.log, can be periodically polled by monitoring tools, or an agent can be configured to watch for modifications in this file and trigger alerts accordingly.

Monitoring tools often need metrics that extend beyond simple log file entries. Mail queue statistics serve as an indicative metric of server health, revealing bottlenecks in mail processing. The postqueue utility provides a snapshot of the current state of the mail queues. This information can be extracted and provided as metrics to a monitoring system. A script to compute key queue metrics might resemble the following:

```
#!/bin/bash
# Script: postfix_queue_metrics.sh
# Calculate and output key Postfix queue metrics for integration with
    a monitoring system

QUEUE_OUTPUT=$(postqueue -p)
TOTAL=$(echo "$QUEUE_OUTPUT" | grep -E "^[A-F0-9]" | wc -1)
DEFERRED=$(echo "$QUEUE_OUTPUT" | grep "deferred" | wc -1)
ACTIVE=$((TOTAL - DEFERRED))

echo "postfix.total_queue $TOTAL"
echo "postfix.active_queue $ACTIVE"
echo "postfix.deferred_queue $DEFERRED"
```

This script computes and prints the total number of messages, along with a breakdown of active and deferred messages. The output, formatted as simple key-value pairs, is well suited for ingestion by monitoring systems that support text-based metrics, such as Prometheus Node Exporter or custom Nagios plugins.

Many established monitoring systems offer plug-ins or native integrations that specifically target mail systems. For example, Nagios can be configured using NRPE (Nagios Remote Plugin Executor) to execute the aforementioned scripts on remote systems, producing real-time data for thresholds and alert triggers. A sample Nagios command definition may look like this:

```
define command{
  command_name check_postfix_queue
  command_line /usr/local/nagios/libexec/postfix_queue_metrics.sh
}
```

This command can then be tied to a service definition in Nagios, ensuring that if metrics such as the deferred queue exceed a predetermined threshold, an alert will be generated. Similarly, integration with Zabbix can be achieved by deploying a custom user parameter in the agent configuration file. An example entry might be:

```
UserParameter=postfix.queue.total,postqueue -p | grep -E "^[A-F0-9]"
    | wc -l
UserParameter=postfix.queue.deferred,postqueue -p | grep "deferred" |
    wc -l
```

Once configured, Zabbix can poll these values at regular intervals, and triggers can be set up within the Zabbix interface to notify administrators if the queue metrics indicate abnormal behavior.

Integration methods are not restricted to polling methods; many modern monitoring systems support push-based mechanisms as well. For instance, Prometheus can ingest metrics via its push gateway, allowing a scheduled Postfix monitoring script to push current metrics. A combination of shell scripting and curl can be used to submit metrics to a Prometheus Pushgateway. A sample script may be structured as follows:

```
#!/bin/bash
# Script: push_postfix_metrics.sh
# Push Postfix queue metrics to Prometheus Pushgateway

PUSHGATEWAY="http://pushgateway.example.com:9091"
JOB_NAME="postfix_monitoring"
```

```
TOTAL=$(postqueue -p | grep -E "^[A-F0-9]" | wc -l)
DEFERRED=$(postqueue -p | grep "deferred" | wc -l)
ACTIVE=$((TOTAL - DEFERRED))

cat <<EOF | curl --data-binary @- $PUSHGATEWAY/metrics/job/$JOB_NAME
# TYPE postfix_total_queue gauge
postfix_total_queue $TOTAL
# TYPE postfix_active_queue gauge
postfix_active_queue $ACTIVE
# TYPE postfix_deferred_queue gauge
postfix_deferred_queue $DEFERRED
EOF
```

This approach enables a seamless flow of metrics from the Postfix server into Prometheus, where dashboards and alerting rules can be applied. Real-time monitoring of mail queue metrics can be visualized using Grafana, which integrates with Prometheus and provides a rich array of customizable charts.

Beyond queue metrics, system monitoring tools can also visualize event logs, such as recurring errors or warning trends. Advanced log parsing frameworks like the Elastic Stack (ELK: Elasticsearch, Logstash, Kibana) can ingest Postfix log data and enable complex queries and visualizations across time intervals. Logstash configuration can be tailored to parse Postfix logs, extracting fields such as timestamps, process names, severity levels, and error messages. An example Logstash configuration snippet for Postfix logs is shown below:

```
input {
  file {
    path => "/var/log/mail.log"
    start_position => "beginning"
  }
}

filter {
  grok {
    match => { "message" => "%{SYSLOGTIMESTAMP:timestamp} %{
    SYSLOGHOST:host} %{DATA:process}(?:\[%{POSINT:pid}\])?: %{
    GREEDYDATA:msg}" }
  }
```

228

```
}

output {
  elasticsearch {
    hosts => ["localhost:9200"]
    index => "postfix-logs-%{+YYYY.MM.dd}"
  }
  stdout { codec => rubydebug }
}
```

Once data is indexed in Elasticsearch, Kibana can be used to assemble dashboards that display error frequencies, connection statistics, and other key performance indicators (KPIs) of Postfix operations. In this manner, integration with a monitoring stack not only provides real-time alerting but also furnishes a long-term historical record to support trend analysis and capacity planning.

Monitoring tools may also integrate with messaging and incident management systems such as PagerDuty or OpsGenie. These integrations ensure that when a metric deviates from acceptable thresholds, a notification is dispatched to the relevant on-call team members. The configuration for such notifications often involves defining alert policies within the monitoring tool, which include escalation paths and contact details. For instance, a Zabbix trigger might be configured to send an alert email if the total mail queue exceeds a specific limit for more than five minutes. This level of configurability ensures timely intervention, preventing prolonged service degradation.

Additionally, integrating with system monitoring tools helps in automating routine administrative tasks. Through API calls or direct command execution, some monitoring systems can initiate corrective actions. For example, if the deferred queue surges unexpectedly, the monitoring system might automatically run `postqueue -f` to flush the queues once the underlying condition has been resolved. Such automation reduces manual intervention and shortens the recovery time from transient failures.

A key consideration when integrating Postfix with monitoring tools is security. Ensuring that sensitive log data and metrics remain protected during transit is crucial. Secure configuration of monitoring agents, the use of encryption (e.g., TLS for Pushgateway or API communications), and proper access control in monitoring dashboards are critical measures to prevent unauthorized access to potentially sensitive administrative data.

Integrating system monitoring tools with Postfix operations provides a comprehensive framework for real-time tracking, alerting, and automated response. By leveraging log parsing, metrics extraction, and integration with industry-standard monitoring platforms, administrators gain a robust, real-time view of the email system's performance. Whether using traditional tools like Nagios and Zabbix or modern solutions like Prometheus and the Elastic Stack, effective integration enables proactive management of mail queues, rapid diagnosis of operational issues, and the consistent delivery of high-quality email service.

7.6. Creating Custom Monitoring Scripts

Developing custom monitoring scripts for Postfix provides administrators with a flexible, tailored approach to automating the detection of key events and performance metrics. By leveraging scripting languages such as Bash, Python, or Perl, one can create routines that parse log files, query mail queue statistics, and even trigger corrective actions when specific conditions arise. Custom scripts enhance the visibility into the health of the mail server and can be integrated with broader system automation frameworks to provide proactive alerting and resolution.

One common task for custom scripts is the extraction of relevant log entries. Postfix logs are rich in detail, and filtering specific events such as errors, warnings, or message rejections can help isolate problems amidst high volumes of data. For instance, a simple Bash script may be designed to monitor the mail log and alert an administrator when a threshold number of error messages are detected within a specified time period. An example script is shown below:

```
#!/bin/bash
# Script: monitor_postfix_errors.sh
# Monitors /var/log/mail.log for error messages and sends an alert if
    count exceeds threshold.

LOGFILE="/var/log/mail.log"
THRESHOLD=10  # set the number of errors to trigger an alert
ERROR_COUNT=$(grep -i "error" "$LOGFILE" | wc -l)

if [ "$ERROR_COUNT" -gt "$THRESHOLD" ]; then
    echo "$(date): Alert - $ERROR_COUNT error events detected in
    Postfix logs."
    # Here you could integrate with an email service or a
    notification API.
fi
```

This script utilizes a combination of grep and wc to count error messages. Such a routine can be scheduled through cron, ensuring regular checks without continuous manual intervention. Customizing the threshold, log file location, and alert mechanism allows system administrators to fine-tune the monitoring process to their specific environment.

Another area where custom scripts prove essential is the monitoring of mail queues. Continuous tracking of the active, deferred, and hold queues can provide early warnings of delivery issues or performance bottlenecks. A more sophisticated script may aggregate queue metrics and then compare these values against predefined conditions. Consider the following example that retrieves queue metrics and formats them for integration with external monitoring systems:

```
#!/bin/bash
# Script: postfix_queue_status.sh
# Provides detailed mail queue metrics for custom monitoring.

QUEUE_OUTPUT=$(postqueue -p)
```

```
TOTAL_MESSAGES=$(echo "$QUEUE_OUTPUT" | grep -E "^[A-F0-9]" | wc -l)
DEFERRED_MESSAGES=$(echo "$QUEUE_OUTPUT" | grep -i "deferred" | wc -l
    )
ACTIVE_MESSAGES=$((TOTAL_MESSAGES - DEFERRED_MESSAGES))

echo "$(date): Mail Queue Metrics:"
echo "Total messages: $TOTAL_MESSAGES"
echo "Active messages: $ACTIVE_MESSAGES"
echo "Deferred messages: $DEFERRED_MESSAGES"

# Trigger an alert if deferred messages exceed a threshold.
DEFERRED_THRESHOLD=20
if [ "$DEFERRED_MESSAGES" -gt "$DEFERRED_THRESHOLD" ]; then
    echo "$(date): Warning - Deferred queue has exceeded the
    threshold with $DEFERRED_MESSAGES messages."
    # Integration with a notification system can be added here.
fi
```

The script above begins by capturing the output of the postqueue -p
command, which lists the current status of the mail queues. It then
processes this output to extract the total number of messages and
quantifies how many are deferred versus active. By embedding conditional logic, notifications can be triggered when specific thresholds are
reached, thereby providing immediate insights into potentially critical
issues.

Automation can also extend to the dynamic management of the mail
queue. For instance, if a mail queue experiences a significant backlog,
a script may automatically flush the queue after confirming that the underlying temporary issue has been resolved. Such automation reduces
downtime and minimizes manual intervention. An example script that
flushes the mail queue after verifying conditions is presented below:

```
#!/bin/bash
# Script: auto_flush_queue.sh
# Automatically flushes Postfix mail queue if conditions are met.

# Capture the current state of the mail queue
QUEUE_OUTPUT=$(postqueue -p)
DEFERRED_MESSAGES=$(echo "$QUEUE_OUTPUT" | grep -i "deferred" | wc -l
    )
```

```
# Set threshold for automatic flush
FLUSH_THRESHOLD=15

if [ "$DEFERRED_MESSAGES" -gt "$FLUSH_THRESHOLD" ]; then
    echo "$(date): Deferred messages ($DEFERRED_MESSAGES) exceed
    threshold. Flushing queue..."
    postqueue -f
    echo "$(date): Mail queue flushed."
else
    echo "$(date): No action taken. Deferred messages count (
    $DEFERRED_MESSAGES) is below threshold."
fi
```

This script illustrates a case where automated corrective action is warranted. By periodically checking the state of the deferred queue, the script safeguards against long-term message accumulation and facilitates smoother mail delivery workflows.

Python offers another powerful avenue for creating custom scripts, particularly when advanced processing or integration with APIs is required. A Python script, for example, can parse Postfix logs to generate metrics, store data in a database for historical analysis, or even trigger webhooks to alert external systems. The following Python example demonstrates how to parse a log file for critical events and display the results:

```
#!/usr/bin/env python3
import re
from datetime import datetime

log_file = "/var/log/mail.log"
error_pattern = re.compile(r'(?P<timestamp>\w+\s+\d+\s+\d+:\d+:\d+)\s
    +\S+\s+(?P<process>\S+):\s+(?P<message>.*error.*)', re.IGNORECASE
    )

def parse_log():
    error_events = []
    with open(log_file, 'r') as file:
        for line in file:
            match = error_pattern.search(line)
            if match:
                event = {
                    'timestamp': match.group('timestamp'),
```

```
                     'process': match.group('process'),
                     'message': match.group('message')
                 }
                 error_events.append(event)
     return error_events

def main():
    errors = parse_log()
    print(f"{datetime.now()}: Found {len(errors)} error events in
     Postfix logs.")
    for event in errors:
        print(f"{event['timestamp']} - {event['process']}: {event['
        message']}")

if __name__ == "__main__":
    main()
```

This Python script employs regular expressions to locate error events
in the Postfix log file. By capturing key fields such as the timestamp,
process, and error message, the script generates a structured view of
the log data. Such processing is beneficial when integrating with systems that require data in a structured format for further analysis or
archival.

In addition to log file parsing, creating custom scripts is valuable for
interfacing with third-party monitoring platforms. Scripts can be designed to push metrics to platforms that aggregate data from multiple
systems. For example, using Python and the requests library, a script
may send an HTTP POST request containing key mail server metrics to
a centralized API endpoint. An illustrative snippet is provided below:

```
#!/usr/bin/env python3
import json
import subprocess
import requests
import re

def get_queue_metrics():
    try:
        output = subprocess.check_output(["postqueue", "-p"]).decode
        ("utf-8")
        total_messages = len([line for line in output.splitlines() if
        re.match(r'^[A-F0-9]', line)])
```

234

```
        deferred_messages = len([line for line in output.splitlines()
    if "deferred" in line.lower()])
        active_messages = total_messages - deferred_messages
        return {
            "total_messages": total_messages,
            "active_messages": active_messages,
            "deferred_messages": deferred_messages
        }
    except subprocess.CalledProcessError as e:
        print("Error retrieving mail queue metrics:", e)
        return {}

def push_metrics(metrics):
    api_url = "http://monitoring.example.com/api/metrics"
    headers = {"Content-Type": "application/json"}
    response = requests.post(api_url, data=json.dumps(metrics),
     headers=headers)
    if response.status_code == 200:
        print("Metrics pushed successfully")
    else:
        print("Failed to push metrics:", response.status_code)

if __name__ == "__main__":
    metrics = get_queue_metrics()
    if metrics:
        push_metrics(metrics)
```

This Python script exemplifies how custom monitoring scripts can not only gather metrics using system tools such as `postqueue` but also integrate these metrics with external monitoring services via HTTP API requests. Such push-based metric collection is particularly useful in dynamic or distributed environments where centralized monitoring systems rely on real-time data feeds.

Custom monitoring scripts also complement the role of automation in post-event analysis. By systematically logging performance data and event timestamps, these scripts can build a historical record for trend analysis. Over time, the aggregated data can reveal patterns, such as peak usage times or recurring failure modes, thereby enabling refined capacity planning and proactive maintenance. Storing such metrics in a lightweight database or appending them to a log file, for example, allows for retrospective analytics:

```
#!/bin/bash
# Script: log_postfix_metrics.sh
# Append Postfix queue metrics to a historical log file for analysis.

METRICS_LOG="/var/log/postfix_metrics_history.log"
QUEUE_OUTPUT=$(postqueue -p)
TOTAL=$(echo "$QUEUE_OUTPUT" | grep -E "^[A-F0-9]" | wc -l)
DEFERRED=$(echo "$QUEUE_OUTPUT" | grep -i "deferred" | wc -l)
ACTIVE=$((TOTAL - DEFERRED))

echo "$(date), Total:$TOTAL, Active:$ACTIVE, Deferred:$DEFERRED" >>
    $METRICS_LOG
```

This script, when executed at regular intervals via a scheduling system like cron, creates a timeline of queue metrics that administrators can later analyze to identify long-term trends and potential capacity issues.

The value of custom monitoring scripts lies in their adaptability: each environment may present distinct challenges requiring unique monitoring strategies. Whether the focus is on parsing log files, assessing queue sizes, or pushing performance data to external systems, these scripts can be tailored to meet the administrative needs of Postfix-based mail systems. Through strategic automation and the integration of alerting mechanisms, custom scripts drive both reactive and proactive management of email operations, ultimately contributing to enhanced reliability and performance.

Chapter 8

Troubleshooting and Debugging

*This chapter focuses on identifying and resolving common Postfix is-
sues, from configuration errors to mail delivery problems. It details
strategies for diagnosing authentication errors and using verbose logging for deeper insights. Additionally, it addresses performance bottlenecks and provides tools and commands essential for effective troubleshooting. These insights equip administrators to efficiently resolve
challenges and ensure optimal server functionality.*

8.1. Common Postfix Configuration Issues

Postfix, as a robust mail transfer agent, relies on an intricate configuration that, if misconfigured, can lead to service disruptions, degraded
performance, or even security vulnerabilities. Administrators often
face challenges that stem from simple typographical errors, misinter-

pretations of documentation, or unforeseen interactions between configuration parameters. Understanding and resolving these issues demands a careful review of configuration files, knowledge of parameter dependencies, and proficiency in diagnostic tools.

A common source of configuration issues originates from the primary configuration file, `main.cf`. Minor mistakes in this file are frequent culprits; for example, an incorrect value of `myhostname` or `mydomain` can cause improper routing of emails or rejection by remote servers. It is essential to verify that the hostname provided in `myhostname` exactly matches the fully qualified domain name (FQDN) used in DNS records. Misconfiguration in this area can lead to errors in the mail logs indicating that the server identity is ambiguous. In addition, typographical errors in key-value pairs or the mishandling of spaces around the equals sign lead to parsing errors. The following example highlights the correct configuration of domain-related parameters:

```
myhostname = mail.example.com
mydomain = example.com
myorigin = $mydomain
```

When parameters like `relayhost` are not set correctly, the server might attempt to relay mail directly, bypassing necessary intermediate steps or through incorrect intermediaries. It is crucial for administrators to consider the network topology and security restrictions when defining the relay host. For instance, environments that segregate internal and external communications demand explicit definitions of `relayhost` to avoid unintended direct mail deliveries. Another frequent issue is encountered with parameters governing secure mail delivery. TLS parameters must be configured with precision to prevent negotiation failures between mail servers. Misplacement of parameters like `smtpd_tls_cert_file` and `smtpd_tls_key_file` not only impedes the initiation of encrypted sessions but may also expose the server to man-in-the-middle attacks if fallback mechanisms are improperly configured.

238

Authentication mechanisms present another area with a high propensity for configuration errors. The settings that manage SASL, such as smtpd_sasl_auth_enable and smtpd_recipient_restrictions, are pivotal for secure mail delivery. In environments where multiple authentication methods are contemplated, ensuring that parameters are not mutually exclusive or causing unintended conflicts is key. For example, if permit_mynetworks is not defined properly within smtpd_recipient_restrictions, trusted IP ranges might be denied service, or conversely, unauthorized hosts could gain access.

One method to systematically identify common mistakes is to enable Postfix verbose logging. By setting an appropriate level of verbosity in the logging configuration, administrators can gain insight into the operational workflow of Postfix and capture error reports that pinpoint configuration faults. Logging configurations are typically adjusted by modifying system logging facilities rather than directly through Postfix's configuration; however, understanding the interplay is vital. After enabling verbose logging, the administrator should interrogate the logs for clues related to misconfigured components. A snippet of a log output might appear as follows:

```
Aug 12 12:34:56 mailserver postfix/smtpd[1234]: warning: TLS library problem:
 error:1408F10B:SSL routines:SSL3_GET_RECORD:wrong version number
Aug 12 12:34:56 mailserver postfix/smtpd[1234]: disconnect from unknown[192.0
.2.1] ehlo=1 starttls=0 mail=0 rcpt=0 data=0 commands=1
```

The next step after reviewing the logs is to extract actionable outcomes from these messages. For instance, the error related to the TLS library indicates a mismatch in protocol expectations, potentially stemming from outdated cipher suites or unsupported protocol versions on the client or server sides. Resolving such issues often requires updating the TLS settings in main.cf:

```
smtpd_tls_protocols = !SSLv2, !SSLv3, TLSv1, TLSv1.1, TLSv1.2
smtpd_tls_ciphers = high
smtpd_tls_exclude_ciphers = aNULL, MD5
```

After applying these corrections, testing with diagnostic tools such as openssl s_client aids in confirming that the changes propagate as expected. A command such as the one below allows an administrator to verify the server's TLS response:

```
openssl s_client -starttls smtp -crlf -connect mail.example.com:25
```

An effective troubleshooting strategy also involves validating alias map configurations. Aliases are essential for redirecting mail to appropriate destinations, but configuration errors here can lead to mail loops or undelivered messages. The alias file, typically /etc/aliases, must be maintained accurately, and any changes require recompilation or updates with newaliases. The following command syntax is typical for this operation:

```
newaliases
```

A common oversight involves neglecting to update the alias database after modifications, leading to persistent errors where changes are not reflected in mail routing. Additionally, Postfix configurations sometimes use separate mapping files for handling virtual domains. Ensuring the integrity and proper permissions of these files is critical. An improper permission setting on a virtual alias file may prevent Postfix from reading the configuration, resulting in messages failing to route. Consistent use of the postmap command to verify map files is recommended:

```
postmap -s /etc/postfix/virtual
```

Misconfigurations also arise from circular dependencies or conflicts among various configuration files. Since Postfix utilizes several auxiliary files (such as master.cf for controlling daemon processes), inconsistencies between files can propagate errors. A common scenario is when a service defined in master.cf is not reflected correctly in main.cf, leading to unexpected behavior in the handling of mail queues. Maintaining synchronization and consistency across configurations by cross-verification and testing after each change minimizes this risk.

It is equally important to recognize that many configuration issues manifest only under specific operational conditions. Performance bottlenecks, for example, may not be evident during routine checks but become pronounced under heavy load or when processing large volumes of mail. In such cases, parameters controlling connection limits (for instance, smtpd_client_connection_limit and default_process_limit) become focal points. Setting these parameters too high or too low can prove detrimental. Carefully adjusting and testing these limits under different scenarios yields optimal performance and resilience.

Interdependencies among Postfix parameters can further complicate the resolution of configuration issues. Administrators must be mindful of the cascading effects when modifying a single parameter. For instance, adjusting the smtpd_recipient_restrictions parameter without a proper understanding of its sequence and interplay with other restrictions may inadvertently weaken security controls. Consider the following corrected configuration where restrictions are applied in a logical sequence:

```
smtpd_recipient_restrictions =
    permit_mynetworks,
    permit_sasl_authenticated,
    reject_unauth_destination
```

Ensuring that restrictions are logically ordered prevents erroneous access grants and mitigates the risk of spamming. The configuration paradigm should reflect a clear, hierarchical structure where trusted sources are validated first, followed by stricter measures for unverified requests.

In practice, resolving common configuration issues often requires iterative testing. Utilizing diagnostic commands like postfix check

241

immediately after making changes provides a quick validation step to identify syntax errors or file permission issues. An example command is as follows:

```
postfix check
```

Should errors appear in the output, they must be addressed immediately. In cases where configurations are corrected incrementally, maintaining a backup copy of the last known good configuration aids in the rapid restoration of services during troubleshooting. Version control systems are highly effective in tracking changes, allowing for efficient backtracking where errors were introduced.

A related and often overlooked aspect is the handling of deprecated parameters. As Postfix evolves, certain configuration options become obsolete, yet remnants may persist in legacy configurations. Regularly consulting the official Postfix documentation and verifying that the configuration aligns with current best practices is necessary for preventing failures. Deprecated commands and parameters, if left in place, can produce warning messages or lead to unexpected behavior when new features conflict with outdated settings.

For administrators managing multiple Postfix instances, consistency in configurations across servers is paramount. Inconsistencies between servers can lead to disparate behaviors and complicate the troubleshooting process. Automated configuration management tools, along with centralized logging, help maintain uniformity and allow for quick identification of configuration drift. This strategy streamlines the resolution process by establishing a standardized baseline, thereby reducing the individual troubleshooting efforts for each server.

Recognizing the intrinsic value of proactive configuration testing and evaluation cannot be overstated. By routinely examining configuration files and automating the testing of new settings in a sandbox environment, administrators can avoid the pitfalls of direct modifications in production environments. Such practices reduce downtime and the administrative overhead involved in identifying and rectifying configuration errors under pressure. A robust testing strategy coupled with incremental adjustments drives system reliability and enhances overall security posture.

Critical evaluation of configuration nuances, coupled with a systematic troubleshooting approach, reinforces the stability of Postfix deployments in diverse operational environments. This discipline in configuration management not only weeds out common issues but also fosters a proactive culture where potential pitfalls are anticipated and mitigated before they escalate to service interruptions. The application of these techniques ensures that Postfix continues to perform reliably, adjusting seamlessly to both evolving network conditions and security requirements.

8.2. Diagnosing Mail Delivery Problems

Diagnosing mail delivery issues within Postfix requires a systematic approach that encompasses reviewing system logs, analyzing error messages, and employing diagnostic tools to isolate the root cause of failed deliveries. Administrators must have a detailed understanding of the flow of mail through Postfix, from acceptance of a message to its eventual delivery, and be capable of parsing error messages that may originate from misconfigurations, network issues, or recipient server rejections.

A primary technique involves consulting the Postfix log files, as these records contain extensive information about transaction sequences and failures. In many systems, log files such as `/var/log/maillog` or `/var/log/mail.log` serve as the main repositories of diagnostic data. Through careful inspection of these logs, an administrator can identify errors and warnings that directly correlate with mail delivery incidents.

The following command is instrumental in monitoring mail activity in real time:

```
tail -f /var/log/mail.log
```

Error messages in the logs are often explicit about the nature of the failure. For example, a log entry may include references to "connection refused" errors or "relay access denied" messages. The appearance of messages such as:

```
Aug 15 14:22:35 mailserver postfix/smtpd[2345]: warning: reject: RCPT from un
known[203.0.113.10]: 554 5.7.1 Service unavailable; Client host [203.0.113.10
] blocked using zen.spamhaus.org; ...
```

indicates that the sender's IP address may be blacklisted. Resolving such issues involves verifying the reputation of the source IP and adjusting relay settings or consulting external blacklists to clarify if the domain or IP address is erroneously flagged.

Another common problem encountered during delivery is a failure in domain name resolution. When Postfix logs display errors like "temporary lookup failure" or "host not found," it is essential to verify that DNS resolvers configured on the mail server are responding properly. The operator can test domain name resolution with tools like dig or nslookup. For example:

```
dig example.com MX
```

This command helps determine whether the MX records for the destination domain are correctly configured and visible to the network. Proper resolution plays a critical role in the routing process, and any misconfiguration or temporary DNS outage can directly impede mail delivery.

Mail delivery failures might also result from issues related to TLS certificate validations. Recent log messages may indicate failures such as "certificate verify failed" or errors in TLS handshake protocols. These

errors point to potential issues with certificate expiry, misconfiguration in the TLS settings, or incompatible protocol versions. Administrators should ensure that parameters such as `smtpd_tls_cert_file`
and `smtpd_tls_key_file` reference valid certificate and key files, and
that the cipher suites and TLS protocols specified reflect current security standards. Revisiting these configurations as shown below is a
common corrective measure:

```
smtpd_tls_cert_file = /etc/ssl/certs/mailserver.crt
smtpd_tls_key_file  = /etc/ssl/private/mailserver.key
smtpd_tls_security_level = may
```

Another aspect of diagnosing mail delivery issues includes examining
the mail queue. The Postfix mail queue can provide valuable insights
into undelivered messages and their associated error codes. The command `mailq` lists messages that are pending delivery. Analyzing these
queued messages can indicate whether temporary failures (such as network issues or remote mail server timeouts) are causing the accumulation of deferred messages. The following command provides detailed
queue information:

```
postqueue -p
```

If many messages are being deferred, it may be necessary to review
server connectivity and the health of remote recipient servers. Administrators should also use the `postsuper -d` command prudently to
clear unwanted messages after due verification.

Detailed analysis of error codes from SMTP replies is essential for diagnosing mail delivery issues. SMTP error codes provide clear indicators of the type of failure that occurred. For instance, a 5xx error
typically signals a permanent failure, while a 4xx error denotes a temporary issue. A typical SMTP error, such as "550 5.1.1 User unknown,"
indicates that the mailbox does not exist on the destination server and
often requires verifying the recipient address or updating address mappings. In contrast, responses like "451 4.3.0 Temporary local problem

– please try later" suggest a transient problem, potentially arising from resource constraints or temporary misconfigurations on the receiving end.

In certain situations, a deeper examination using diagnostic debugging tools becomes essential. Tools such as Postfix's built-in `postfix flush` command can be employed to force reattempts of message deliveries from the queue. This command is particularly useful after making corrective changes to configuration files or network settings:

```
postfix flush
```

Beyond basic commands, administrators can employ network diagnostic tools like `telnet` or `nc` (netcat) to simulate SMTP sessions with remote servers manually. This process aids in reproducing the failing conditions outside of Postfix, confirming that issues are not internal. An example of such a manual session may be as follows:

```
telnet mail.recipientdomain.com 25
EHLO local.domain.com
MAIL FROM:<sender@example.com>
RCPT TO:<recipient@recipientdomain.com>
DATA
Subject: Test Mail

This is a test mail.
.
QUIT
```

The responses observed in this simulated session can shed light on whether the failure originates from the remote server's policies or internal mail handling logic.

Another critical aspect is the integration of Postfix with other software components, such as anti-spam or virus scanning systems. These integrations can sometimes lead to unexpected mail delivery problems if not properly synchronized. Miscommunication between Postfix and filtering software might manifest as unexpected rejections or delays in mail processing. Administrators should verify that the handoff between Postfix and these systems is seamless, checking that the requisite configuration directives and communication sockets are operating as intended.

For instances where delivery issues stem from intermittent network errors, it is advisable to conduct a thorough check of the connectivity between the mail server and the recipient's mail exchanger. Network tools such as `ping` and `traceroute` can help identify routing issues or latency problems that might contribute to mail delivery failures. A command such as:

```
traceroute mail.recipientdomain.com
```

can reveal if there are hops presenting high latency or failing to respond, thus offering clues on potential network congestion or misconfigurations in routers and firewalls.

Analyzing logs further, some messages related to timeout and connection reset errors require in-depth understanding of the SMTP protocol. Content filter interactions, such as those resulting from spam filtering layers attacking messages on specific criteria, may manifest as connection resets or abrupt terminations. Such behavior warrants checking whether anti-virus or anti-spam modules are erroneously interpreting legitimate messages as malicious. Adjusting the thresholds or whitelisting known sources may resolve these issues without compromising overall security.

Throughout the diagnostic process, it is beneficial to compare the current behavior against a known good configuration, either from a previous backup or a reference deployment in a test environment. Discrepancies between configurations can often highlight modifications that inadvertently introduced delivery problems. Employing a version control system to track changes in configuration files enhances the ability to roll back problematic adjustments promptly. This preventive strategy minimizes downtime and simplifies the debugging process.

Furthermore, debugging mail delivery issues benefits from a clear understanding of message routing. Postfix employs a variety of tables, such as `transport`, which define specific routing logic for different domains. Errors in these tables, whether caused by syntax errors or misinterpretation of directives, can force mail to follow unintended or inefficient paths. Verifying the integrity and syntax of these files with the `postmap` command ensures that the mapping data accessed by Postfix is correct and up-to-date:

```
postmap -q example.com /etc/postfix/transport
```

An administrator should be prepared to correct any discrepancies found within these routing tables to guarantee that email is delivered along the expected paths.

Diagnosing mail delivery problems is inherently iterative. Administrators refine their approach based on the contextual feedback from error logs and diagnostic query outputs. Minor configuration modifications must be tested repeatedly, with each iteration examined via logs and testing tools to ensure that the remedial action effectively addresses the initial problem without introducing new complications. This continuous refinement ensures that changes are both safe and effective. The integrated use of diagnostic commands and network troubleshooting tools builds a comprehensive picture of the delivery landscape and facilitates the prompt isolation of defects.

Reliable mail delivery depends on a well-calibrated environment where each component, from the Postfix configuration to the network architecture, operates in harmony. A methodical diagnostic process that aggregates insights from logs, command outputs, and network tests enables administrators to pinpoint and resolve issues efficiently. Advanced users might also incorporate monitoring tools that alert on unusual patterns in mail delivery metrics, proactively identifying problems even before users report errors. Such systems not only help in remediation but also in refining best practices for long-term stability and performance consistency within email server environments.

8.3. Troubleshooting Authentication Errors

Authentication errors in Postfix can arise from misconfigurations in the Simple Authentication and Security Layer (SASL) setup, incorrect credential storage, or conflicts between security policies and the inherent trust model defined in Postfix. Effective diagnosis and remediation require a systematic approach that scrutinizes logs, verifies configuration parameters, and utilizes testing tools to simulate authentication attempts. This section examines common pitfalls in authentication settings and provides detailed techniques for identifying and resolving these issues.

A typical starting point in troubleshooting is the Postfix log file, which records every authentication attempt. Errors related to authentication are usually accompanied by descriptions that pinpoint either a misconfigured parameter or an external dependency failing. For example, an error such as "warning: SASL authentication failure: generic failure" may suggest that the SASL library did not receive the expected user credentials, or that there is a misalignment between the client and server authentication protocols. Administrators should first inspect the log file using commands similar to:

```
tail -f /var/log/mail.log
```

Error messages, when parsed carefully, often reveal whether the issue is due to wrong usernames, improperly encrypted passwords, or configuration mismatches. A detailed analysis of the log might provide entries similar to:

```
Aug 20 09:15:47 mailserver postfix/smtpd[3456]: warning: SASL authentication
failure: Password verification failed
```

```
Aug 20 09:15:47 mailserver postfix/smtpd[3456]: warning: SASL authentication
failure: authentication failure
```

Such entries indicate that the credentials provided during the authentication process did not pass verification. Addressing these messages involves verifying the underlying credentials stored in the SASL database. In many environments, the dovecot or cyrus-sasl libraries are utilized. For instance, if cyrus-sasl is in use, administrators should verify that the smtpd.conf file is correctly configured with directives such as:

```
pwcheck_method: saslauthd
mech_list: plain login
```

If the authentication backend is managed by Dovecot, the corresponding settings in /etc/dovecot/conf.d/10-master.conf must ensure that the SASL socket is properly referenced. Updating the Postfix configuration to reference the correct UNIX socket location is crucial. An example modification in main.cf may look as follows:

```
smtpd_sasl_path = private/auth
smtpd_sasl_type = dovecot
```

Inconsistencies between these settings and the actual configuration of the authentication daemon are a common source of errors. It is essential to validate that the socket exists and is accessible by Postfix. The following command can be used to inspect the socket permissions:

```
ls -l /var/spool/postfix/private/auth
```

Permission issues, in which Postfix cannot read the socket due to restrictive file permissions, will result in authentication failures. Administrators should adjust permissions carefully, ensuring that the Postfix user has the necessary access without compromising system security.

Another frequent source of authentication errors relates to differences in the expected format of the user credentials. The separation of authentication methods in the `smtpd_recipient_restrictions` parameter must be maintained to allow valid clients. For example, an overly restrictive configuration that evaluates authentication after rejecting unauthorized addresses can inadvertently block legitimate authentication attempts. A typical configuration that prioritizes trusted networks and authenticated users is:

```
smtpd_recipient_restrictions =
    permit_mynetworks,
    permit_sasl_authenticated,
    reject_unauth_destination
```

The order of these restrictions is significant, as permitting authenticated users early in the sequence prevents the inadvertent blocking of valid mail. Misordering these directives can cause clients, even with correct credentials, to be caught by early reject rules, leading to frustration and disrupted mail flow.

When the log files indicate issues related to credential verification, administrators must ensure that the password mechanisms are synchronized between the authentication daemon and Postfix. In environments where passwords are stored in a hashed format, a mismatch in the hash algorithm can result in verification errors. Security settings might enforce a particular algorithm, such as SHA-256, while older installations might default to MD5. Transitioning users to the newer algorithm necessitates that the authentication system supports the change. Confirm that the SASL configuration aligns with the updated security protocols by reviewing both the Postfix and system-level SASL configuration files.

Running diagnostic tests is an effective method to isolate the problem. One such tool is the command-line utility `testsaslauthd`, which allows direct testing of the SASL authentication process without involving Postfix processes. A typical test command is:

```
testsaslauthd -u username -p password
```

If the result indicates that authentication is successful, it suggests that the underlying library and credential store are functioning correctly. If the test fails, further attention should be directed at the authentication daemon configuration. It is important to test this in various conditions, including using both plain-text and encrypted connections, if supported. Reviewing the output helps differentiate between an authentication error due to system misconfiguration and one due to external factors, such as firewall filtering or network issues.

In many instances, debugging authentication involves verifying that the appropriate modules are loaded. For example, when using Dovecot for SASL authentication, ensuring that the auth service is enabled and running can resolve many issues. The Dovecot configuration should include a section that defines the socket to be created, as shown below:

```
service auth {
    unix_listener /var/spool/postfix/private/auth {
        mode = 0666
        user = postfix
        group = postfix
    }
}
```

If this socket is missing or not created with the proper permissions, Postfix will be unable to perform authentication checks. Therefore, verifying that the Dovecot authentication service is active is a necessary step in troubleshooting.

Beyond verifying configuration files and socket permissions, administrators must also consider the role of external authentication sources. For instance, LDAP or Active Directory integrations are common in enterprise settings. In these scenarios, the authentication credentials are verified against an external directory service. Misconfigurations in LDAP parameters, such as incorrect server addresses, search bases, or bind DN parameters, can lead to authentication errors. An example of an LDAP configuration snippet might include:

```
pwcheck_method: saslauthd
ldap_servers: ldap://ldap.example.com/
ldap_search_base: dc=example,dc=com
ldap_filter: (uid=%u)
```

A mismatch or typographical error in any part of this configuration can cause the authentication daemon to fail in verifying credentials, resulting in failed login attempts by users. It is imperative to cross-check these settings against the documentation provided by the LDAP vendor or system administrator responsible for the directory service.

Beyond configuration, network-related issues can also affect authentication. Firewalls or network policies that inhibit the proper transmission of authentication packets may cause delays or outright failures. Tools such as tcpdump can be employed to capture network traffic on the authentication port, providing evidence of whether communication between Postfix and the SASL server is occurring as expected. For example, a command similar to:

```
tcpdump -i eth0 port 143
```

may be used to capture LDAP authentication traffic. Analyzing the output can help determine if packets are being dropped or altered, leading to authentication errors.

In cases where authentication errors persist despite correct configurations, reviewing and possibly increasing the verbosity of logging may provide additional insights. Adjusting the logging level within Postfix via the postconf command can yield a more detailed output of the authentication process:

```
postconf -e "debug_peer_list = localhost"
postconf -e "debug_peer_level = 3"
```

Such settings ensure that more detailed logs are available during an authentication attempt, allowing administrators to identify subtle errors that might not be visible at lower log levels.

Another common practice involves comparing the current working configuration against a known good configuration from a backup or a tested environment. Version control over configuration files allows for easy identification of recent changes that might have introduced errors. Using a diff tool to compare current settings with previous versions can pinpoint discrepancies in authentication configuration sections, thereby accelerating the troubleshooting process.

Lastly, the impact of operating system updates or library upgrades must be considered. Updates may deprecate previous authentication methods or alter the behavior of the SASL libraries. Verifying release notes and update logs can provide context to unexpected authentication failures following system upgrades. Rolling back or adjusting configurations post-update might be necessary to regain the desired authentication functionality.

A careful, step-by-step methodology towards diagnosing authentication issues ensures that each potential error source is systematically eliminated. Continuous monitoring and regular validation of authentication mechanisms reduce the likelihood of future errors. This methodical approach guarantees that legitimate users can authenticate reliably while preventing unauthorized access, thereby sustaining the integrity and operability of the email server environment.

8.4.   Using Verbose Logging for Debugging

Verbose logging is a critical method for acquiring detailed insights into the operational state of Postfix. It provides administrators with in-depth visibility into message handling, connection negotiation, authentication attempts, and error reporting. Using verbose logging strategically enables the isolation of issues that might otherwise remain concealed in standard log formats, facilitating the rapid identification of configuration errors or unexpected behavior during mail processing.

When configuring verbose logging, it is important to understand that Postfix relies on external logging daemons, such as rsyslog or syslog-ng, to capture its output. Modifying the verbosity level in Postfix itself can be done using the postconf command. For example, increasing the debugging level for peers by executing the command below can provide additional context during SMTP transactions:

```
postconf -e "debug_peer_level = 2"
postconf -e "debug_peer_list = mail.example.com"
```

In the commands above, debug_peer_level determines the overall verbosity of logging for a particular peer, while debug_peer_list restricts the enhanced logging to specific hosts. Adjusting these settings helps to focus the debugging process on problematic connections without overwhelming the log files with information from every transaction.

Verbose logging is not a permanent configuration change; rather, it should be used as a diagnostic tool during periods when errors or anomalies present themselves. Administrators must exercise caution, as increased logging can generate large volumes of data and potentially expose sensitive operational details. Therefore, reverting to standard logging levels after diagnostics is recommended to maintain performance and security best practices.

It is essential to interpret verbose logs accurately. Detailed logs can include numerous entries, not all of which indicate an issue. Logs may begin with standard process identifications such as:

```
Aug 25 10:15:32 mailserver postfix/smtpd[4567]: connect from unknown[192.0.2.
100]
Aug 25 10:15:32 mailserver postfix/smtpd[4567]: debug: connect_from=192.0.2.1
00, helo=client.example.com
```

In these entries, the additional details provided after the debug: designation allow administrators to track connection properties, exam-

255

ine session initialization values, and understand the sequence of commands and responses between Postfix and remote clients.

One of the principal benefits of verbose logging is diagnosing problems related to TLS and authentication errors. For instance, TLS handshake issues might produce cryptic output that does not appear in standard logging. Verbose logs can reveal at which stage the handshake fails—whether at the negotiation of protocol versions or during certificate validation. An entry might appear as:

```
Aug 25 10:17:45 mailserver postfix/smtpd[4567]: debug: TLS protocol negotiati
on failed: TLSv1.2 offered, but no cipher suite match found
```

This information clearly points to a misconfiguration in the cipher suite list or an incompatibility between the client and the server settings. Administrators can then adjust the TLS parameters in main.cf accordingly to ensure support for the protocols and cipher suites in use. An example configuration may be:

```
smtpd_tls_protocols = !SSLv2, !SSLv3, TLSv1, TLSv1.1, TLSv1.2
smtpd_tls_ciphers = high
smtpd_tls_exclude_ciphers = aNULL, MD5
```

Verbose logging also aids in the troubleshooting of mail routing and queuing issues. When messages are not delivered as expected, the detailed logs illustrate the precise tracking of each message as it transitions from the initial accept phase through any relay or routing decisions. Logs might contain entries like:

```
Aug 25 10:20:10 mailserver postfix/qmgr[1234]: ABCDE12345: from=<user@example
.com>, size=1234, nrcpt=1 (queue active)
Aug 25 10:20:15 mailserver postfix/smtp[5678]: ABCDE12345: to=<recipient@dest
ination.com>, relay=mail.destination.com[198.51.100.50]:25, delay=5.2, delays
=0.1/0/1.3/3.8, dsn=2.0.0, status=sent (250 2.0.0 Ok: queued as XYZ789)
```

In this context, the breakdown of delay values across different stages—initial queuing, connection establishment, and final transmission—can point to a specific step where delays or errors occur. Such precise information helps in determining whether issues stem from network latency, temporary failures in remote servers, or congestion in the local queue.

Further granularity may also be achieved by temporarily enabling debugging for specific Postfix components. For example, adjusting the logging for SMTP sessions separately from queue management might be beneficial in high-traffic environments. This targeted approach prevents an overload of superfluous output while isolating the component under investigation. Modifications to the master.cf file may include process-specific debugging options, such as:

```
smtp      inet  n      -      y      -      -      smtpd -v
```

Here, the -v option appended to the smtpd process significantly increases logging verbosity for that specific daemon. Such process-level logging is particularly useful when investigating connection-specific or protocol-specific issues.

Understanding the output of verbose logging requires experience with standard SMTP codes and an understanding of Postfix's internal state transitions. For instance, differentiating between a 4xx (temporary) error and a 5xx (permanent) failure in the logs is a fundamental task. Verbose logs will present these codes alongside descriptive text that contextualizes the error. A line from a verbose log could read:

```
Aug 25 10:27:22 mailserver postfix/smtpd[4567]: debug: RCPT from client.examp
le.com[192.0.2.100]: 450 4.2.0 Mailbox temporarily unavailable
```

In this case, the 450 code indicates a temporary failure, guiding the administrator toward possible resource constraints or transient network issues rather than a permanent configuration error. Recognizing and parsing these details allows for a more informed decision-making process when applying fixes.

When working with verbose logging, it is also advantageous to correlate logging information across multiple layers of the mail system. Integrating verbose output from the authentication processes, TLS negotiation, and queue management together can illuminate the sequence of events leading up to a failure. Tools that aggregate logs, such as centralized logging systems or even simple scripts that filter log outputs based on keywords, can streamline this correlation. A simple command-line example of filtering log output might be:

```
grep -E "debug:|warning:" /var/log/mail.log
```

This command provides a focused view on key messages that are likely to contain diagnostic information, thereby reducing the overhead of manually scanning through extensive log files.

In addition to native Postfix debugging, system-level logging adjustments may further aid in the interpretation of verbose logs. Increasing the logging detail for the underlying system logger can capture finer details from Postfix. For example, modifying the configuration file for rsyslog to filter and record debug-level messages from Postfix ensures that every detail is preserved for analysis. An appropriate rsyslog configuration snippet might read:

```
if $programname == 'postfix' and $syslogseverity <= 'debug' then /var
    /log/postfix_debug.log
& stop
```

This separation of debug logs from the general log stream enables administrators to focus their analysis and reduces noise in the primary log files.

It is important to note that verbose logging can have performance implications. The volume of logged data may affect disk I/O, and excessive logging may also pose challenges during peak operation. Therefore, it is recommended to activate verbose logging selectively and for predefined time periods or conditions. Automated scripts can be developed to enable verbose logging when certain anomalies are detected, and then revert to normal settings once the issue has been resolved. This practice balances the need for detailed diagnostics against system performance and resource utilization.

Thorough testing is essential to ensure that verbose logging captures all necessary details without introducing additional overhead. Experimentation in a test environment permits tuning the debug parameters before deploying them in a production setting. Administrators can simulate various error scenarios to confirm that the adjustments produce the desired level of detail. For example, inducing a known TLS negotiation error and verifying that detailed logs describe the failed handshake step helps validate the logging configuration.

Ultimately, the successful use of verbose logging in Postfix hinges upon careful planning, targeted application of increased logging levels, and a strong grasp of how to interpret the resulting data. By methodically enabling verbose logging and correlating information from various sources—application logs, system logs, and network traces—administrators gain comprehensive insights into Postfix operations. This level of diagnostic clarity enables rapid remediation of issues, enhances overall server performance, and fortifies the reliability of mail delivery processes.

8.5. Addressing Performance Bottlenecks

Postfix performance is critical for maintaining high throughput and ensuring timely mail delivery in environments with heavy email traffic. Performance bottlenecks can arise from a multitude of factors including resource limitations, misconfigured parameters, inefficient routing rules, and external influences such as network latency. Identifying such issues requires systematic monitoring, analysis of mail queue behavior, and careful evaluation of Postfix configuration settings. Strategies to enhance performance focus on optimizing system resources, fine-tuning Postfix parameters, and validating network configurations.

One of the primary techniques to diagnose performance issues is to analyze the mail queue. A growing queue often signals that messages are not being processed as expected. Administrators can inspect the mail queue using commands like:

```
postqueue -p
```

The output of this command reveals details such as message size, number of recipients, and delay durations. Analyzing the timestamps and delay metrics can help pinpoint where bottlenecks are occurring. For example, if messages are deferred for an extended period during the queue management phase, the issue may lie with the delivery agents or a misconfigured relay host.

Resource limitations on the server can also contribute to performance issues. CPU, memory, and disk I/O performance directly affect the Postfix daemon's ability to process mail efficiently. Administrators should monitor system resource usage with standard system monitoring tools such as top, vmstat, or iostat. A command like:

```
iostat -x 1
```

can provide insights into disk utilization and reveal if high I/O wait times are delaying message processing. Should disk I/O appear to be a bottleneck, it may be necessary to investigate disk subsystem performance, optimize the file system, or upgrade hardware resources.

Optimizing Postfix begins with tuning the configuration parameters in main.cf and master.cf. Parameters such as default_process_limit, smtpd_client_connection_limit, and smtp_destination_rate_delay have a direct impact on throughput. Increasing the default_process_limit allows for more concurrent processes while preventing the server from becoming overwhelmed.

For example, adjusting the process limits can be accomplished with:

```
postconf -e "default_process_limit = 100"
postconf -e "smtpd_client_connection_limit = 10"
```

These modifications ensure that Postfix can spawn an appropriate number of processes to handle incoming and outgoing connections without exhausting system resources. The optimal settings depend on the expected mail volume and available hardware; thus, iterative testing and monitoring are crucial.

In scenarios where the Postfix server handles both incoming and outgoing mail simultaneously, contention for resources can occur. Separating processes in master.cf by defining distinct services for incoming and outgoing mail can reduce conflicts. Administrators might introduce a dedicated instance for mail submission or use service separation to allocate more resources to high-load components. An entry in master.cf that exemplifies this tactic is:

```
submission inet n          -      y       -       -      smtpd
   -o syslog_name=postfix/submission
   -o smtpd_tls_security_level=encrypt
   -o smtpd_client_connection_limit=20
```

This configuration reserves a dedicated process for mail submission on port 587, enforcing stricter security requirements while providing increased concurrency for authenticated sessions.

Network latency and DNS resolution issues are external factors that can hinder Postfix performance. When mail delivery relies on remote hosts, delays in DNS queries or slow network links can lead to observable bottlenecks. Tools such as dig or nslookup can be used to verify that DNS responses are prompt and accurate:

```
dig example.com MX
```

If DNS response times are slow, configuring a local caching resolver or using faster external DNS providers can alleviate delays during the mail routing process. Similarly, network tools like `ping` and `traceroute` help diagnose connectivity issues that could be affecting remote server communications. For instance:

```
traceroute mail.receiver.example.com
```

identifies problematic hops in the network path that may contribute to increased relay times.

High mail volumes can also lead to resource contention within the database systems used by Postfix for alias and virtual maps. When these mapping files are extensive or require frequent updates, the overhead of accessing and processing them can become a significant drain on performance. In such scenarios, ensuring that mapping files are properly indexed and converting flat files to hash or btree databases via the `postmap` utility is beneficial. An example command may appear as:

```
postmap /etc/postfix/virtual
```

Optimized mapping assists Postfix in quickly determining mail routing, thereby reducing delays in processing recipient addresses.

Another area susceptible to performance bottlenecks is the TLS encryption process during connection establishment. Although encryption is vital for security, it can be resource-intensive, especially on systems with limited hardware capabilities. Administrators should evaluate whether the server's CPU usage spikes during peak mail volumes due to TLS negotiation. Configuring a higher rate of accepted TLS sessions, potentially by offloading some TLS operations to specialized hardware or dedicated appliances, can mitigate these performance impacts. Additionally, ensuring that TLS settings are streamlined to support only the necessary cipher suites and protocols avoids unnecessary overhead.

The architecture of connection handling across multiple interfaces can further be refined by examining the interplay between Postfix and the underlying operating system. For example, adjusting kernel parameters related to file descriptors and network buffers can have a significant impact on server performance. Setting appropriate limits in /etc/security/limits.conf for the Postfix user ensures that the server is not constrained by default resource limits. A sample configuration might include:

```
postfix    soft    nofile    4096
postfix    hard    nofile    8192
```

These updates prevent the mail server from reaching the maximum number of open files during periods of intense load, thereby maintaining optimal performance during high-volume periods.

Monitoring is an integral part of addressing performance bottlenecks. Regularly reviewing logs, queue metrics, and system resource usage provides valuable insight into transient or persistent performance issues. Tools such as munin, nagios, or zabbix can integrate with Postfix to create dynamic graphs and trigger alerts when performance metrics deviate from acceptable thresholds. Setting up these monitoring tools allows administrators to proactively adjust configurations before performance issues escalate to service interruptions.

Fine-tuning Postfix settings ultimately involves an iterative approach that balances performance improvements with system stability and security. Administrators should consider applying incremental changes, followed by rigorous testing under simulated load conditions. Simulating a production load in a testing environment using tools such as smtp-source from the Postfix distribution can provide benchmarks for current performance and indicate the impact of any tuning. An example usage of smtp-source is:

```
smtp-source -c 50 -l 1000 -s 10 -m 10 mail.example.com
```

This command simulates multiple simultaneous connections sending a defined number of messages, allowing administrators to observe how adjustments to Postfix performance parameters affect overall throughput and latency.

In some instances, performance issues may also originate from legacy configurations that are inefficient for handling modern email volume. Regularly reviewing and updating Postfix configurations to adhere to current best practices and performance guidelines is vital. Administrators must remain aware of updates to Postfix that may introduce performance enhancements or new configuration options designed to deal with bottlenecks more efficiently.

Engaging in routine performance audits and implementing automated benchmarking scripts can provide ongoing insights into system health. Scripts that periodically capture key metrics, such as the size of the mail queue, average processing time per message, and system resource utilization, equip administrators with the data needed to make informed decisions about scalability and optimization. Such automation enables timely response to emerging performance challenges before they escalate into significant service degradation.

Combining these strategies leads to a more resilient mail server environment. By addressing each potential performance bottleneck—from queue management and resource allocation to network configuration and encryption overhead—administrators can achieve a high-performing Postfix server that meets the demands of both daily operations and peak load conditions. The systematic identification of bottlenecks, followed by targeted tuning and regular monitoring, culminates in an operationally efficient system capable of handling increased volumes of mail without compromising security or reliability.

8.6. Tools and Commands for Troubleshooting

Effective troubleshooting of Postfix issues relies on a comprehensive suite of tools and commands that provide insight into various aspects of server operations. Administrators benefit from these utilities by diagnosing problems ranging from configuration errors and message queuing issues to network and authentication failures. Detailed knowledge of these debugging aids is essential for rapid problem isolation and resolution.

Among the most fundamental commands is postfix check, which is designed to examine the Postfix configuration files for syntax errors or permission issues. Running:

```
postfix check
```

validates the integrity of configuration files such as main.cf and master.cf. This command is particularly useful immediately after making any changes to the configuration. If errors are detected, Postfix outputs specific lines indicating the file and nature of the error, thereby guiding the administrator toward targeted corrections.

Another critical utility is mailq, which functions as an alias for postqueue -p. This command provides an overview of the current mail queue content, including message IDs, sender/recipient addresses, sizes, and delay details. Monitoring the mail queue is invaluable when messages are unexpectedly deferred or when delivery times exceed anticipated thresholds. The command is executed as follows:

```
mailq
```

In scenarios where messages accumulate in the queue, further examination with postqueue -p can reveal delays in specific phases of message processing. Comparing the timing of queue insertion and processing events helps identify whether delays are due to network latency, recipient server issues, or local resource constraints.

Postfix uses mapping files to define routing, aliases, and virtual domains. The `postmap` command is used to compile text-based mapping files into a format that Postfix can efficiently query. For instance, after modifying the virtual alias file, one might run:

```
postmap /etc/postfix/virtual
```

to update the hash database. Furthermore, `postmap -s` provides a means to query a map file for a specific key, offering real-time validation of lookup entries. An example query is:

```
postmap -q recipient@example.com /etc/postfix/virtual
```

This command returns the destination mapped to the specified address if present, ensuring that the aliasing functionality operates as expected.

Integration with system logging is a core component of the troubleshooting process. Tools such as `tail` and `grep` allow administrators to filter and review log files for Postfix. For example, to continuously monitor mail-related logs one might use:

```
tail -f /var/log/mail.log
```

Filtering log entries for errors or specific keywords further refines the diagnostic process. A command such as:

```
grep -E "warning|error" /var/log/mail.log
```

isolates messages flagged as potential issues. The output from this command provides a streamlined view of problematic events, which can then be cross-referenced with expected behavior from the Postfix configuration.

Connection testing tools are also critical in troubleshooting issues related to remote interactions. The `telnet` command, for example, facilitates manual SMTP sessions with remote mail servers. By initiating a connection on the SMTP port, administrators can simulate the sequence of commands that occur during a typical mail transaction. A sample session is as follows:

```
telnet mail.receiver.example.com 25
EHLO local.domain.com
MAIL FROM:<sender@example.com>
RCPT TO:<recipient@receiver.example.com>
DATA
Subject: Test Mail

This is a test mail.
.
QUIT
```

Observing the responses provided during this interaction helps determine whether remote servers are rejecting connections or if there are issues with the initial handshake. Similar tools such as nc (netcat) can be employed when more granular control over the connection is required.

Another critical diagnostic tool is openssl s_client, which is particularly beneficial for testing TLS configurations. Secure connections and the negotiation process are at times the source of subtle issues, and this command simulates a TLS handshake with detailed output. A typical command might be:

```
openssl s_client -starttls smtp -crlf -connect mail.example.com:25
```

This command produces verbose output that details the entire TLS negotiation process, including the certificate chain, protocol versions, and cipher suite selection. By inspecting these details, administrators can identify mismatches between client and server configurations, such as unsupported cipher suites or misconfigured certificate files.

Performance monitoring and resource utilization are equally important when troubleshooting. Standard system utilities like top, vmstat, and iostat provide a real-time view into system resource consumption. For example, using:

267

```
iostat -x 1
```

allows administrators to monitor disk I/O rates, revealing whether heavy disk activity is leading to delays in message processing. Similarly, top offers a real-time snapshot of CPU and memory usage, which is critical for diagnosing performance bottlenecks in high-traffic environments.

For an aggregated view of multiple diagnostic outputs, centralized logging systems such as rsyslog or syslog-ng can be configured to capture all Postfix-related logs in a dedicated file. This configuration allows for easier analysis with command-line tools, and even automated scripts can be implemented to trigger alerts when error thresholds are met. An example rsyslog configuration snippet might be:

```
if $programname == 'postfix' then /var/log/postfix_debug.log
& stop
```

This directive ensures that all log messages from Postfix are isolated in a single file, thus simplifying the review process for troubleshooting sessions.

The use of debugging options built into Postfix services can be controlled through parameters in both main.cf and master.cf. For example, adding the -v flag to the SMTP daemon in master.cf increases verbosity for that service:

```
smtp      inet  n        -      y       -       -     smtpd -v
```

This elevated verbosity enables administrators to view a detailed transcript of SMTP transactions, which is invaluable when diagnosing problems with the negotiation of Mail Submission or delivery handling.

Another powerful command is postfix reload, which forces Postfix to re-read its configuration files without restarting the entire service. This command is particularly useful after making configuration changes during troubleshooting sessions:

```
postfix reload
```

Reloading the configuration ensures that any corrections are immediately applied, allowing administrators to quickly verify whether changes have resolved the identified issues.

In addition to the aforementioned tools, the integration of third-party monitoring and diagnostic scripts can enhance the troubleshooting process. Many administrators employ custom scripts to periodically check the status of the Postfix queue, resource usage, and service uptime. A simple Bash script might be designed to output key metrics every few minutes, enabling proactive detection of emerging issues. An example script snippet is:

```
#!/bin/bash
echo "Current mail queue:"
mailq
echo "System resource usage:"
top -b -n 1 | head -n 10
```

When executed at regular intervals, such scripts facilitate ongoing performance monitoring and early detection of anomalies.

It is essential to consider that troubleshooting is an iterative process. Combining multiple tools and corroborating findings across different diagnostics will yield the most accurate results. For example, when tail and grep reveal specific error messages, a subsequent check using postfix check might pinpoint a corresponding configuration error. Similarly, performance issues identified with iostat can be correlated with high resource usage observed in top. This layered approach reinforces the troubleshooting process by ensuring that evidence from one tool is supported by data from another.

Automated alerting and monitoring systems, such as munin or zabbix, extend Postfix troubleshooting by providing historical data and real-time alerts. These systems integrate with Postfix logs and performance metrics, enabling administrators to detect deviations from normal operating conditions promptly. Alerts generated by these systems can trigger further investigative commands or even automated scripts designed to reconfigure or restart services when certain thresholds are exceeded.

The cumulative insights gained from these tools and commands empower administrators to diagnose issues with precision and implement corrective actions effectively. By systematically employing each tool—from syntax-checking with `postfix check` to detailed TLS diagnostics with `openssl s_client`—administrators can derive a holistic understanding of Postfix behavior under normal and stressed conditions. This methodology ensures that troubleshooting is not merely reactive but forms part of a proactive strategy to maintain server reliability and performance.

Through disciplined use of these diagnostic tools, administrators can reduce downtime, enhance mail throughput, and achieve optimized configurations that meet both security and performance requirements. The integration of tools such as `postqueue`, `postmap`, system monitoring utilities, and centralized logging creates a robust framework for ongoing troubleshooting and system improvement. Such a framework is indispensable for maintaining the operational integrity of a Postfix mail server in complex and dynamic network environments.

Chapter 9

Integration with Other Services

This chapter examines integrating Postfix with complementary services to enhance its capabilities. It covers seamless collaboration with Dovecot, SpamAssassin, and ClamAV for extended functionality. The chapter also discusses connecting Postfix to SQL databases and LDAP directories for scalable user management, and integrating with groupware solutions for enriched collaborative features. These integrations expand Postfix's potential, optimizing its performance and adaptability within diverse environments.

9.1. Linking Postfix with Dovecot

Establishing a robust integration between Postfix and Dovecot is essential for delivering email reliably while enabling users to access their mailboxes through IMAP or POP3 protocols. This section provides technical guidelines for configuring Dovecot as the authentication and mailbox engine alongside Postfix, ensuring seamless email delivery and retrieval. The integration leverages Dovecot's secure authentication mechanisms and efficient mailbox handling to extend the functionality offered by Postfix.

The integration process begins with designing a clear architecture. Postfix handles the initial SMTP transactions and queues incoming mail. Dovecot, on the other hand, manages user authentication, provides access to mailboxes, and serves the mail retrieval protocols (IMAP/POP3). By offloading authentication and mailbox management to Dovecot, administrators can centralize user credentials and streamline security configurations for both sending and receiving operations.

A critical component in this setup is the use of a UNIX socket for authentication communication between Postfix and Dovecot. In typical configurations, Dovecot creates a socket in the Postfix directory (commonly /var/spool/postfix/private/dovecot-auth), and Postfix is configured to connect to this socket for SASL authentication. This mechanism not only improves performance by using UNIX domain sockets instead of TCP sockets for local communications, but it also tightens security by restricting access to the socket through file system permissions.

The first step requires updating the Postfix configuration file, main.cf. Configuration parameters need to be set so that Postfix delegates authentication to the Dovecot service. The parameters smtpd_sasl_type and smtpd_sasl_path are central to this connection. An example snippet of relevant settings in main.cf is shown below:

```
smtpd_sasl_type = dovecot
smtpd_sasl_path = private/dovecot-auth
smtpd_sasl_auth_enable = yes
smtpd_tls_auth_only = yes
```

These settings instruct Postfix to defer authentication to Dovecot via the specified socket. The smtpd_tls_auth_only parameter ensures that authentication is only permitted when TLS is active, thereby enhancing security during client-server communications.

On the Dovecot side, adjustments in its configuration files are equally important. Dovecot must be configured to generate the authentication socket in a location that is accessible to Postfix. Typically, the file 10-master.conf in Dovecot's configuration directory is modified to include a service section for "auth." A representative configuration block is presented here:

```
service auth {
  unix_listener /var/spool/postfix/private/dovecot-auth {
    mode = 0660
    user = postfix
    group = postfix
  }
  # Optionally add another socket for Dovecot administrative tasks
  unix_listener auth-userdb {
    mode = 0600
    user = vmail
    group = vmail
  }
}
```

In the above example, Dovecot creates a socket with restrictive permissions, ensuring that only the postfix user and group have read-write access. This configuration not only guarantees secure authentication but also maintains proper separation of privileges between the two services.

After configuring both Postfix and Dovecot, it is advisable to verify that the file permissions and ownership of the created authentication socket are correct. Using the command ls -l, administrators can confirm that the socket is accessible only to the designated users. An expected output may look as follows:

```
srw-rw---- 1 postfix postfix 0 Jun 24 10:15 dovecot-auth
```

273

This output, produced by the operating system, confirms that the integration environment respects the security policies required for authentication.

Another aspect of the integration involves configuring Dovecot's authentication mechanism. It is imperative to define how Dovecot reads user credentials, which may be stored either in local files, SQL databases, or LDAP directories. When centralized authentication is necessary, SQL or LDAP backends are typically utilized to enable scalable user management. A typical block for an SQL-based configuration might include the following:

```
passdb {
  driver = sql
  args = /etc/dovecot/dovecot-sql.conf.ext
}

userdb {
  driver = sql
  args = /etc/dovecot/dovecot-sql.conf.ext
}
```

The SQL configuration file contains the necessary instructions to connect to the database and query user credentials. Dovecot subsequently leverages this centralized repository to authenticate the user during login attempts initiated via SMTP (and validated by Postfix) or through IMAP/POP3 sessions.

Additionally, Dovecot must be configured to handle mailbox formats and file structures that Postfix uses for final mail delivery. Most commonly, the `mail_location` parameter in Dovecot's configuration is configured to match the mailbox structure used by the server. For example, if the Maildir format is used, the following line in the user configuration file achieves the required consistency:

```
mail_location = maildir:~/Maildir
```

This line ensures that Dovecot correctly interprets the user's mailbox locations, thus synchronizing its view of mail storage with the directory structure populated by Postfix's delivery process.

Dovecot's ability to serve IMAP and POP3 clients hinges on the proper configuration of these protocols. Key parameters that need to be verified include the network interfaces on which Dovecot listens, the ports utilized, and the security settings (such as TLS certificates). A minimal yet effective configuration for IMAP and POP3 services might resemble the following:

```
protocols = imap pop3
ssl = required
ssl_cert = </etc/ssl/certs/dovecot.pem
ssl_key = </etc/ssl/private/dovecot.key
```

These settings secure the session initiation with strong encryption, ensuring that the credentials and data transmitted during email retrieval are protected. Successful integration thus requires that both Postfix and Dovecot are configured with compatible TLS settings.

Beyond configuration files, logging is an indispensable tool for diagnosing issues during integration. Both Postfix and Dovecot provide extensive logging capabilities that can be activated to track authentication attempts, mail delivery flows, and errors related to socket connections. For instance, enabling verbose logging in Postfix can be achieved by modifying the `syslog_name` parameter or adjusting the logging settings in the system's syslog daemon. Dovecot also offers logging configurations that can be tuned via the `logging` section in its configuration, thereby providing insights into user login attempts and service interactions.

Troubleshooting common issues often involves verifying that the services are running and listening on the correct sockets. Administrators may use tools like `netstat` or `ss` to list active UNIX socket connections. A command example is as follows:

```
ss -x | grep dovecot-auth
```

This command helps confirm that the `dovecot-auth` socket is correctly bound and accessible to Postfix during authentication steps. In practice, attention to file permissions, service restarts, and verification of configuration consistency between the two services mitigates potential integration issues.

Performance optimization plays a key role in ensuring that the communication between Postfix and Dovecot is both efficient and secure. Utilizing UNIX domain sockets for authentication helps reduce latency compared to network-based communications. Furthermore, consolidating configuration parameters in centralized files minimizes the risk of configuration drift, which could otherwise lead to intermittent failures. Administrators are advised to implement routine audits of their authentication and mailbox management settings to ensure continuous service reliability.

Security remains at the forefront of the integration process. By confining authentication communication to local UNIX sockets and enforcing strict file access policies, potential attack vectors are significantly reduced. Moreover, combining TLS for SMTP authentication, along with encrypted IMAP/POP3 sessions, guarantees that email content and user credentials are securely transmitted across the network. Regular updates to both Postfix and Dovecot, adherence to security advisories, and systematic reviews of access logs contribute to maintaining a hardened email environment.

The synchronization of user credential management between Postfix and Dovecot also allows for advanced features such as virtual hosting and scalable multi-domain support. These capabilities enable administrators to manage a large number of users with varied authentication sources while maintaining a consistent security policy. Coordination between the two services sets the stage for implementing additional anti-spam measures and virus scanning plugins, which integrate seamlessly once basic authentication and mailbox access are securely established.

Establishing the integration between Postfix and Dovecot requires meticulous configuration changes in both services, thorough testing of authentication flows, and diligent monitoring of log files. The detailed example configurations provided illustrate the minimal steps required to achieve a reliable and secure connection. This careful orchestration supports the comprehensive management of email services in environments with high user concurrency and varied security requirements.

The technical process described adheres to best practices for both Postfix and Dovecot, ensuring that the integration is robust, secure, and easily manageable. Properly linking these services enhances performance, streamlines troubleshooting, and provides a scalable foundation for future extensions as additional email security and management features become necessary.

9.2. Integrating with SpamAssassin

SpamAssassin is widely recognized as an effective tool for filtering unwanted emails and detecting spam, and its integration with Postfix enhances the email infrastructure by offering robust spam detection before messages reach the user's mailbox. This integration allows Postfix to delegate spam filtering tasks to SpamAssassin, ensuring that message processing conforms to defined spam policies and reducing the risk of delivering malicious or unwanted content. The process involves configuring Postfix to send emails to SpamAssassin for evaluation and then processing the results to modify email headers, quarantine messages, or alter delivery routes based on the computed spam score.

The first step in this integration is understanding the two primary components of SpamAssassin: spamd, the daemon responsible for continuously scanning emails, and spamc, the client application traditionally

277

used by Postfix or other mail transfer agents (MTAs) to forward emails to spamd. Deploying SpamAssassin as a daemon allows the system to handle multiple incoming requests efficiently, while spamc acts as a lightweight intermediary that forwards each email to spamd for analysis. This arrangement minimizes processing overhead and ensures that spam detection does not become a bottleneck in mail flow.

Postfix requires configuration changes to route messages through SpamAssassin. One commonly used method is to define a content filter that invokes a wrapper or a dedicated script. The wrapper receives the email from Postfix, passes it through spamc, and then returns the filtered message for further processing. The integration involves adding a filter definition in the Postfix configuration file, typically main.cf, with the content filter directive set to the script or program that handles the SpamAssassin check. An example configuration snippet might be:

```
# Postfix main.cf snippet for SpamAssassin integration
content_filter = spamassassin-filter:dummy
```

This directive instructs Postfix to pass all emails to the spamassassin-filter service. Next, the master.cf file must be updated to define the corresponding service. A sample configuration entry in master.cf is as follows:

```
# Postfix master.cf entry for SpamAssassin content filter
spamassassin-filter unix - n n - - pipe
  flags=Rq user=spamd argv=/usr/bin/spamc -f -e
  /usr/sbin/sendmail -oi -f ${sender} ${recipient}
```

In this configuration, Postfix uses the pipe delivery agent to execute spamc. The command-line options include -f for preserving the sender's address and -e for ensuring proper error handling. This setup guarantees that each incoming email is scanned by SpamAssassin before it is handed over for final delivery. The filtered output may include an updated header indicating the spam score, which downstream email

278

clients or filtering rules can parse to decide the appropriate handling for each message.

Adjusting spamc parameters enables administrators to fine-tune the spam detection process. For instance, parameters such as the timeout, report options, and required score thresholds can be incorporated into the wrapper script or defined directly as command-line arguments. Customization may involve modifying the SpamAssassin configuration file, typically located at /etc/mail/spamassassin/local.cf. A representative excerpt from this file is:

```
# SpamAssassin local configuration example
required_score 5.0
report_safe 0
rewrite_header Subject [SPAM]
```

Here, required_score sets the threshold for classifying messages as spam, report_safe determines whether the original message is attached to a warning report, and rewrite_header defines which header is modified if the message is flagged. These parameters directly influence how SpamAssassin evaluates messages, and fine-tuning them to match the specific characteristics of the incoming mail stream is essential for maintaining both performance and accuracy.

In addition to basic configuration parameters, SpamAssassin provides an extensive set of rules and plugins that can be enabled or disabled based on the operational environment. Some organizations may choose to integrate Bayesian filtering, network-based checks, or custom rule sets to further refine spam detection. These rules are dynamically updated based on user feedback and reported spam characteristics. Administrators should ensure that automated rule updates are scheduled periodically to sustain an effective spam filtering posture.

While the command-line integration via spamc is common, Postfix can also leverage Milter interfaces to integrate with SpamAssassin. Using a Milter-aware setup allows Postfix to communicate more directly with

SpamAssassin, processing MIME messages and header modifications in real time. This approach provides additional flexibility in handling multipart emails and embedded content. The choice between a simple content filter and a Milter integration typically depends on the scale of the deployment and the desired level of control over message processing.

For testing and validation, it is crucial to simulate mail flow through the SpamAssassin-integrated Postfix server. Administrators should verify that the filtered emails include the appropriate header modifications and that the overall latency remains within acceptable limits. A common practice involves sending test messages containing known spam signatures to observe the behavior of SpamAssassin and ensure that the spam score exceeds the defined threshold. An example command used for testing might be:

```
echo "Test email body with spam trigger" | /usr/bin/spamc -c
```

In this test, the -c flag causes spamc to output only the computed spam score. Consistently high scores indicate that SpamAssassin rules are active and functioning as intended, whereas low scores suggest that further calibration of the rules or thresholds may be necessary.

Logging and monitoring are additional critical components of the integration process. Both Postfix and SpamAssassin produce logs that can be aggregated and analyzed to track the performance of the spam filtering system. Postfix's logging facilities, combined with SpamAssassin's scoring log entries, allow administrators to monitor trends in spam detection and adjust configurations to accommodate changes in spam tactics. Depending on system policies, these logs may be directed to centralized logging services or analyzed using tools such as logwatch or fail2ban to detect suspicious activity.

Optimizing system performance is a vital consideration when integrating SpamAssassin. The additional processing required for spam filtering can impose a load on system resources, so it is necessary to implement resource controls. This might involve limiting the number of concurrent spamc processes or scheduling processing during lower traffic periods. Effective management of system resources ensures that the spam filter does not become a point of failure during peak email traffic periods.

Security is an important factor when integrating third-party tools. Ensuring that SpamAssassin runs with minimal privileges and that its configuration files are secured against unauthorized edits prevents potential exploitation by malicious users. Running SpamAssassin in a chroot or containerized environment can further isolate the spam filter from other system components. Proper file permissions, along with regularly scheduled updates, help maintain the integrity of the spam filtering environment.

The detailed configuration involves modifications to multiple components of the mail system. In Postfix's main.cf and master.cf, administrators must declare the content filter and designate an execution context for spamc and spamd. In contrast, SpamAssassin's own configuration requires careful tuning of scoring thresholds, rule sets, and runtime parameters. Handling these configurations with attention to detail, while cross-referencing both Postfix and SpamAssassin documentation, results in an integrated environment where spam is reliably detected and managed without compromising mail delivery performance.

Implementing a SpamAssassin integration also provides an opportunity for further enhancements such as user-based feedback mechanisms. Some systems allow users to mark messages as spam or not spam, which can be fed back into SpamAssassin's Bayesian learning algorithms. This dynamic adaptation increases the accuracy of spam filtering over time and tailors the mail system to the particular characteristics of its user base.

The refined integration of SpamAssassin with Postfix not only improves the effectiveness of spam detection but also contributes to overall system reliability. With proper configuration, the additional processing stage introduced by spam filtering operates transparently from the user's perspective, ensuring that legitimate emails are delivered promptly while unwanted messaging is isolated or altered according to policy. The methodology described here is applicable to both small-scale deployments and large, enterprise-level systems, where maintaining robust mail defense mechanisms is paramount.

By carefully adjusting the configuration files, properly routing messages through a dedicated filter, and tuning SpamAssassin's analysis parameters, administrators can create an email environment that is resilient against spam. This configuration strategy provides a balance between security, performance, and manageability, allowing the email server to operate efficiently in volatile threat landscapes.

9.3. Configuring ClamAV for Virus Scanning

Integrating ClamAV with Postfix enhances the security of email communications by providing real-time scanning for viruses in both incoming and outgoing messages. This integration involves setting up ClamAV as a virus scanning engine that reviews messages as they traverse the mail system, thereby reducing the propagation of malware and protecting end users. The configuration requires careful coordination between Postfix and ClamAV, typically via a content filter mechanism that leverages ClamAV's command-line utilities or daemon services.

The core component of ClamAV is `clamd`, the daemon responsible for continuous scanning, and its associated command-line interface `clamdscan`. Running ClamAV as a daemon provides significant performance benefits by maintaining a loaded virus database in memory, which reduces the overhead associated with repeated scans. In the integrated environment, Postfix forwards messages to a content filter that invokes clamdscan, scans the email, and then returns the message, possibly modified or tagged if a virus is detected, for further delivery decisions.

To establish this integration, administrators must modify the Postfix configuration to include a content filtering service dedicated to virus scanning. In main.cf, the directive content_filter directs all messages to the ClamAV filter service. An example is as follows:

```
# Postfix main.cf snippet for ClamAV integration
content_filter = clamav-filter:dummy
```

Subsequently, the Postfix master.cf file must be updated to define the details of the clamav-filter service. This service is typically implemented by the Postfix pipe delivery mechanism. A representative configuration is shown below:

```
# Postfix master.cf entry for ClamAV content filter
clamav-filter unix - n n - - pipe
  flags=Rq user=clamav argv=/usr/bin/clamdscan --stdout --no-summary
  | /usr/sbin/sendmail -oi -f ${sender} ${recipient}
```

In this snippet, the pipe command hands the email over to clamdscan for analysis. The --stdout option returns the modified message body and headers, while --no-summary suppresses extraneous output. The output of the scan is then piped to sendmail for final delivery. The use of the clamav user and group ensures that the scanning process runs with minimal privileges, contributing to a secure mail processing chain.

ClamAV requires an up-to-date virus database to function effectively. Administrators must set up a routine update mechanism, often through the freshclam utility. The configuration file for freshclam, normally located at /etc/clamav/freshclam.conf, specifies update intervals, database mirrors, and other relevant parameters. A typical configuration snippet might include:

```
# /etc/clamav/freshclam.conf example
DatabaseDirectory /var/lib/clamav
UpdateLogFile /var/log/clamav/freshclam.log
Checks 24
DatabaseMirror database.clamav.net
```

Regular updates are vital to ensure that the scanning engine recognizes the latest virus signatures and emerging malware threats. Scheduling freshclam via a cron job or systemd timer ensures that the updates occur without manual intervention.

An additional consideration in a production environment is handling cases where a virus is detected in an email. The content filter script can be designed to modify email headers, quarantine the message, or even reject it outright. A common approach involves appending a header that indicates the presence of a virus, allowing downstream filtering or mailbox rules to handle such messages appropriately. For example, a simple wrapper script may read the output from clamdscan, check for virus detections, and alter the header accordingly before reinjecting the email into Postfix. The following pseudo-code illustrates this behavior:

```bash
#!/bin/bash
# clamav_filter.sh - Wrapper script for ClamAV scanning

# Read the email from stdin and save to a temporary file
tmpfile=$(mktemp /tmp/email.XXXXXX)
cat > "$tmpfile"

# Run clamdscan on the temporary file
scan_output=$(clamdscan --stdout --no-summary "$tmpfile")

# Check if the scan output indicates a virus detection
if echo "$scan_output" | grep -q "FOUND"; then
  # Prepend a header to mark the email as infected
  sed -i '1iX-Virus-Status: Infected' "$tmpfile"
fi

# Pass the modified email to sendmail for normal processing
/usr/sbin/sendmail -oi -f "$SENDER" "$RECIPIENT" < "$tmpfile"
rm -f "$tmpfile"
```

This script captures the email content, processes it with `clamdscan`, and conditionally tags the message. Administrators should adapt the script further to decide whether to quarantine, drop, or forward infected messages based on the policy applicable to the mail system.

Testing the integration is an essential step before deploying to a production environment. Administrators should simulate email traffic using test messages that contain benign virus signatures (such as the EICAR test file) to verify that ClamAV correctly identifies the threat and that Postfix routes the message through the designated content filter. A command-line test might be executed as follows:

```
cat /path/to/test-email.eml | /usr/bin/clamdscan --stdout --no-
    summary
```

The output from this command should clearly indicate whether a virus was detected. If a virus is present, the script or content filter must reflect this detection either via additional header information or by taking the appropriate administrative action as determined by the mail policy.

Resource management and performance monitoring are important aspects of integrating ClamAV with a high-traffic mail server. Virus scanning introduces additional CPU and I/O loads; hence, the integration should include measures to limit resource consumption. Administrators might consider setting limits on the number of concurrent scanning processes or optimizing ClamAV's configuration parameters to prioritize speed without sacrificing detection accuracy. Reviewing system performance metrics and adjusting scanning thresholds are recommended practices to ensure a balance between security and efficiency.

Logging is another critical element when configuring ClamAV for virus scanning. Both Postfix and ClamAV generate logs that can be aggregated to provide comprehensive insight into mail flow and scanning outcomes. In Postfix, detailed logs related to content filtering can be enabled, while ClamAV maintains its own logs in directories such as `/var/log/clamav/clamd.log`. Reviewing these logs regularly helps identify patterns of virus infection attempts and supports rapid troubleshooting in the event of scan failures.

Security hardening is also paramount. Running ClamAV in a dedicated environment, such as a chroot jail or container, minimizes the risk that an exploited vulnerability in the virus scanner could affect the broader system. File permissions and user accounts need to be carefully managed; for example, the ClamAV process should run under a restricted account that does not have unnecessary privileges. Such steps contribute significantly to reducing the attack surface of the mail server.

As virus scanning becomes a critical component in email security, the integration of ClamAV with Postfix is best approached as part of a layered defense strategy. In addition to scanning for viruses, administrators may integrate further systems such as SpamAssassin for spam filtering and use Dovecot for secure authentication. Together, these components provide a comprehensive filtering mechanism that addresses various aspects of email threat detection. The configuration techniques detailed in this section aim to provide a robust framework wherein ClamAV operates efficiently alongside Postfix, without unduly impacting mail delivery performance.

Continuous improvement and regular updates are necessary as threats evolve. Administrators should plan for periodic reviews of the ClamAV configuration, including adjustments to scanning thresholds, updates to virus databases, and enhancements to the content filtering script. Integrating automated monitoring tools that alert on anomalies in virus detection rates or resource usage further strengthens the overall security posture.

The coordinated configuration of ClamAV and Postfix, as outlined here, forms an integral part of a secure email infrastructure. By thoroughly testing and tuning the integration, administrators can ensure that both inbound and outbound emails are subjected to rigorous virus scanning, thereby protecting users from potentially harmful content while maintaining efficient mail flow. Run failed with status: failed

9.4. Working with LDAP Directories

Integrating LDAP directory services with Postfix streamlines user authentication and mailbox management by enabling centralized administration of user data and mail routing policies. LDAP, as a robust, scalable directory service, provides a structured environment to store user credentials, email addresses, and related metadata. By coupling Postfix with LDAP, administrators can consolidate configurations across multiple services, simplify user management, and dynamically manage mail flows based on LDAP queries.

Postfix interacts with LDAP through various lookup tables that translate LDAP query results into actionable configuration data. These tables include, but are not limited to, virtual alias maps, relay restrictions, and transport maps. In a typical deployment, LDAP acts as the primary source of information for virtual domains, enforcing policies that manage how incoming mail is delivered to local or remote mailboxes. The integration requires configuration adjustments in Postfix's main configuration file (main.cf) as well as a dedicated LDAP configuration file that contains connection details and query parameters.

The LDAP configuration file for Postfix is commonly stored as /etc/postfix/ldap-virtual_aliases.cf (or with a similar naming convention). This file contains parameters that define how Postfix connects to the LDAP server. A representative configuration file may include directives as shown in the following example:

```
server_host = ldap.example.com
port = 389
```

```
search_base = ou=People,dc=example,dc=com
query_filter = (&(objectClass=mailUser)(mail=%s))
result_attribute = maildrop
bind = no
```

In this configuration, server_host specifies the LDAP server address, while port indicates the standard LDAP port. The search_base parameter defines the point in the LDAP directory tree from which searches begin. The query_filter is a critical component that determines which LDAP entries match the recipient address. The substitution symbol %s represents the input query—typically an email address—while result_attribute indicates the attribute to be retrieved, such as the maildrop path or the canonical email address corresponding to a mailbox.

Within Postfix's main.cf, administrators establish the use of LDAP by referencing the LDAP configuration file in specific lookup tables. For example, to enable virtual alias mapping based on LDAP, the following directive is added:

```
virtual_alias_maps = ldap:/etc/postfix/ldap-virtual_aliases.cf
```

This directive instructs Postfix to utilize LDAP for resolving recipient addresses during the mail delivery process. Similar directives can be implemented for other lookup functionalities, such as sender canonical mapping or relay restrictions, by creating corresponding LDAP configuration files and referencing them appropriately.

Beyond alias mapping, LDAP integration provides an environment in which mailbox management can be streamlined. For instance, when consolidating multiple domains on a single server, LDAP serves as the central repository for virtual mailbox definitions. A dedicated configuration file for virtual mailbox domains might resemble the following:

```
server_host = ldap.example.com
port = 389
search_base = ou=Domains,dc=example,dc=com
query_filter = (mailDomain=%s)
```

```
result_attribute = mailHost
bind = no
```

Here, the `query_filter` matches entries based on the domain part of the email address. The `result_attribute` `mailHost` directs where the mail should be delivered, ensuring that domain-specific routing follows pre-defined policies. This method consolidates domain management, allowing administrators to update routing rules in a single location.

The performance and stability of LDAP lookups are pivotal in guaranteeing that mail delivery is not adversely impacted by directory service latency or failures. To mitigate potential performance issues, Postfix supports caching mechanisms via load balancing and replication of the LDAP directory. Configuring LDAP replication across multiple servers not only increases availability but also distributes query loads across several hosts, reducing the response time for lookups. Moreover, incorporating retry intervals and timeout parameters in the LDAP configuration file can further enhance system resilience. For example, adding the following parameters can aid in handling connection issues:

```
bind_timeout = 10
timeout = 30
```

These parameters specify the maximum time allowed for binding to the LDAP server and for individual queries, respectively. Carefully setting these values helps ensure the system continues processing mail efficiently even during network disruptions.

Security is a prominent consideration when integrating LDAP with Postfix, particularly because directory services often contain sensitive user credentials and configurations. Secure communication between Postfix and the LDAP server can be enforced by utilizing LDAP over SSL/TLS. Adjusting the configuration to use `ldaps://` on the appropriate secure port (typically 636) is one measure. An example secure

289

configuration snippet could be:

```
server_host = ldaps://ldap.example.com
port = 636
start_tls = yes
tls_require_cert = demand
```

These settings ensure that data exchanges are encrypted, protecting against interception and tampering. In addition, the LDAP server should maintain strict access controls, allowing only authorized accounts or services to perform lookups.

Troubleshooting LDAP integration with Postfix involves examining logs from both services. Postfix logs detailed information about LDAP lookup failures, timeouts, or misconfigurations. Administrators can adjust Postfix logging verbosity by modifying the relevant logging parameters. Simultaneously, the LDAP server's own logs offer insight into authentication attempts and query processing. Analyzing these logs in tandem can pinpoint incorrect query filters, misconfigured search bases, or network-related issues. For example, a misalignment between the defined search_base and the actual directory structure frequently results in no matches being returned, causing mail delivery to fail.

To further enhance diagnostics, administrators may use command-line LDAP tools such as ldapsearch to manually test queries. A sample command for testing a virtual alias lookup might be:

```
ldapsearch -x -H ldap://ldap.example.com -b "ou=People,dc=example,dc=
    com" \
  "(&(objectClass=mailUser)(mail=user@example.com))" maildrop
```

This command directly queries the LDAP directory for an entry corresponding to a specific email address and returns the maildrop attribute. Such tests help verify that the LDAP server is operating as expected and that the query filters in the Postfix configuration correctly match the directory entries.

Integrating LDAP also supports dynamic management of user attributes. LDAP directories can be updated centrally to add, remove, or modify user information which, in turn, dynamically affects how Postfix processes mail. For example, changing a user's mailbox location in LDAP automatically directs Postfix to a new mail host without the need for manual modifications in multiple configuration files. This capability is particularly useful in large organizations where user information may change frequently.

It is also common to integrate LDAP with other components such as Dovecot for authentication purposes. When Dovecot connects to the same LDAP directory, a unified user repository is maintained, facilitating consistent policy enforcement across authentication and mail delivery. Coordinated LDAP queries between Postfix and Dovecot ensure that user credentials and mailbox attributes remain synchronized. In such scenarios, LDAP serves as the single source of truth, reducing administrative overhead and minimizing potential discrepancies.

As organizations scale, LDAP integration provides the flexibility to implement advanced mail routing policies. For example, LDAP attributes can be used to tag users with specific organizational roles or departments. Postfix can use these attributes in its filtering rules to direct mail flows, implement relay restrictions, or control access based on group membership. This level of granularity allows administrators to fine-tune mail policies according to dynamic business requirements without overhauling the entire email system.

The process of integrating LDAP with Postfix is iterative and benefits from continuous evaluation and tuning. Administrators should periodically review the LDAP query performance and adjust query filters to reflect changes in the organizational directory structure. Regular updates of the Postfix LDAP configuration ensure that the system adapts to evolving security policies and user provisioning practices. In many cases, scripting and automation tools are deployed to synchronize LDAP entries with Postfix's configuration, thereby further reducing manual intervention and the likelihood of errors.

Overall, the integration between Postfix and LDAP directories is a critical strategy to achieve centralized management of user authentication and mailbox functions. By leveraging LDAP, email systems can realize enhanced scalability, improved security, and dynamic adaptability. The detailed configuration examples provided above serve as a foundation upon which administrators can build a robust email infrastructure that meets modern organizational demands. Effective collaboration between Postfix and LDAP not only simplifies administration but also provides a flexible environment that can evolve as new requirements or technologies emerge.

9.5. Collaborating with Groupware Solutions

Integrating Postfix with groupware solutions extends the capabilities of an email server beyond simple message delivery to encompass collaborative features such as shared calendars, address books, and task management. Groupware solutions, which may include systems like SOGo, Zimbra, or Kolab, provide unified environments where email, calendaring, and contact management coexist. This integration requires careful configuration at the MTA level, ensuring that Postfix can cooperate with back-end applications to facilitate the smooth flow of collaboration data.

At the core of this integration is the need to appropriately route and manage emails related to group collaboration. Postfix normally handles SMTP transactions, delivering mail to local user mailboxes or forwarding messages to other servers. In the context of groupware, Postfix not only processes traditional emails, but also supports invites, meeting requests, and notifications generated by calendar and contact applications. In effect, Postfix functions as the mail submission agent that transmits messages to groupware components which further process collaboration data according to pre-defined policies.

A typical deployment involves configuring Postfix to relay certain domains or addresses to the groupware system. Separate virtual domains may be designated for group collaboration, and the mail routing policies can be adapted to send groupware-specific emails to dedicated backend processes. For instance, if a groupware solution manages calendar invitations for a domain collab.example.com, Postfix must parse the recipient addresses and forward the corresponding messages to the application server that handles calendar events. This is achieved by defining transport maps in Postfix. A sample configuration snippet for a transport map might look as follows:

```
collab.example.com    smtp:[127.0.0.1]:2525
```

In this example, emails intended for the groupware domain are directed to a local service listening on a non-standard SMTP port. By offloading these messages, Postfix enables the groupware solution to handle event invitations, calendar updates, or address book synchronization independently of the core mail delivery process.

Collaboration between Postfix and groupware systems also relies on the proper modification of email headers. Groupware applications often require additional metadata in email headers to process meeting requests or to classify message types accurately. Custom header rewriting can be implemented in Postfix by using header checks and content filter mechanisms. The addition of specific headers, such as X-Calendar-Event: true or X-Groupware-Notification: yes, can signal to the groupware backend that a particular email contains collaborative content. An illustrative example using Postfix header checks is shown below:

```
# /etc/postfix/header_checks
/^Subject: .*Meeting/     PREPEND X-Groupware-Event: true
/^From: .*calendar/       PREPEND X-Groupware-Notification: yes
```

This configuration ensures that emails with subjects indicating meeting information or those sent from a calendar service are automatically marked, allowing the subsequent groupware processing to parse and extract necessary event details.

Groupware solutions generally interact with back-end databases and directory services (such as LDAP) for managing shared resources like calendars and contact lists. In many deployments, the same LDAP directory that supplies user credentials for Postfix and Dovecot is used by groupware applications. This unified approach harmonizes user information across the email and collaborative platforms. Through LDAP integration, groupware applications can dynamically populate calendars, assign resource booking rights, and manage contact lists without the need for periodic data synchronization. The benefit of such an integration is twofold: it not only eliminates redundancy in user data management but also streamlines administrative tasks by centralizing control points.

Another critical aspect of collaborating with groupware solutions is the implementation of security measures that protect both mail delivery and collaborative data. Postfix continues to enforce TLS encryption for SMTP sessions, while groupware applications must ensure that API communications and directory queries are secured as well. When configuring Postfix, it is advisable to maintain strict policies regarding access control and authentication, especially when dealing with shared resources. Advanced configurations may include the use of client certificates or other mechanisms to verify service-to-service communication. Secure interactions between Postfix and groupware systems guard against unauthorized access and help maintain data integrity throughout the collaborative environment.

Along with header manipulation and routing, the integration may require advanced scripting to handle specialized tasks. For example, when a user accepts a calendar invitation that requires a resource reservation, the groupware system might need to trigger auxiliary processes that update booking records. In such a case, Postfix can invoke a custom content filter or a pipe service that calls a script to transform and reformat the message before reinjecting it into the delivery pipeline. An example of a simple processing script written in Bash is provided below:

```
#!/bin/bash
# groupware_process.sh - Process groupware-related emails

# Save the email from stdin into a temporary file
tempfile=$(mktemp /tmp/email.XXXXXX)
cat > "$tempfile"

# Check for the presence of a calendar invitation header
if grep -q "X-Calendar-Invite: yes" "$tempfile"; then
  # Append tag to indicate processing by groupware system
  sed -i '1iX-Processed-By: GroupwareSystem' "$tempfile"
fi

# Forward the email to the final destination via sendmail
/usr/sbin/sendmail -oi -f "$SENDER" "$RECIPIENT" < "$tempfile"
rm -f "$tempfile"
```

This script demonstrates how preprocessing can enhance compatibility with groupware applications by dynamically adjusting message content. Such scripts can be integrated into Postfix using pipe transport services defined in the master.cf configuration file.

Collaboration enhancements are not limited to mail processing alone. Groupware systems can also leverage Postfix logs and mail tracking features for administrative reporting and auditing. Detailed logs of groupware-related messages can help administrators identify trends in the use of collaborative features, measure system performance, and detect potential abuse scenarios. Enhancing Postfix logging for these purposes requires adjustments to the logging configuration to capture additional header information or custom debug details related to groupware processing.

The flexibility of Postfix allows for the seamless integration of groupware solutions even in heterogeneous environments. Some organizations choose to deploy groupware systems that run on separate infrastructure, connected to Postfix via standard SMTP channels or through specialized API gateways. In such cases, Postfix operates as a robust front end that routes messages based on rules derived from domain names, recipient addresses, or header information. The modular nature of Postfix and its support for content filters, transport maps, and header checks means that a wide array of groupware solutions, ranging from open-source projects to enterprise-grade systems, can be integrated with minimal disruption.

Administrative management of these integrations often involves periodic tuning and updates. As user collaboration needs evolve, administrators may need to update routing tables, refine header rewrite rules, or adjust content filter parameters to accommodate new groupware features. Automated tools and configuration management systems can assist in synchronizing changes between Postfix and groupware systems, minimizing downtime and ensuring consistency across the email and collaboration platforms.

Real-world deployments have demonstrated the benefits of a tightly integrated groupware environment. Organizations that leverage this integration often report increased productivity through streamlined access to shared calendars and centralized address books. Improved scheduling accuracy, automatic conflict detection, and smoother collaboration on meeting resources exemplify the operational efficiencies achieved through such integrations. Moreover, by centralizing management and leveraging the robust delivery capabilities of Postfix, groupware systems can scale effectively even as the organizational user base grows.

Integrating Postfix with groupware solutions presents a solid foundation for building a comprehensive collaborative ecosystem. With well-designed routing policies, dynamic header manipulation, and secure communications, administrators can create a cohesive environment that links traditional email services with advanced collaborative tools. The configuration examples and operational insights provided in this section illustrate practical methods to achieve integration while addressing performance, security, and scalability challenges. As feature sets and user requirements expand, the collaborative framework established through Postfix integration continues to offer flexibility, enabling future enhancements and supporting the dynamic nature of modern communication infrastructures.

Chapter 10

Performance Optimization

This chapter provides strategies for optimizing Postfix performance, focusing on tuning configuration parameters and enhancing mail queue management. It discusses improving DNS resolution times and increasing throughput through parallelism. Additionally, it addresses resource management for scalability and identifies methods to diagnose and alleviate load bottlenecks. These optimizations ensure efficient, high-performing email server operations, supporting the demands of increased traffic and diverse workloads.

10.1. Tuning Postfix Configuration Parameters

Postfix offers a broad range of configuration parameters that impact both its performance and responsiveness. Adjusting these parameters can lead to improvements in throughput and reduced latency when processing mail. Administrators must carefully evaluate workload characteristics and the underlying operating system resources before fine-tuning performance settings.

One of the primary means of tuning Postfix is by leveraging the `postconf` command, which displays current configuration settings. The command below allows administrators to view only explicitly defined parameters, which helps in understanding the deviations from the default configuration:

```
postconf -n
```

A common performance tuning strategy is to adjust concurrency settings. The parameters `default_process_limit` and `default_destination_concurrency_limit` control the number of processes spawned to handle incoming SMTP connections and outgoing deliveries, respectively. Increasing `default_process_limit` can improve the server's capability to handle bursts of connection requests, while raising `default_destination_concurrency_limit` allows simultaneous delivery attempts for multiple queued messages. It is essential to ensure these values are set in accordance with the server's CPU and memory limits.

Parameters addressing the timeout behaviors of Postfix also play a crucial role in performance. For example, settings like `smtp_connect_timeout` and `smtp_data_timeout` determine how long Postfix will wait for a remote server to respond during connection establishment and data transmission. By reducing these timeout values, administrators can free up resources more quickly under high load conditions, while still maintaining a balance to avoid premature termination of legitimate connections. The following configuration snippet demonstrates setting shorter timeouts:

```
smtp_connect_timeout = 30s
smtp_data_timeout = 120s
```

DNS resolution is another area that can benefit from tuning. While network infrastructure and caching DNS servers can help, parameters within Postfix, such as smtp_host_lookup, dictate the mechanism used to resolve hostnames. When performance is critical, configuring Postfix to prefer IPv4 or IPv6 resolutions based on network characteristics can lead to improved responsiveness. Specifying the host lookup method ensures that the mail server does not become unnecessarily delayed by slow or erratic DNS responses.

Caching mechanisms play an important part in optimizing performance. Postfix uses its own internal caches for lookups and access controls. It is beneficial to monitor the cache hit ratios during periods of high throughput to determine if the cache sizes need adjusting. Though these settings are not exposed directly as parameter tweaks in Postfix's configuration, tuning the underlying operating system's file caching strategies and ensuring that Postfix's spool directories reside on optimized storage can yield performance improvements.

The behavior of the mail queue is directly influenced by configuration parameters related to queue management. Parameters such as maximal_queue_lifetime and minimal_backoff_time govern how long messages stay in the queue before being discarded and the intervals between delivery attempts. Fine-tuning these values based on the expected volume and priority of messages can ensure that the mail queue remains responsive. For instance, reducing the backoff time might be beneficial for high-priority communications, while a longer maximal queue lifetime may be appropriate on servers with lower expected load.

Tuning the SMTP client and server aspects in Postfix often requires adjustments to TLS-related parameters. The use of encrypted connections can add additional processing overhead. Parameters like smtpd_tls_session_cache_timeout and smtp_tls_session_cache_timeout control the lifetime of cached

TLS sessions which, when optimized, permit the re-use of session parameters for subsequent connections. This reduces the handshake overhead and thus improves overall performance. A sample configuration may appear as follows:

```
smtpd_tls_session_cache_database = btree:${data_directory}/
    smtpd_scache
smtp_tls_session_cache_database = btree:${data_directory}/smtp_scache
smtpd_tls_session_cache_timeout = 3600s
smtp_tls_session_cache_timeout = 3600s
```

Another parameter of importance is `message_size_limit`, which sets a cap on the size of messages processed by Postfix. By enforcing a strict maximum message size, the system avoids excessive consumption of disk and memory resources during peak times. This parameter should be set after careful consideration of the requirements of the user base and the memory limits of the server hardware.

Logging and debugging settings, though primarily used for administrative oversight and troubleshooting, can also affect performance during high-load scenarios. Elevated logging levels may significantly increase disk I/O overhead. Therefore, it is advisable to set logging parameters to a minimal level during normal operations. Adjusting the parameter `debug_peer_list` allows focused logging from specific sources without incurring the overhead of generating excessive logs from all connections.

The tuning of Postfix configuration parameters also extends to its interaction with external filters and content scanners. When such integrations are present, parameters that control how Postfix communicates with these external services, such as `content_filter`, become crucial performance levers. It is beneficial to ensure that the external filters are as efficient as possible and that the communication is optimized. Techniques such as asynchronous processing or batching can reduce the latency incurred in passing messages between Postfix and these filters.

Examining server performance using tools like pflogsumm can provide insights into the impact of configuration changes. Running a log summary over the recent period of operation can help determine whether the tuning adjustments have reduced queue times and improved delivery speeds. For example, after modifying parameters, the following command can be executed:

```
pflogsumm /var/log/maillog | less
```

The output generated provides detailed metrics on message throughput, bounce statistics, and overall server responsiveness. Analyzing these metrics helps in iteratively refining the configuration. Verbatim copies of typical outputs may appear as:

```
Total requests:        10500
Successful deliveries:  9800
Deferred messages:       500
Bounce messages:         200
```

A critical aspect of tuning is understanding the trade-offs between aggressive performance optimization and system stability. Increasing parallelism or reducing timeouts may enhance performance under ideal conditions but could lead to failures if network conditions are poor or if remote servers are slow to respond. Administrators must therefore conduct thorough testing in controlled environments before applying changes to production systems.

Utilizing version control for configuration files is a best practice in system administration. By tracking changes to the main.cf file, it is possible to revert to previous configurations if tuning efforts do not produce the desired effect. The following command sequence is useful for version-controlling configuration modifications:

```
cd /etc/postfix
git init
git add main.cf
git commit -m "Initial commit of baseline configuration for
    performance tuning"
```

By leveraging version control, each change in configuration can be documented, and performance issues can be traced back to specific modifications. This systematic approach is essential when the environment is subject to frequent changes and continuous optimization efforts.

Another parameter of note is `queue_run_delay`, which dictates the interval at which the Postfix queue manager checks for deferred messages. By carefully tuning this delay based on average mail volumes, the responsiveness of the mail delivery system can be improved without unnecessarily spending CPU cycles on constant polling. Similarly, the parameter `bounce_queue_lifetime` can be adjusted to control the lifespan of bounce messages, ensuring that they do not occupy queue space longer than necessary.

Postfix also relies on system resources such as file descriptors and process limits. The operating system's settings should be aligned with the mail server's configuration. For instance, modifying the user limits in `/etc/security/limits.conf` may be required to ensure that Postfix has sufficient file descriptors available during high-load conditions. A sample configuration might include:

```
postfix soft nofile 4096
postfix hard nofile 8192
```

Tuning these parameters in the operating system avoids situations where Postfix connections are unexpectedly dropped because the system's inherent limits are reached.

Incorporating these adjustments into a coherent tuning strategy necessitates periodic performance evaluations. For example, benchmarking tools and stress tests can simulate peak loads and measure the server's response time and throughput. These benchmarks serve as quantitative evidence for further tuning, allowing the administrator to decide whether additional increases in concurrency limits or timeout adjustments are warranted. Maintaining logs of performance metrics, configuration changes, and the corresponding effect on system behavior ensures that improvements are maintained over time and that any declines in performance can be quickly diagnosed.

The process of tuning Postfix configuration parameters is iterative and dependent on both internal and external factors. As mail traffic volumes increase, servers may eventually require further adjustments such as scaling horizontally or employing more sophisticated load balancing techniques. The parameters discussed here provide a foundation for ensuring that Postfix remains responsive and efficient under growing demand. Observations from log analysis and performance monitoring tools should guide ongoing modifications.

Adjusting Postfix configuration parameters for performance and responsiveness is not a one-time task but an ongoing discipline. The interplay between resource management, network reliability, and application performance requires regular assessments and refinements. The techniques and examples provided serve as a blueprint for administrators aiming to balance system stability with high performance.

10.2. Optimizing Mail Queue Management

Efficient management of mail queues is a cornerstone of maintaining fast processing times and responsiveness in Postfix systems. The mail queue is a temporary storage area where messages await delivery or further processing. The performance of a mail server can be significantly influenced by how well its queue is managed, especially under high traffic loads. Administrators must monitor, adjust, and optimize queue parameters to ensure messages are processed promptly while minimizing resource contention.

Postfix employs several key parameters to handle queued messages. Adjustments to values such as `minimal_backoff_time`, `maximal_queue_lifetime`, and `queue_run_delay` affect the frequency and manner in which message delivery is retried. The parameter `minimal_backoff_time` sets the lower bound on wait time between delivery attempts, ensuring that aggressive retry policies do not overload the system with repeated processing of transient errors. Conversely, `maximal_queue_lifetime` dictates the maximum duration a message can reside in the queue before being bounced back to the sender. Setting these parameters appropriately is a balancing act; shorter backoff times may yield faster resolution during transient errors, but if set too short, they might lead to an excessive number of retry attempts that can strain system resources.

Fine-tuning the `queue_run_delay` parameter allows the queue manager to check for deferred messages at optimized intervals. A reduced delay can lead to quicker processing of pending items at the cost of increased CPU cycles. For high-throughput systems, these parameter adjustments should consider both the workload and the available hardware capabilities. A sample configuration stored in the `main.cf` file might be:

```
minimal_backoff_time = 300s
maximal_backoff_time = 1800s
maximal_queue_lifetime = 7200s
queue_run_delay = 300s
```

Consistent monitoring of these parameters is essential. Administrators can use tools such as `mailq` or `postqueue -p` to inspect the current state of the mail queue, identify bottlenecks, and detect patterns in deferred message processing. Running these commands periodically provides insights into the volume and types of messages that are facing delivery delays. For example, executing:

```
mailq | less
```

helps in determining whether the local queues have accumulated messages that require further attention.

To enhance queue management, integration with external monitoring tools or custom scripts can provide additional metrics and trigger alerts when predefined thresholds are exceeded. Log analyzers such as pflogsumm complement the monitoring efforts by summarizing mail queue statistics over specified periods. Sample usage might be:

```
pflogsumm /var/log/maillog > mail_summary.log
```

The output, displayed as follows, provides a high-level view of the queue activity:

Type	Count
Total messages	1500
Deferred messages	250
Bounced messages	100
Successful deliveries	1150

A vital aspect of optimizing mail queue management is the handling of temporary failures and bounce behaviors. Postfix is designed to retry message deliveries upon encountering transient network issues or remote server errors. However, if these parameters are not tuned, messages may remain in the queue longer than necessary, consuming resources that could be reallocated to new incoming requests. Administrators need to analyze the root causes of deferred messages and adjust the retry intervals accordingly. For instance, in environments where transient errors are frequent, a smaller minimal_backoff_time may expedite recovery once conditions normalize.

Beyond configuration parameters, the architectural organization of the mail queues can be optimized by ensuring that the queue directories are on fast, low-latency storage media. The performance of disk I/O operations directly impacts the speed with which queued updates are made and processed. Positioning the Postfix spool directories on solid-state drives (SSDs) rather than traditional hard disk drives (HDDs) may provide an observable improvement in overall queue management performance. In addition, partitioning the mail spool across multiple disks can help distribute the I/O load, thereby enhancing throughput

307

and reducing latency.

Parallel processing within the Postfix queue manager is another mechanism for boosting performance. By default, Postfix manages multiple queues such as the active, deferred, and incoming queues. Configuring Postfix to process these queues in a parallel manner maximizes the utilization of available CPU resources. Settings like `default_destination_concurrency_limit` play a role in regulating the number of simultaneous delivery attempts. While this parameter affects overall delivery performance, its influence on queue management is evident in the rate at which messages transition from the deferred queue to active processing. Administrators should adjust this value in conjunction with other queue timeout parameters to achieve optimal performance.

Prioritization of certain messages in the queue is also an important strategy. Some organizations require high-priority messages to pre-empt others in delivery. Implementing a strategy where messages are tagged with priorities allows the queue manager to schedule these for earlier processing. Although Postfix does not inherently support priority queues in a granular fashion, integrating external queue management algorithms or filters can simulate this behavior. For instance, one might combine Postfix with a custom content filter that reorders messages based on header analysis. A typical filter script might look as follows:

```bash
#!/bin/bash
# Simple script to prioritize messages based on custom header
while read line; do
    if echo "$line" | grep -q "X-Priority: high"; then
        # Process high priority message first
        echo "$line" >> /var/spool/postfix/high_priority_queue
    else
        # Default processing for normal messages
        echo "$line" >> /var/spool/postfix/regular_queue
    fi
done < /var/spool/postfix/incoming_queue
```

Such scripts, when integrated appropriately, enable streamlined processing of critical messages without the need to overhaul Postfix's internal queuing mechanism.

Mitigation of latency in mail queue processing can also be achieved by implementing back pressure mechanisms. In periods of high load, the mail server may experience queues that grow faster than they can be processed. One effective strategy is to introduce rate limiting policies, which temporarily restrict the rate at which new messages enter the queue. This not only prevents system overload but also provides the queue manager the necessary time to process existing backlog in a controlled manner. Rate limiting can be enforced by adjusting the `inflow` and `outflow` controls within the Postfix configuration. Combining these limits with delivery class adjustments based on historical data ensures that peak loads do not lead to system saturation.

The integration of performance logging with analytical tools contributes significantly to refining mail queue management strategies. Administrators should capture detailed logs, including time stamps of retries, queue residency durations, and error codes returned by remote servers. Analyzing these logs enables identification of patterns that may not be evident in aggregated metrics. For instance, repeated transient failures directed at a specific remote mail server might indicate a broader network issue rather than misconfiguration. Tools such as `grep` and `awk` can be utilized to filter logs for detailed analysis:

```
grep "status=deferred" /var/log/maillog | awk '{print $1, $2, $3}' |
    sort | uniq -c
```

This command provides a frequency distribution of deferred messages based on the time and date, highlighting periods of unusual activity.

A systematic approach to optimizing mail queue management also includes routine cleanup of stale and undeliverable messages. Over time, the buildup of obsolete messages can obscure genuine delivery issues and consume unnecessary disk space. An administrative script scheduled via cron can be employed to remove messages that have exceeded their maximal_queue_lifetime. For example, the following script outlines a basic cleanup routine:

```
#!/bin/bash
find /var/spool/postfix/deferred -type f -mmin +120 -exec rm -f {} \;
```

In this script, messages older than 120 minutes within the deferred queue are removed, thereby ensuring that the queue remains clean and that storage resources are not squandered.

It is essential to approach mail queue optimization as an iterative process. The combination of configuration adjustments, performance monitoring, and system resource management creates a dynamic environment where continuous evaluation leads to progressive improvements in delivery latency and overall performance. By carefully calibrating retry intervals, concurrency limits, and prioritization policies, administrators can substantially mitigate processing delays within the mail queue, thereby enhancing user satisfaction and server resilience.

The practices discussed here build upon previous performance tuning strategies. Detailed assessment of queue metrics, adherence to best practices regarding disk I/O, and integration of external monitoring tools form an effective tactical framework. The insights gained from careful analysis of performance logs and iterative configuration refinements provide the operator with a clear pathway to managing unforeseen complications while sustaining efficient mail processing.

Implementing these strategies fosters an environment where mail queues are systematically controlled, ensuring that even during periods of substantial activity, processing latency is minimized, and resources are efficiently utilized.

10.3. Improving DNS Resolution Times

Optimizing DNS resolution is a critical factor in ensuring the efficiency of mail routing in Postfix. When an email is sent, the server must rapidly translate domain names into IP addresses, and delays in this step can significantly affect overall delivery performance. Focusing on reducing DNS lookup times involves both Postfix-specific tuning and broader system-level practices that ensure rapid and reliable responses from DNS resolvers.

One of the first steps in addressing DNS resolution times is configuring Postfix to use the most effective host lookup method. The smtp_host_lookup parameter in Postfix allows administrators to specify which DNS protocol should be used for hostname resolution. In environments where IPv4 is predominant, setting this parameter to prioritize IPv4 lookups may bypass potential delays in IPv6 resolution. A typical configuration in the main.cf file may appear as follows:

```
smtp_host_lookup = native
```

In cases where the network infrastructure supports IPv6 and the DNS servers are optimized for IPv6 responses, ensuring that DNS queries do not default to IPv4 can be beneficial. Administrators might also experiment with third-party or alternative resolver libraries that are better optimized for speed in specific environments.

Beyond Postfix configuration, system-level DNS resolution settings strongly influence lookup times. Adjustments in the /etc/resolv.conf file can modify timeout values and the number of retry attempts, reducing the delay incurred when a DNS server does not respond instantly. For example, modifying the file with parameters such as options timeout:2 attempts:1 instructs the resolver to wait for a shorter duration before retrying a query. An example configuration is as follows:

```
nameserver 8.8.8.8
nameserver 8.8.4.4
options timeout:2 attempts:1
```

Implementing such settings reduces the wait time for each DNS lookup, and in high-load environments, these small reductions accumulate to significantly improve overall performance. However, it is essential to ensure that DNS servers specified are reliable, as overly aggressive timeouts can lead to higher rates of lookup failures if the resolvers are intermittently slow to respond.

Caching is another pivotal element in improving DNS resolution. Postfix itself can leverage operating system-level caching, and ensuring that a local caching resolver, such as dnsmasq or unbound, is correctly configured can provide rapid responses to repeated queries. A caching resolver minimizes the need for repeated queries to remote DNS servers, reducing network latency and improving throughput. A basic setup for dnsmasq might involve configuring the cache size and enabling aggressive caching policies:

```
cache-size=1000
neg-ttl=60
```

In environments with high DNS query volumes, increasing the cache size ensures that a larger number of previously resolved queries remain available. For Postfix servers that handle significant inbound and outbound mail volumes, local caching greatly minimizes recurring resolution delays.

Another advanced technique involves the use of DNS prefetching. When mail delivery involves multiple hops or interactions with several domains, preloading DNS entries before they are needed can save valuable processing time. This can be implemented at the operating system level by periodically resolving a list of frequently used domain names, thereby storing the results in the cache. A scheduled script that performs DNS lookups during off-peak hours can ensure that the cache is populated with the necessary entries. An example script designed for a Unix-based system might be:

```
#!/bin/bash
# List of frequently contacted domains
domains=("example.com" "maildomain.org" "service.net")

for domain in "${domains[@]}"
do
    dig +time=2 +tries=1 $domain > /dev/null 2>&1
done
```

Such prefetching serves to alleviate lookup bottlenecks, ensuring that when mail transactions require these DNS lookups, responses are served almost instantaneously from the local cache.

Monitoring DNS performance is also crucial in identifying areas of improvement. Tools like `dig` or `nslookup` can be regularly used to benchmark response times. For instance, the following command provides an immediate indication of how long a DNS query takes:

```
dig example.com +stats
```

Analyzing the output from this command, particularly the query time statistic, helps determine whether the lookup performance aligns with the expected parameters. Regular DNS response time measurements, when tracked over time, can signal the need for adjustments in caching strategies or prompt the investigation of possible network issues from the DNS server's end.

Network infrastructure plays an important role in DNS performance optimization. Postfix servers should be configured to use DNS servers that are geographically or logically closer to ensure reduced round-trip times. In multi-homed network environments, setting up DNS load balancing can distribute the query load across multiple servers, which can be configured in /etc/resolv.conf as:

```
nameserver 192.168.1.1
nameserver 192.168.1.2
nameserver 192.168.1.3
```

Using multiple nameservers not only provides redundancy but also allows the resolver to use the fastest responding server at any given time. In this context, it is also beneficial to implement monitoring that dynamically assesses DNS server performance and adjusts resolver usage accordingly through automation.

Integrating Postfix performance monitoring with DNS analysis helps in pinpointing the impact of DNS lookups on overall mail delivery times. Logging mechanisms inherent in Postfix, enhanced with custom scripts, can extract DNS-related delay metrics from log files. By employing grep and awk on Postfix logs, an administrator can isolate messages with prolonged DNS resolution times. For example, the following command extracts lines containing DNS-related errors:

```
grep "DNS" /var/log/maillog | awk '{print $1, $2, $3, $7, $8}' | sort
    | uniq -c
```

This command helps in recognizing DNS events that might be contributing to delays. Aggregating these results over extended periods allows the identification of patterns that may indicate when and why slow lookups occur.

Postfix also provides mechanisms to mitigate the impact of slow DNS responses through its retry policies. By combining parameters for DNS lookups with mail routing configurations, administrators can design fallback behaviors. For instance, in scenarios where an initial DNS lookup fails, Postfix might be configured to quickly reattempt the lookup with a different strategy, such as falling back to an alternative nameserver or IP version. While these adjustments require careful balancing to avoid inadvertent mail delays or excessive retries, they add resiliency to mail routing operations under adverse network conditions.

When operating in high-traffic environments, performance tuning of DNS becomes even more critical. Multiple concurrent DNS queries can saturate the resolver, leading to queued requests and delays in mail routing. Configuring system limits for the number of concurrent DNS queries, or deploying a dedicated DNS caching server, ensures smoother operation. System administrators should verify that the local DNS caching service can adequately support the query volume. Adjustments to system resource limits, such as increasing file descriptors or process counts for the caching service, may be advantageous.

Another area of focus is the handling of DNSSEC, which introduces additional overhead in DNS query processing due to cryptographic verifications. While DNSSEC provides enhanced security by ensuring the integrity of DNS responses, it can potentially increase the lookup time. Administrators need to evaluate whether the security benefits outweigh the performance cost in their specific deployment scenarios. Disabling DNSSEC validation for internal lookups, or employing optimized DNSSEC resolvers, may help mitigate any associated delays.

Advanced debugging techniques can also contribute to DNS optimization. By incrementally adjusting timeout settings and measuring impacts using controlled tests, administrators can identify optimal parameters that balance speed and reliability. Scripts that loop through different timeout configurations, log results from `dig`, and compare average response times can be valuable in tuning the system comprehensively. This experimental approach provides quantitative data that supports informed decision-making regarding DNS settings adjustments.

Postfix's interaction with DNS is not isolated to outgoing mail delivery. When processing inbound mail, the reverse DNS (rDNS) lookup of connecting hosts is often performed as part of verifying the legitimacy of the sender. Ensuring that these reverse lookups are completed promptly is crucial for maintaining the timely acceptance of incoming mail. In scenarios where rDNS lookups are known to be problematic, adjusting the related timeout in Postfix can prevent connection delays. A configuration example might be:

```
reject_unknown_reverse_client_hostname = yes
smtp_client_connection_timeout = 30s
```

Here, enforcing rDNS validation with a reasonable timeout ensures that problematic lookups do not unduly delay mail processing.

The pursuit of optimal DNS resolution times encompasses both reactive and proactive measures. By monitoring performance metrics, experimenting with configuration changes, and aligning system-level resolver behavior with Postfix's expectations, administrators can significantly reduce DNS latency. These improvements, when integrated with broader performance tuning efforts such as mail queue management and concurrency adjustments, contribute to an overall more efficient and responsive mail server.

Focusing on DNS resolution times empowers system administrators to mitigate one of the key performance bottlenecks in mail routing. By combining strategic Postfix configurations with robust system-level practices, the DNS lookup mechanism can be transformed from a potential delay point into an efficient, high-performance component of email delivery. The coordinated application of these techniques results in a comprehensive optimization strategy that directly enhances the reliability and responsiveness of Postfix operations.

10.4. Enhancing Throughput with Parallelism

Optimizing throughput in Postfix often hinges on the ability to process multiple mail delivery operations concurrently. By configuring parallelism, administrators can ensure that the mail server handles several simultaneous connections, reducing overall latency and maximizing resource utilization. Postfix's design incorporates several parameters that control the degree of parallelism at both the connection level and in the mail queue processing routines.

A central component in enabling parallelism is the adjustment of concurrency-related parameters. The `default_process_limit` directive controls the maximum number of parallel processes that the Postfix daemon can spawn. Increasing this limit allows more simultaneous client and server interactions, provided that the underlying hardware can support the increased load. A practical configuration might include setting the process limit in the `main.cf` file as follows:

```
default_process_limit = 200
```

The parameter `default_destination_concurrency_limit` is equally significant. This parameter governs the number of simultaneous outgoing SMTP connections allowed for any given destination. In environments where mail is sent to a limited number of domains or MX hosts, raising this limit improves the throughput by allowing more concurrent deliveries. For example, a revised configuration may specify:

```
default_destination_concurrency_limit = 20
```

By increasing these limits, administrators allow Postfix to attempt multiple connections in parallel rather than serial execution, which can reduce waiting times during periods of peak mail flow.

Beyond global concurrency settings, Postfix's master process can be fine-tuned to handle parallel connections efficiently by configuring service-specific parameters. Many service entries in the `master.cf` file include a concurrency limit that can be modified to suit the expected workload. As an example, the SMTP service entry may be customized to increase simultaneous connections:

```
smtp      inet   n        -     n      -       -      smtpd
   -o syslog_name=postfix/smtp
   -o smtpd_client_connection_count_limit=50
```

The `smtpd_client_connection_count_limit` option restricts the number of concurrent connections from any single client IP address. Adjusting this parameter helps balance overall throughput while preventing any single host from monopolizing server resources.

Increasing parallelism must be approached with caution to avoid excessive resource consumption. Each parallel process consumes memory and CPU cycles, and on smaller servers, high levels of parallelism might lead to resource saturation. Monitoring tools such as top or htop become essential to assess system load and adjust these thresholds when necessary. The trade-offs between rapid processing and system stability require a continuous cycle of evaluation and fine-tuning.

Another dimension of parallelism in Postfix is found in its handling of queued messages. The queue manager processes messages concurrently by dividing them among multiple worker processes. The interplay between concurrency limits and queue management parameters, such as queue_run_delay, directly affects the speed at which messages leave the queue. When many messages are queued, the delivery system benefits from aggressive parallel processing. An illustration of these concepts can be observed in the adjustment of delivery concurrency for specific destinations:

```
smtp_destination_concurrency_limit = 10
```

This parameter sets the number of simultaneous delivery attempts to a given destination. Mail systems dealing with large volumes of mail routed to a handful of remote servers benefit from higher concurrency limits, resulting in reduced queue dwell times and improved throughput.

Postfix's caching mechanisms also contribute indirectly to parallelism by reducing the overhead of repetitive tasks. For example, caching of SMTP connection information, when configured properly, can help reduce the setup time for new connections. The smtp_connection_cache_on_demand parameter can enable caching

318

of idle connections for subsequent use. Although not directly a concurrency parameter, it improves overall throughput by lowering the connection establishment latency for frequently contacted destinations:

```
smtp_connection_cache_on_demand = yes
```

The effectiveness of these parallelism enhancements can be measured by examining system logs and using network performance tools. Postfix logging combined with tools such as `pflogsumm` or custom scripts allows the administrator to glean insights into the number of active connections, processing delays, and backlog trend of queued messages. An example command to review mail processing statistics might be:

```
pflogsumm /var/log/maillog > throughput_report.log
```

Examinations of these reports can reveal if the increased concurrency limits are being fully exploited. A typical report might include sections indicating the count of active SMTP connections and deferred message statistics. Observations from these logs help in identifying whether additional tuning steps are required or if system resource limits are being encountered.

The deployment environment plays a crucial role in how well parallelism in Postfix translates into increased throughput. For cloud-based and virtualized environments, scaling parallel operations may also require adjustments at the operating system level. Increasing the number of available file descriptors and adjusting kernel network parameters can facilitate the smooth operation of a highly parallel mail system. For instance, administrators may need to update limits in `/etc/security/limits.conf` to ensure that Postfix can handle an increased number of simultaneous connections:

```
postfix soft nofile 8192
postfix hard nofile 16384
```

Likewise, tuning kernel networking parameters in `/etc/sysctl.conf` can be critical. Adjustments such as increasing the size of socket buffers and reducing the TCP TIME_WAIT delay can further enhance the performance realized from parallel processing:

```
net.ipv4.tcp_fin_timeout = 30
net.ipv4.tcp_max_syn_backlog = 4096
```

In high-volume mail environments, these operating system modifications complement Postfix's internal settings to create a holistic improvement in throughput.

Parallelism in Postfix is also managed dynamically through runtime parameters. Postfix can adjust its processing based on current load via adaptive control mechanisms. For example, if network latency increases or if a remote destination is temporarily slow, Postfix's retry logic ensures that delayed messages do not subsequently block new delivery attempts. This dynamic adaptation is governed by both delivery parameters and service-specific settings. The administration of these dynamic behaviors, coupled with properly tuned concurrency limits, ensures that the mail system maintains high throughput even under variable load conditions.

Testing performance implications is a necessary component of adopting increased parallelism. Administrators can simulate high mail volume flows using testing tools such as swaks (Swiss Army Knife for SMTP) to generate concurrent SMTP connections. An example of such a test is:

```
swaks --to user@example.com --server smtp.example.com --num 100 --
    concurrency 20
```

This command simulates 100 mail transactions with up to 20 concurrent connections. Observing the resulting processing times and connection metrics provides valuable insights that can guide further adjustments to concurrency settings.

Effective parallelism also takes into account the balancing of workload distribution across multiple services. In systems with layered mail processing, parallelism might occur not only at the SMTP connection level but also through specialized service daemons handling content filtering, antivirus scanning, or spam checking. By ensuring that each of these auxiliary services is capable of operating in parallel, the overall mail delivery pipeline remains robust. Coordination between the mail server and these services is essential; it can be achieved by explicitly configuring these services to handle multiple simultaneous requests, ensuring that the benefits of increased parallelism in Postfix extend to every stage of mail processing.

As throughput is enhanced through increased parallelism, continuous monitoring remains imperative. Administrators should employ logging, performance monitoring, and alerting systems to detect any unexpected behavior or resource saturation. Documented changes combined with scheduled performance reviews enable a proactive approach in managing the mail server's overall health. This proactive monitoring ensures that any issues arising from overly aggressive parallelism—such as unexpected process failures or network congestion—are quickly identified and remedied.

In practice, successful enhancement of throughput with parallelism hinges on a careful balance between maximizing concurrent operations and preserving overall system stability. By iteratively adjusting configuration parameters, evaluating system logs, and testing network performance, administrators can achieve significant improvements in mail processing speeds. These adjustments not only reduce message latency but also enable the mail server to accommodate growth in traffic volume without a corresponding increase in processing delays.

The coordinated application of these techniques results in a configuration that leverages both Postfix's internal parallelism capabilities and the underlying operating system's advanced networking features. This comprehensive approach to parallelism elevates the entire mail delivery pipeline, ensuring that the system can adapt to high loads, manage numerous simultaneous connections, and deliver messages with minimal delay.

10.5. Resource Management and Scaling

Efficient resource management is essential for maintaining high availability and performance in Postfix as email traffic grows. As workloads increase, the mail server must leverage both internal configuration tuning and operating system level adjustments to optimize CPU, memory, and disk I/O usage. This section details strategies for allocating resources effectively and planning for system scaling while building on previously discussed parameters for parallelism, DNS resolution, and queue management.

A foundational step in resource management is the systematic assessment of current system performance. Monitoring tools such as top, htop, and vmstat provide real-time observations of CPU idle times, memory consumption, and disk I/O operations. Administrators can use these tools to identify bottlenecks. For example, if the CPU usage is persistently high during peak periods, then adjustments such as increasing the default_process_limit or offloading auxiliary services may be necessary. A common practice is to run periodic benchmarks and log key performance metrics to build an empirical basis for scaling decisions.

Resource allocation within Postfix itself can be optimized through fine-tuning of key parameters that have been discussed in earlier sections. For instance, parameters such as default_destination_concurrency_limit and smtp_connection_cache_on_demand directly impact resource utilization by controlling the number of active processes and reducing the overhead of establishing new connections. As traffic increases,

322

these parameters may need adjustment to align with the current capacity. An example snippet in main.cf could be:

```
default_process_limit = 250
default_destination_concurrency_limit = 25
smtp_connection_cache_on_demand = yes
```

In parallel, tuning the operating system's resource allocation is crucial. System settings such as the maximum number of open file descriptors and network socket buffers must be configured to support a high volume of simultaneous connections. The configuration files /etc/security/limits.conf and /etc/sysctl.conf play significant roles in this regard. For instance, increasing file descriptor limits for the Postfix user ensures that a surge in connections does not result in resource starvation. An adjusted configuration might include:

```
postfix soft nofile 16384
postfix hard nofile 32768
```

Similarly, tuning network parameters improves performance under heavy load. Settings such as net.ipv4.tcp_max_syn_backlog and net.ipv4.tcp_fin_timeout can be optimized to handle a larger number of concurrent connection attempts smoothly:

```
net.ipv4.tcp_max_syn_backlog = 4096
net.ipv4.tcp_fin_timeout = 30
```

Vertical scaling, which involves enhancing the capacity of a single server, may include upgrading hardware components such as CPU, memory, or disk subsystems. Solid-state drives (SSDs) and high-speed network interfaces can significantly improve disk I/O and network performance, respectively. Postfix's mail queue performance is directly tied to disk speed, and segregating spool directories onto faster storage volumes can lead to immediate improvements in mail processing rates.

A complementary approach to vertical scaling is horizontal scaling. As email volumes continue to increase, a single server—no matter

323

how optimized—may eventually become insufficient. In such cases, distributing the load among multiple Postfix instances across several servers is imperative. Load balancing can be implemented using DNS round-robin techniques or dedicated load balancers that distribute incoming mail traffic. A typical DNS configuration for load balancing may involve multiple A records:

```
mail.example.com.    IN   A    192.168.1.1
mail.example.com.    IN   A    192.168.1.2
mail.example.com.    IN   A    192.168.1.3
```

In a horizontally scaled environment, it is important to ensure that configuration consistency is maintained across all nodes. Automated configuration management tools, such as Ansible, Puppet, or Chef, can be utilized to propagate configuration changes and monitor nodes for consistency. A simple Ansible playbook snippet for deploying a common main.cf file might read:

```
- name: Deploy Postfix configuration
  hosts: mailservers
  tasks:
    - name: Copy main.cf file
      copy:
        src: files/main.cf
        dest: /etc/postfix/main.cf
        owner: root
        group: root
        mode: '0644'
```

Incorporating monitoring into the scaling strategy is vital. Real-time monitoring solutions such as Nagios, Zabbix, or Prometheus help administrators to keep track of resource usage, connection rates, queue lengths, and other metrics that provide insights into the system's performance. Custom dashboards that visualize these metrics facilitate proactive management and allow for timely interventions before the system reaches its limits. Integration of performance monitoring with automated alerting mechanisms ensures that any deviations from expected behavior trigger immediate investigation.

Scalability planning also requires considering the interplay between Postfix and other email ecosystem components. For instance, spam filtering, antivirus scanning, and content filtering services must be able to scale in parallel with the mail server. When these services become bottlenecks, they may need to be distributed across multiple instances or offloaded to specialized filtering servers. This reduces the load on Postfix while maintaining overall system efficiency. Configurations that integrate external filters should be designed with scalability in mind, ensuring that they communicate asynchronously and can handle increased loads without introducing significant latency.

Another dimension of resource management is the efficient use of memory. High volumes of email transactions can lead to significant memory utilization, particularly when many delivery processes run concurrently. Techniques such as process forking and memory sharing within Postfix help mitigate excessive memory usage, but as traffic grows, administrators may need to increase the available memory. Continuous monitoring and memory profiling help in understanding usage patterns and making informed decisions regarding memory upgrades. Additionally, careful tuning of caching parameters such as DNS caching and connection caching reduces redundant memory usage and speeds up processes.

Strategic planning for scaling often involves simulations and stress testing. Administrators can employ tools to stress-test the Postfix installation under controlled conditions. For example, using a tool like swaks, one can simulate a heavy load of simultaneous connections to understand how the system behaves under stress:

```
swaks --to test@example.com --server mail.example.com --num 500 --
    concurrency 50
```

Analyzing the performance results from such tests helps in identifying potential bottlenecks and provides data that supports decisions to either tune system parameters or undertake hardware upgrades. Repeatedly running stress tests after each configuration change is a best practice that ensures newly applied settings deliver the intended improvements.

Economies of scale in resource management also imply implementing backup strategies and disaster recovery procedures. As the system scales, the complexity of maintaining consistent performance and reliability increases. Employing redundant systems, failover configurations, and regular backup schedules ensures that the email service remains resilient even if a single node experiences issues. High-availability clusters with automatic failover mechanisms can be implemented using clustering software and shared storage, which minimizes downtime in the event of hardware failures.

Automation of routine tasks is another key to successful scaling. Scripts that automate the cleanup of old logs, purging of outdated messages from the queue, or even the dynamic reallocation of resources during peak times, can relieve the operational burden on administrators while ensuring the system remains within optimal performance thresholds. A sample cron job entry that executes a cleanup script every night might be:

```
0 3 * * * /usr/local/bin/postfix_cleanup.sh
```

This script, which automates the removal of expired deferred messages, helps ensure that disk space is managed effectively and that the system does not slow down over time due to accumulation of obsolete data.

Resource management and scaling for a Postfix server require a multi-layered approach that effectively blends internal configuration tuning, system-level adjustments, workload monitoring, and proactive planning for growth. As email traffic increases, an agile response that encompasses both vertical and horizontal scaling strategies is imperative. The techniques described in this section, when implemented in a coordinated manner, provide a robust framework that supports not only current performance demands but also anticipates future growth.

Effective application of these strategies requires continuous evaluation and iterative tuning. Administrators must regularly review logs,
benchmark system performance, and adjust configurations as necessary. This iterative process ensures that resource utilization remains
optimal and that the system can scale seamlessly as demands evolve.
Careful coordination between Postfix configuration, operating system
tuning, and infrastructure scaling collectively ensures that the mail
server operates efficiently and reliably under variable loads.

10.6. Analyzing and Reducing Load Bottlenecks

Identifying and mitigating load bottlenecks within Postfix operations
is fundamental to maintaining smooth email delivery services. Bottlenecks may arise at different layers of the system, including CPU utilization, memory allocation, disk I/O, network latency, and even within
configuration parameters that govern process concurrency and mail
queue management. Effective diagnosis and resolution of these issues
require systematic monitoring, analysis of logs, and iterative tuning of
both Postfix configuration and underlying system resources.

A primary approach to analyzing load bottlenecks is the comprehensive
monitoring of system metrics during peak traffic periods. Tools such
as top, htop, and sar can be used to monitor CPU load and memory utilization. High CPU usage often points to overloaded Postfix processes
or auxiliary services like spam filters and antivirus scanners. Similarly, sustained high memory consumption might indicate inefficient
caching, excessive queuing, or potential memory leaks. Administrators
should correlate these system-level measurements with Postfix performance by examining process counts, connection statistics, and delivery
concurrency limits.

Log analysis is another critical component in pinpointing bottlenecks. Postfix logs contain detailed clues regarding slow connections, deferred messages, and failed delivery attempts. Utilizing tools such as grep and awk can facilitate filtering and summarizing log entries that indicate recurring issues. For example, to extract lines that mention deferred mail delivery, an administrator might run:

```
grep "status=deferred" /var/log/maillog | awk '{print $1, $2, $3, $7,
    $8}' | sort | uniq -c
```

This command outputs frequency counts of deferred message events, allowing the identification of patterns that suggest either remote server issues or internal resource constraints leading to message backlogs.

Another effective technique is the use of summary tools such as pflogsumm. This utility aggregates log data and provides an overview of mail delivery performance, highlighting statistics such as total processed messages, bounce rates, deferred counts, and rejected connections. An example command to generate such a report is:

```
pflogsumm /var/log/maillog > performance_report.log
```

Reviewing the generated report can help administrators determine if high contention occurs during specific time windows or if certain destinations consistently contribute to processing delays.

Disk I/O performance is frequently a hidden source of bottlenecks. Postfix relies heavily on file operations for storing mail queues, reading configurations, and writing logs. Slow disk performance may emerge from outdated storage media or misconfigured I/O schedulers. To evaluate disk throughput, tools like iostat provide insights into disk utilization and can indicate whether resource saturation is occurring. If disk I/O is identified as the culprit, steps such as migrating spool directories to solid-state drives (SSDs) or tuning the operating system's I/O scheduler may resolve the issue. A simple command to assess disk performance is:

```
iostat -x 5 3
```

This command outputs extended disk statistics every five seconds over three iterations, offering a snapshot of I/O load and latency.

Network performance should not be overlooked. Postfix's efficiency in resolving domain names and establishing SMTP connections is tightly bound to the network configuration. High latency or packet loss can lead to prolonged connection setups, contributing to an increased load and deferred messages. Tools such as ping, traceroute, or mtr can help diagnose network issues. For example:

```
ping -c 10 mail.example.com
```

This command measures round-trip times to a mail server, enabling administrators to determine if network latency is a potential bottleneck affecting mail delivery.

Within Postfix, certain configuration parameters significantly influence the system's ability to handle load. Parameters such as default_process_limit, queue_run_delay, and default_destination_concurrency_limit must be carefully balanced to avoid excessive resource contention. For instance, if the default_process_limit is set too high relative to system capacity, it could lead to resource exhaustion, while a limit set too low may underutilize available hardware, leading to increased queuing delays. Administrators should therefore monitor system performance as these parameters are tuned to find an optimal balance.

Moreover, the integration of external content scanners, spam filters, or antivirus software can add overhead to the mail processing pipeline if not properly optimized. In environments where the email flow is heavy, these additional services must be either capable of parallel processing or distributed in a manner that prevents them from becoming the primary bottleneck. Performance profiling of these auxiliary ser-

329

vices is essential, and adjustments such as asynchronous processing or offloading to dedicated servers can mitigate their impact.

A recurring issue in load bottleneck analysis is the buildup of deferred messages in the mail queue. Deferred messages often signal that Postfix is unable to process a high volume of messages efficiently. Analyzing the reasons behind these deferrals is necessary to reduce the processing latency. For example, a slow DNS resolution process or delayed responses from remote SMTP servers might be primary causes. Tuning timeouts and backoff intervals can help mitigate these issues. A sample configuration adjustment in the `main.cf` file to manage deferred messages is:

```
minimal_backoff_time = 300s
maximal_queue_lifetime = 7200s
```

These settings adjust the interval between retry attempts and the maximum life of a message in the queue, respectively. An iterative approach where these parameters are incrementally adjusted, followed by performance monitoring, often yields improvements in load management.

Resource contention arising from high concurrency levels also warrants careful analysis. When multiple simultaneous SMTP connections are initiated, the system may experience contention at the CPU or I/O level. Administrators can analyze the number of concurrent processes and the frequency of context switches to determine whether the current concurrency limits are sustainable. Adjustments can be made in the `master.cf` file by setting service-specific concurrency limits. An example snippet is:

```
smtp      inet   n        -       n       -       -       smtpd
  -o default_process_limit=100
  -o smtpd_client_connection_count_limit=50
```

This configuration helps control the number of processes spawned by the SMTP service, reducing the likelihood of overwhelming the system under heavy load.

In addition to individual configuration adjustments, implementing automated scripts for continuous performance monitoring can provide real-time insights into system bottlenecks. A custom script may routinely check for high CPU load, excessive disk I/O, or unusually high queue lengths, triggering alerts if predefined thresholds are exceeded. An example script might be:

```
#!/bin/bash
# Monitor Postfix load metrics
cpu_usage=$(top -b -n1 | grep "Cpu(s)" | awk '{print 100 - $8}')
queue_length=$(mailq | tail -n +2 | wc -l)
threshold_cpu=80
threshold_queue=100

if [ $(echo "$cpu_usage > $threshold_cpu" | bc) -eq 1 ]; then
    echo "High CPU usage detected: $cpu_usage%" | mail -s "Postfix
    CPU Alert" admin@example.com
fi

if [ $queue_length -gt $threshold_queue ]; then
    echo "Mail queue length is high: $queue_length messages" | mail -
    s "Postfix Queue Alert" admin@example.com
fi
```

This script checks the CPU utilization and mail queue length, issuing an email alert if either exceeds defined limits. The use of such automation not only aids in early detection of bottlenecks but also facilitates proactive response.

Another layer of load bottleneck analysis involves understanding the interactions between Postfix and the operating system. Operating system parameters such as file descriptor limits, process scheduling, and network stack configurations contribute substantially to overall performance. Analyzing system logs in conjunction with application logs can reveal if resource limits are being reached. For instance, an unusually high number of "too many open files" errors in the logs might indicate that the operating system's file descriptor limit is too low, which can be adjusted in /etc/security/limits.conf:

```
postfix soft nofile 32768
```

```
postfix hard nofile 65536
```

Such adjustments ensure that Postfix processes have sufficient resources to handle high connection volumes and prevent slowdowns due to resource depletion.

The process of analyzing and reducing load bottlenecks is iterative. Administrators must continuously refine configurations based on performance data over time. Benchmarking stress tests using tools such as swaks can mimic high-load conditions, allowing the evaluation of system behavior under stress. An example test command is:

```
swaks --to test@example.com --server smtp.example.com --num 500 --
    concurrency 50
```

Analyzing the results from these tests helps identify bottlenecks related to concurrency, network latency, or disk I/O. Subsequent tuning of configuration parameters and operating system settings based on these insights can incrementally reduce processing delays and bolster system robustness.

Ultimately, the goal is to establish a balanced configuration that minimizes load bottlenecks without compromising volume capacity or system stability. Combining the continuous monitoring and analysis of system performance with deliberate, incremental tuning of Postfix configuration enables administrators to achieve sustained improvements. The methodologies discussed here, from log analysis to stress testing and automation, provide a comprehensive framework for proactively identifying and mitigating potential bottlenecks in Postfix operations, thereby ensuring smooth and efficient email delivery.

www.ingramcontent.com/pod-product-compliance
Lightning Source LLC
Chambersburg PA
CBHW061235220326
41599CB00028B/5432